Business Studies AS

The Complete Companion

OCR

25

Jenny Wales

•

Neil Reaich

Published in 2004 by:
Nelson Thornes Ltd
Delta Place
27 Bath Road
CHELTENHAM
GL53 7TH
United Kingdom

04 05 06 07 08/ 10 9 8 7 6 5 4 3 2 1

A catalogue record for this book is available from the British Library

ISBN 0 7487 7533 1

Illustrations by Harry Venning and IFA Design Ltd, Plymouth, Devon
Page make-up by IFA Design Ltd, Plymouth, Devon

Printed and bound in Spain by Graficas Estella

Contents

Acknowledgements

The publishers would like to thank Chris Sammons and Stephen Wood for their input and advice on the examining elements of the text.

The authors would like to thank the following businesses for their support in writing this book:

DJ Wildrich, Yeo Valley, Wadsworth's Brewery, Harriet Kessie Hairdressing, CMRC, Carphone Warehouse, Virgin Mobile, The Big Pit, Dan yr Ogof Show Caves, The Co-op in Aldbourne, Discarray, Indulge, Chester Zoo, Claire Wilson and Terry Warlock.

Art Directors & Trip Photo Library: p188 (top)
BP plc 2003: p20
Cadburys plc: p106
Corbis Images/ Patrik Giardino: p182 (left)
Future Network plc: p164, p174
John Walmsley/ Education Photos: p71
Microsoft: p168
Nature Picture Library: p74
Press Association/ Barry Batchelor: p80
Rex Features Ltd/ Richard Young: p98, Rex Features Ltd/ Jeremy Sutton-Hibbert: p114, p116, Rex Features Ltd/ John Wright: p118 Rex Features Ltd/ Frank Casimiro: p122
Sue Sharp: p111
Thomson Holidays: p96
Virgin Mobile Telecoms Ltd/Copyright © Virgin Mobile Telecoms Ltd 1999-2003: p154

Picture research by Sue Sharp.

How to use this book

In your Complete Companion you will find all the support you need for your AS Business Studies. Each topic has been broken down into sections which are each covered on two pages so they can be easily understood and build a comprehensive understanding of the specification

starSTUDY

The 'Star study' is a short case study which aims to help you work out what the theory really means. The questions are not just comprehension but ask you to make connections so you understand the theory and can put it to work.

Text

The links in the icon tell you what these sections are about. They tie the theory together with the real world and provide analysis and evaluation of the ideas.

IN THE KNOW

'In the know' provides all the knowledge you need. It is the basis for all your answers in the exam. The rest of the material on each page helps you to put these ideas to work so that you can apply it in different situations.

Critical thinking

In exams you get good grades when you show you can analyse and evaluate business ideas in different situations. The 'Critical thinking' questions give you the opportunity to practise these skills in the context of the ideas on the page

KEY TERMS

You will find definitions under the heading 'Key terms'. They are explained further and used in context in other places on the page.

Next steps

'Next steps' asks you to use the concepts and ideas in situations you know about. It might be your school or college, a business you know well or your local area.

Assessment

There are assessment opportunities throughout the book. These combine case study exercises to practice using the knowledge and skills you have acquired with real exam questions. They all provide you with assistance. The practice questions all have help! which give you hints and tips about answering the questions. The exam questions show you the concepts and ideas which are being used in the case studies. Identifying these is very important because it gives you clues to how to answer the questions.

Nature of business

Classification of business

Objectives and strategy

Part 1
Businesses, their objectives and environment

What does business do?

Specification Content

What businesses do:
meet the needs of stakeholders:
customers, managers, creditors,
owners/shareholders, employees
and the community

starSTUDY

Making magic

DJW designs and installs audio-visual experiences. The Premier League Hall of Fame and Explore@Bristol are among its customers. The business started life by providing the audio-visual expertise for the Motor Museum in Beaulieu, Hampshire, where it is based. It then found there were other people who wanted to buy the services that it offered. It now employs 13 people and has a range of experts it can call on for specialist jobs. Most of the employees live in the local area.

The business buys all sorts of things – from hi-tech equipment to jars of coffee – from a range of suppliers.

Sometimes DJW needs to borrow money from the bank. It might want to use the money to buy some new equipment. There are times when customers haven't paid their bills on time so the business needs to borrow to fill the gap.

The business, which was set up by David Willdich, is owned by its shareholders who are members of the family. This small group of shareholders puts money into the company and shares the profits.

David and his wife Lynn, who is responsible for finance, work hard to make DJW a success because they enjoy running the business and want to make a profit. This means ensuring that each installation covers its costs – and makes a little more.

Businesses and stakeholders

WHO ARE THE STAKEHOLDERS?

Stakeholders all have an interest in an organisation. They may:

- work within the business – employees and managers.
- have financial relationships – lenders, suppliers and customers.
- be affected by the way the business functions – people in the local community and beyond.
- own the business or hold shares in it.

Sometimes the interests of stakeholders might conflict. When a business wants to expand, it may put pressure on the local environment. Owners may put pressure on employees to increase profits.

Stakeholders may wear different hats. Employees are often members of the local community. Expansion, for example, will secure jobs but will make the roads busier and put pressure on local schools. What should they do?

MEETING STAKEHOLDER OBJECTIVES

The primary function of any business is to make a profit for the owners or shareholders. If this is not achieved over a period, the business will cease to exist and other stakeholders will lose out as jobs will be lost and suppliers will find that their order books get thinner.

Businesses have different priorities in dealing with stakeholders. Carphone Warehouse, for example, puts customers and employees at the top of the list because they think that this is critical for success in the phone business.

Often the most powerful stakeholder wins attention. A vociferous campaign in the local community, for example, can prevent a business from making an unpopular decision. The business may want to protect its reputation because negative stories in the media can drive customers away.

Working with stakeholders

Companies, large and small, are aware that stakeholders need to be looked after. They know that a good reputation is important and once it is lost, it is hard to regain.

Stakeholder	How to look after them	Effect
Customers	Sell a good product at a fair price	They will keep coming back
Employees	Good working conditions	Produce better results
Suppliers	Pay them on time	Supply what the business needs, when it needs it
Creditors	Pay back loans regularly	Lend willingly – the next time
Shareholders	Make a good profit	Keep their money in the business
Community	Look after people and the environment	Support if you want to expand or make other changes

1 Make a list of the people and organisations that have an interest in DJW.

2 Explain why each one is interested in this business.

3 Can you think of anyone else who might be interested in what the business does? Explain why.

BP is the UK's largest company and has activities all over the world. Its stakeholders are many and varied because of the nature of the business. Chemicals and oil production affect people in many ways so the company must work with its stakeholders to try to avoid conflict. Like all big companies, it has policies on working with stakeholders and is aware that objectives might conflict. Instead of fighting with organisations like Greenpeace, it tries to work with them to achieve ends that satisfy everyone. Despite much care, it doesn't always get it right.

Suppliers to any company feel under pressure to sell their products at the lowest possible price because if others do it more cheaply, they might lose the business. Some companies have started working more closely with suppliers in order to give security and develop a relationship which makes both businesses work better.

KEY TERMS

Stakeholders are people who have an interest in a business. They include employees, managers, customers, creditors, suppliers, owners/shareholders and the community.

Shareholders own a part of the business.

Costs include everything that has to be paid for when making a product.

Profit is the difference between the cost of a product and the price the customer pays.

Critical thinking

BP's Cleaner Fuels strategy includes:

* Making cleaner fuels available in 90 cities throughout the world.
* Working to reduce emissions of the greenhouse gases produced by its manufacturing operations by 10% from a 1990 baseline by 2010.

1 Work out how these activities:
a benefit BP
b benefit the stakeholders.

Evaluate these benefits.

2 Identify a business which you know and work out whether its approach to stakeholders helps it to achieve its objectives.

Next steps

Choose a business that you know about. It could be one you work for, a large business such as McDonalds or a small local company.

1 Who are the stakeholders?

2 Work out the objectives of each stakeholder group.

3 How do you think these objectives affect the way a business works?

4 In what ways might the objectives conflict?

5 What might happen if a business makes a 'wrong' decision?

What businesses need

Specification
Content

*What businesses need:
sources of finance,
labour, customers,
suppliers, organisation*

star**STUDY**
Resources for magic

DJW is a small organisation but it needs all sorts of resources to keep it going. Some of the people it employs use sophisticated electronic equipment to create amazing audio-visual installations. Others are involved in making sure that the business runs smoothly – Lynn looks after finance, Josh is responsible for sales, Paula keeps orders under control and Kevin and John run projects for customers.

Suppliers provide all sorts of things, ranging from computers to coffee. It buys video projectors from Sharp and Sony. Bose supply sound systems. Capacitors, connectors and cables come from RS Components. The everyday office needs are ordered from Roman Office Supplies.

Customers are located across the country and beyond. DJW works very closely with them so that the product really fits the bill. In order to get it right, staff members work in teams on a project.

The original funding for the business came from its shareholders. Sometimes DJW borrows money from the bank in order to bridge the gap between paying for resources and being paid for its installations.

1 Draw a spider diagram to show the range of inputs that DJW needs.
2 Draw another one for a business that you know.
3 Why do you think a business needs finance?
4 How does DJW keep the business running smoothly?
5 Why is it important for a business to be well organised?

Adding value

Businesses **add value** by putting resources together and selling them for more than the cost of the individual items. DJW uses several sophisticated components and some highly skilled people to create products that meet the customers' needs. All businesses must add value if they are to survive. This may be something very simple, such as putting wood together to make a chair or providing a service in a nail salon.

Customers need to be convinced that their purchases are worth the price they pay. It is important, therefore, for a business to manage production and develop its products so that

- each product adds value
- customers want to buy the products.

To achieve this, the business must be well organised. All parts of the business must work together to achieve the objectives. DJW, like all other businesses, must look out for changes in the way their products are made and what customers want if they are to continue to be successful. 'In the know' gives an overview of the part played by each contributor.

What businesses need

IN THE KNOW

CUSTOMERS

No business can survive without customers. They buy the products of a business and are therefore critical to success. It is important to listen to existing and potential customers so that products can be changed to meet their needs. If a business fails to do this, the customers will go elsewhere and profits will fall. The marketing department generally has the responsibility for attracting and keeping customers.

The law protects customers when businesses provide unsatisfactory goods or services. Products must, for example, be safe to use and work as intended.

go to → Find out more on page 68.

SOURCES OF FINANCE

Businesses need finance at all stages of development:

- getting started
- running the business
- keeping ahead of competitors
- growing.

These different situations are often funded in different ways. Sometimes finance can be internal so it comes from within the business. On other occasions, it is external and comes from outsiders.

go to → Find out more on page 17.

LABOUR

Every business needs people. They may make a product, provide a service or help with the organisation of the business. They will need specific skills which may be, for example, technical, financial, marketing or administrative. These skills are often developed while in employment because the world of work moves very quickly and people need training to keep up to date. Many businesses look after their employees because they are expensive to recruit and train. When things go wrong, the law protects the employee.

go to → Find out more on page 66.

SUPPLIERS

All businesses have to buy things in order to make products or provide services. Suppliers must be reliable if the business is to meet the needs of its customers. Businesses work with suppliers in different ways. Some will chop and change because they are looking for the cheapest price for their inputs. Others develop a relationship with a supplier so the inputs are just right. A supplier will then be prepared to help out if there is a sudden demand for the end product and an order must be dealt with quickly.

go to → Find out more on page 199.

Critical thinking

DJW employs administrative people to organise the business and technical people to carry out the contracts it wins. These contracts involve working in different parts of the country on different installations for a range of different organisations. DJW is often working to tight deadlines. Work out what might happen if:

- the costs of a project were underestimated
- the technical people did not check that the suppliers had sent the correct equipment.
- someone with specialist skills left suddenly
- the finance department didn't submit bills for work that had been done.

1 What effect do you think these actions might have on the rest of the business?

2 Why is organisation so important to a business?

Next steps

1 Work out what resources are needed by a business you know. How does it add value?

2 A business cannot survive without customers. Come up with ideas about what can be done to attract new customers and keep existing ones.

3 Why is it important for a business to look after its employees?

4 Why is it important to keep a good relationship with suppliers?

5 Suppliers want to make a profit. Why can there be a conflict between a business and its suppliers?

KEY TERMS

Added value is the difference between the total cost of resources and the price that is charged for the product or service.

Resources are all the things a business needs to make its product.

Sources of finance show where a business can raise money. They may be internal from inside the business or external from sources outside the business.

Good behaviour

star**STUDY**
The new store

Worcester has its fair share of supermarkets but there was a gap in the St John's area on the west side of town. Tesco planned to build a new store on the site of a school, which was badly in need of updating. It proposed to put up £12.6 million to build a new school on another site – a tempting offer for the county council since it knew the school needed a lot of money spent on it.

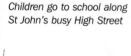

Children go to school along St John's busy High Street

Sainsbury's also put forward a proposal. This involved keeping the school but providing a sports centre, youth club and an all-weather pitch.

Local people were keen on the idea of a new supermarket at this end of town but weren't sure that it should be Tesco because there were already two in the city. They were also anxious about the extra traffic that would come through the area – Sainsbury's plan might bring in more traffic because it was keeping everything on the same site.

It would be great to have a new school but, with Tesco's plan, students would have to travel out of St John's to the new site. There was some concern about the effect that it would have on the local community.

The traders in St John's High Street campaigned ferociously against any supermarket, because they knew it would take their customers away.

1 Which stakeholders live in the local community?

2 How would the new store affect the local community? Draw up a table showing the pros and cons of each scheme.

3 How do you think the following stakeholders would respond to the proposed developments:
   a suppliers
   b creditors
   c shareholders?

4 Which plan would you go for? Why?

Keeping everyone happy

A business's prime objective has to be to keep its shareholders happy. They own the company because they have bought shares in it, so they expect to be paid a share of the profit. This is known as a **dividend** and it is a reward to the shareholders for buying into the business. If they do not receive the reward they expect, they will probably sell the shares and buy into another company instead.

There are other stakeholders who need to be kept happy if the business is going to be successful.

A new store means:
• new jobs
• easy shopping for customers

• more orders for suppliers
• more borrowing from creditors and interest payments
• more traffic in the local area.

It may also mean that the local area benefits. The business wants to persuade people that the new store is a good thing – in Worcester, Sainsbury's and Tesco were in competition, so each company was keen to make a tempting offer to the community.

Both businesses are **accountable** to their stakeholders. Upsetting any of them can lead to problems but often a business has to decide which stakeholders are most important when changes are made.

Accountability in practice

IN THE KNOW

SHAREHOLDERS have bought shares in a business and hope to be paid a dividend each year if the business is making a profit. They must be kept informed of events so they know how the business is going and be given the opportunity to have their say.

SUPPLIERS expect to be paid on time. Most suppliers give a period of credit but some companies delay payment to help their own financial position. Suppliers can add interest if bills are not paid on time but many don't do this because they don't want to upset the customer.

CUSTOMERS can expect to buy products that live up to the claims of the business. If they don't, the law protects them. Customers can turn to the local Trading Standards Officer or the Citizens' Advice Bureau for help if they feel that they have been unfairly treated.

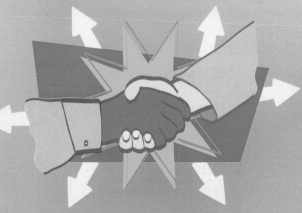

CREDITORS have lent money to the business and expect it to be repaid with the right amount of interest. A bank that has not been paid may call in the loan and the business might fail as a result. It is always sensible for a business to discuss problems, however small, with the bank before the problems get too serious.

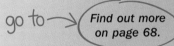 go to → Find out more on page 68.

THE LOCAL COMMUNITY around a business can be critical to its success. By working with them, a business can develop a 'licence to operate'. If a business wants to expand, having a good relationship with the community may make the process much easier. Big businesses like BP have found that working with Greenpeace, for example, helps when environmental issues are at stake.

EMPLOYEES expect to be treated fairly by employers and are protected by the law if things go wrong. The law covers unfair dismissal, discrimination, disability, and health and safety among other areas. Someone who feels that an employer's decision has been unfair can take their case to an Employment Tribunal where a judgement will be made.

go to → Find out more on page 66.

Critical thinking

Vodafone's mobile phone network broke down for a whole day. Customers were not happy!

- Work out who Vodaphone's stakeholders are.
- How was each of them affected by the network failure?
- If you were responsible for communicating with Vodaphone's stakeholders, what would you have done?

KEY TERMS

Dividends are the share of profits paid to shareholders as a return for investing in a company.

Accountability describes the relationship between a business and its stakeholders.

Next steps

1 Draw up a spider diagram for a business you know. Show its stakeholders and its accountability to each one.

2 How do you think this accountability affects the way the business works?

Sorting out the sectors

Specification Content

Economic sectors: primary, secondary, tertiary

star**STUDY**

What does BP do?

BP has oil wells in the main oil fields across the world both on land and at sea.

It turns oil into a variety of products ranging from petrol to plastics.

It sells petrol from stations around the world.

BP pumps oil from the ground, processes it and owns petrol stations to sell the products to the customer. It is an unusual business because it works in the **primary**, **secondary** and **tertiary** sectors.

Many businesses work in two sectors. A farm, for example, produces crops and can sell them from a farm shop. Thorntons makes sweets and sells them from its own shops on the high street.

1 BP's oil wells extract natural resources from the Earth. What other industries produce resources from the land?

2 BP's oil refineries turn one type of product into another. What other industries do this?

3 BP's petrol stations provide a service by selling products to the public. What other industries do this?

The sectors

IN THE KNOW

PRIMARY activity uses resources provided by nature. Businesses that are involved in primary activity change these resources into something more useful to customers.

- A farmer uses land to grow crops or keep animals to feed us.
- A quarry company digs stone for construction work.
- Mining businesses extract minerals from the earth for a wide range of activities.
- A fishing business catches fish for people to eat.

SECONDARY activity turns resources into products for other businesses and end customers. The process can be very simple, like turning wheat into flour, or very complex, like building computers. Many businesses make products that are bought by others to turn into end products. Cars and televisions are full of parts that have been bought in by the manufacturer. Whatever the process, it's all manufacturing.

TERTIARY activity involves providing a service for other businesses and end customers. It includes delivering bread to the shop, providing technical support for computer users and designing buildings. This sector has been growing in the UK and other developed economies.

The pie chart shows how much each sector produces as a percentage of the whole economy.

The pattern of UK industry

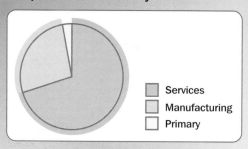

☐ Services
☐ Manufacturing
☐ Primary

What is produced?

All businesses sell products, a term which includes both tangible things and services. These products fall into a variety of categories according to how they are used and who uses them. BP, for example, produces petrol for domestic consumers and chemicals and plastics for industry so it falls into more than one category. Others, like Thorntons, produce one type of product for one market.

IN THE KNOW

Classify the products

SINGLE USE GOODS are products that can only be used once. Thorntons' sweets and BP's petrol are both in this category.

MULTIPLE USE GOODS can be used over a period of time. They include a wide range of products ranging from a magazine to a jar of pickle.

DURABLE CONSUMER GOODS have long lives. All the large items that people buy for their homes fall into this category. It includes cars, televisions and washing machines.

INVESTMENT GOODS are bought by businesses. They are all used to help the production process. Machinery and raw material are obviously included. There is also a wide range of products that are bought by both businesses and consumers but are used for different purposes. A car, bought by a family, is used to transport them about. If a car is bought by a business, it might be used by a member of the sales team to help sell the product. This is an investment good.

SERVICES are bought by both businesses and consumers. They do not involve a tangible product but are still very much in demand. Services include a very wide range of products including cleaning, hairdressing, travel services, accountancy and IT consultancy. Despite not having a physical entity, services still need inputs and a business adds value by putting them together effectively.

Critical thinking

Hotels, beer and more?

A very large company owns hotels – both exclusive and middle market – beer and spirits production and pubs. There is pressure to split the business into separate companies, which sell a narrower range of products.

On track

The railway industry is owned and run by different companies. Some run trains, others are responsible for installing and maintaining the track, signalling and systems for running trains.

1 Which sectors are these businesses working in?

2 What categories of products are they producing?

3 Think of reasons why a company might work across sectors in the hospitality business. Why might it decide to split up?

4 Give reasons why the railway industry should or should not work in this way. Put together a short report explaining your view on railway organisation.

5 Were any of your arguments common to both situations? If so, what were they?

Next steps

Primary	Secondary	Tertiary

1 Draw a table like this one. Add twelve rows.

2 Complete the table with six businesses from your local area and another six with famous names.

3 Are businesses in your local area mainly primary, secondary or tertiary? Make a list of reasons why you think this is so.

4 How does your local area compare with the pie chart showing the national pattern?

5 What sort of products are made by each of the businesses you have included?

KEY TERMS

Primary sector includes farming, fishing, mining and quarrying.

Secondary sector includes all manufacturing activity.

Tertiary sector includes all service industries.

Products include all the output of business including items that have a physical entity and services, which do not.

Services are products, such as shoe repairing, nursing, teaching, computer training and designing, which do not have a physical entity.

Sizing up the business

Specification Content

Typical measures of size: turnover, profit, employees

starSTUDY
Superstores

	Sainsbury's	Tesco
Number of stores	463	729
Number of employees	145,400	195,000
Total sales area	14.35 million sq. ft	18.8 million sq. ft
Turnover	£17,154 million	£20,025 million
Operating profit	£515 million	£1,213 million
Weekly sale per square foot	£17.54	£22.33
Capital employed	£4,909 million	£5,566 million
Market share	11.7%	16.8%

Source: Annual reports

1 If you measured Sainsbury's and Tesco by working out the average turnover per store, employee and square foot, how would they compare?

2 Compare the companies on the basis of operating profit per store, employee and square foot.

3 Capital employed shows how much money has been invested in the business. Work out how much profit each company makes for each pound that has been put into the business.

4 What share of the market does each company have? Why do you think that businesses often work hard to increase their market share?

5 Write a short paragraph explaining which business you think is (a) bigger and (b) more successful. Are there any other measures that you would like to include?

How big?

There is no single easy way to measure the size of a business. Profit is obviously key to any business but a small business can make big profits and large businesses may make small profits. It is always important to compare profits with other factors, such as the amount of money that has been invested in the business. To decide whether a business is large, the business needs to lead in several categories of the measures listed in the table. The group of indicators will vary according to the type of business.

Measures of size

Measure	Use and effectiveness
Number of stores/factories/offices	More useful for retail than other types of business. One large factory may be more profitable than a whole string of shops.
Number of people	Often used to measure businesses but can be misleading because some very large businesses are highly automated and use few people.
Capital employed – the amount of money invested in a business	A useful indicator for businesses which use plant and equipment. Not as effective for personal services as they need more people than equipment. Often used in combination with profit.
Market share	Businesses often push for a bigger market share but there may be high costs involved from promotion, setting up new stores etc. A business might also have a large share of a small market.
Turnover – the sales of a business	A big business usually has a large turnover but a small business that deals in high value products can as well. A business that sells a few Lamboughinis will have a much bigger turnover than one that sells the same number of Minis.
Unit cost – the cost of each item produced	A big business can often produce things more cheaply because it has economies of scale. It will depend on what is being produced. Unit costs of a packet of Polos will be different to a box of Ferrero Rocher. Comparisons must be made between similar products.
Share value	A business with many issued shares is generally large. The value of the shares does not reflect the size of the business. A small business can be successful so people want to buy the shares and the value rises. A big business can be a disaster so people sell shares and the value falls.
Corporate social responsibility	Businesses are increasingly aware of the impact they have on the community. It can be difficult to measure responsibility because it can be hard to evaluate the positive and negative impact of a business. Responsible behaviour can create benefits for both stakeholders and the business. This is often called a win-win situation.

GOOD BUSINESS

Business can be 'good' for all sorts of reasons. If it is good for shareholders it will be making lots of profit and paying high dividends. It can also be good for the community. If so, it will be demonstrating corporate social responsibility. Many businesses have realised that maintaining a good reputation contributes to being successful in the market place. Customers have been known to avoid companies when adverse publicity hits the news. A good reputation is hard to win and very easy to lose. Many large companies now devote a lot of attention to this aspect of the business. Business in the Community, an organisation of leading companies, has developed an index to measure corporate social responsibility. Many listings of businesses now include corporate social responsibility among the features that contribute to success.

Critical thinking

Measure	Burger chain 1	Burger chain 2	Burger chain 3
Number of restaurants	300	500	100
Employees	3,000	4,000	1,200
Turnover per year	£2 million	£6 million	£1 million
Operating profit	£150,000	£650,000	£100,000
Capital employed	£20 million	£30 million	£10 million

Which business do you think is biggest and/or most successful? Explain why.

WWW

www.bitc.org.uk will tell you more about corporate social responsibility and how businesses measure up.

Next steps

Look at the websites of two football clubs. Find as many measures of size and success as you can. Which indicators are most useful when comparing football clubs? Which football club is bigger? Which is more successful? Is there a difference? If so, explain why.

KEY TERMS

Turnover is the value of total sales to customers.

Operating profit is the profit remaining when operating costs and overheads have been deducted.

Capital employed is the long-term finance for the business.

Market share is the proportion of the market held by a business.

Economies of scale mean that costs can be lower for large-scale production than small-scale production.

Corporate social responsibility measures the way a business behaves towards the community.

Making it legal

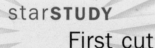

Specification Content

Legal structure:
sole trader, partnership,
private and public limited
companies

starSTUDY

First cut

Harriet Kessie always wanted to run her own hairdressing salon. After a lot of hard work, her dream came true when she opened Harriet Kessie Hairdressing in Edmonton, London.

The business is owned by Harriet and Joseph Cudjoe. Being a small business has its upsides and downsides. Despite all the hard work

it has taken to start her business, Harriet never looks back. 'Every time a door opens you forget the obstacles that have stood in your way.'

Her dreams haven't stopped there. She now plans to develop a high street chain – the first black hair salon with a national profile and training scheme. Harriet enjoys making things happen.

1 Why do you think Harriet and Joseph enjoy running their own business?

2 Why do you think it can be difficult to run a business on your own?

3 Use the information on these two pages to work out

   a what sort of legal structure Harriet and Joseph used when they first set up the business

   b what will change as the business grows

   c why she decided to change the legal structure?

Getting going

Harriet and Joseph run the business as a **partnership**. Many small businesses start as **sole traders** or partnerships because they are easy to set up. They are the most common form of business organisation, but the businesses are usually small and turnover is low. As Harriet's business grows, she will want to think about changing to another type of organisation that suits a bigger business.

IN THE KNOW

Sole traders and partnerships

Sole traders are businesses that are run by one person. The main drawback is that they have **unlimited liability** so, if the business fails, the owner risks losing everything he or she owns to pay off the debts. It does, however, give the owner a lot of freedom because he or she doesn't have to consult anyone.

THE UPSIDE

- The owner is in control
- Freedom to organise work
- Personal relationship with customers
- Fewer legal restrictions

THE DOWNSIDE

- Unlimited liability
- No-one to share decisions
- Only one set of skills

Most plumbers and electricians are sole traders. New businesses – from IT advisors to beauty therapists – also function in this way.

Partnerships are very similar to sole traders but involve more people. A group of people who trust each other make a legal agreement to work together. Trust is very important because all the partners are liable for the actions of the others. As a partnership has unlimited liability, each partner's possessions are at risk if one does something wrong.

A partnership can increase the range of skills in a business but it still remains difficult to raise finance for expansion.

Solicitors, doctors and other professional groups tend to work in partnerships. John Lewis is also a partnership, which is unusual for a large retailer.

Bigger business

As the business grows, Harriet will probably set up a **private limited company**, which means that a small group of shareholders can contribute to the finances and own their share of the company. Setting up a company will reduce Harriet's risk because if it were to go under, she would only lose the money that she has put into the business as she would have **limited liability**.

If her dreams come true and she has a shop on every high street, she may well decide to 'go public'. This means setting up a **public limited company** and selling shares which can then be traded on the Stock Exchange. They can then be bought by anyone and provide more capital for the business.

Private and public limited companies

A company has a legal identity of its own. This brings both rights and responsibilities. It can enter into agreements in its own right. It can be sued if it does wrong. To set up a company you have to register with Companies House and submit the Memorandum and Articles of Association and an annual return. These documents give all the details of what the business does, who is involved and how it will be organised.

The main drawback is loss of control. If people are putting money into your business, they will expect to have a say in what happens. A public company must send detailed accounts to Companies House and its shareholders. It must also hold an Annual General Meeting for shareholders so that everyone knows what is going on. The reporting requirements for a private company are less demanding.

	Private company – Ltd	Public company – Plc
Limited liability	Yes	Yes
Buying and selling shares	Must have permission of existing shareholders	Open to the public
Raising capital	Easier than sole trader	Easier than private company
Control	Tight – in hands of small group of shareholders	In hands of shareholders; may be takeover battles
Legal constraints	Yes	Yes
Value of shares	Stable	Fluctuates according to public view of value

Critical thinking

1 If a business is responsible for using other people's money, it has to be accountable. Explain how each type of legal structure is accountable to people who put their money into a business.

2 Why is accountability important?

Next steps

Find out about the legal structures of the following businesses. Explain each business and its structure.

1 The Virgin Group

2 Richer Sounds

3 Unilever

4 Dixons

5 Your local shop

6 A local builder

KEY TERMS

Sole traders run their own businesses. They have complete control but bear all the risk as they have unlimited liability.

Partnerships are groups of people who decide to run businesses together. They take joint control but have unlimited liability.

A **private limited company** belongs to a small group of shareholders who all have limited liability.

A **public limited company's** shares are traded on the Stock Exchange. All shareholders have limited liability.

Limited liability provides protection for people who own shares in a company. It means they can only lose the money they have put in. Sole traders and partners have unlimited liability.

What is finance for?

starSTUDY
Finance matters

Harriet knew just what she wanted to do. The plans for her hair salon were clear but she had one major problem to surmount. Getting the money together was a challenge.

Harriet had £10,000 in savings and managed to borrow £8,000 through the Business Link scheme, a government organisation that supports local businesses. Lloyds TSB lent her another £8,500, which meant she had enough to turn her ideas into reality.

1 What did Harriet have to pay for before she started her business?
2 What does Harriet have to pay for once the business is running?
3 Why do you think it can be difficult for new businesses to raise money?
4 Why was it easier to borrow money from Lloyds TSB once Business Link had agreed to help her?
5 Why might Harriet need finance for her business in future?

Finance for business

Running your own business gives lots of people a buzz of excitement but often the financial aspects cause sleepless nights. Learning to manage the money is often critical to the success of a new venture.

Harriet needed to raise money because she didn't have enough to get going on her own. She had to be able to pay to set up the salon and then run it. Any business is in the same boat.

Raising finance for a new business can be difficult because people who lend want to be convinced that they will get their money back. As a new business has no track record, lenders have to have confidence in the person and his or her plans. They have to see that the money is going to be put to good use.

Big businesses need to organise finance as well if they are going to develop or grow. Few businesses can afford to stand still or they will be overtaken by more dynamic competitors.

Why raise finance?

SETTING UP THE BUSINESS
To buy equipment and lease a shop, office or factory.

RUNNING THE BUSINESS ON A DAY-TO-DAY BASIS
To pay the bills for everything the business needs, from stock to employees. A shop will need heating and lighting. A business nearly always needs marketing if people are to know about it. The accountant has to be paid. Working capital is the term used to describe this aspect of a business's finances. A business should aim to cover these costs from revenue but when starting up or in difficult times, it may need to raise finance to pay the bills.

EXPANDING
To cover the costs of setting up a new shop or office. Expansion often means increasing the working capital as well. A bigger business will be buying and spending more. It may also mean taking over another business so finance will be needed to buy out the owners.

DEVELOPING
To create new product lines or move into a new market. Getting new products right takes time and money. A business that decides to export its products for the first time will have to explore the market where it plans to sell.

EMERGENCIES
To protect the business in difficult times. Sales might fall if there are economic problems. A new product line might not have sold as much as expected. Bad debts might be mounting.

The business plan

A business that wants to raise money from other people must show them what the business is planning to do, how the money will be spent and the revenue that is expected.

A business plan incorporates all this information. It will contain sections on all the relevant functions from production and human resources to marketing and finance. It needs to be realistic because bank managers are good at spotting when things don't add up.

All businesses need to plan if they are going to achieve their objectives. The planning process will also help people to set objectives. If the economy is booming, a business might set different objectives. If customers' tastes are changing, plans will change.

go to → *Go to pages 26–29 to find out more about objectives.*

Finding finance

Harriet found some of the funds she required from her own resources but she had to look outside the business for the rest. Most businesses work in this way. Once up and running, a business aims to make a profit and some of this can be used to fund developments or help out if things get difficult. Finance from inside the business is known as internal finance. If it is from other people or organisations, it is external finance.

There is a range of sources for both types of finance. A business needs to choose carefully depending on the circumstances.

go to → *Find out more on pages 4–18.*

Next steps

Look at some newspapers or search the Internet for stories about businesses that are expanding. What do you think they will need finance for as they develop?

Internal finance

IN THE KNOW

RETAINED PROFIT

If a business wants to develop it often ploughs back part of its profit. It is a secure way of growing because the business is not borrowing, and is therefore not dependent on anyone else.

SALES OF ASSETS

A business might sell assets that it no longer uses to raise money.

It might also decide to focus on one aspect of its business – as Sainsbury's did when it sold Homebase to raise finance to develop the supermarket chain.

WORKING CAPITAL

A business that is in need of cash may cut its stocks or give customers less time to pay. It will then have more money to use for other things.

KEY TERMS

Working capital is used to carry out the day-to-day running of a business. It pays for the process of turning stock into products, despatching them to customers and waiting for customers to pay.raise finances.

External finance comes from sources outside the business.

Internal finance comes from within the business.

Business plans are made by new and existing businesses to help them achieve objectives and raise finances.

Classification of business

Where does the money come from?

Specification Content

Sources of finance — external

starSTUDY
Harriet Kessie Hairdressing 2015

Harriet's business flourished. She had obviously found a gap in the market. As the years went by, she opened more and more salons across the country. Soon after opening her first shop, Harriet set up a private limited company. As the business grew Harriet Kessie Hairdressing became a public company.

1 What does Harriet have to pay for as she opens each shop?
2 What advantages are there in becoming
  a a private company
  b a public company?
3 Harriet had to raise a lot of money to develop a high street chain. Use the information on internal and external sources of finance to work out where it might come from. Explain why.
4 Draw up a table of the different sources of finance with a column to show how Harriet could use each type.

Raising finance

Any business wanting to raise finance must select the right type for the purpose. If Harriet wants to refurbish a shop, she will have to decide whether to use retained profit or borrow money to pay for it. She will need to ask some questions before making up her mind.

- How long is the finance required for?
- How much is needed?
- What will it cost?
- Will it affect control of the business?
- What is the current financial state of the business?
- Will the use of finance add to revenue?

KEY TERMS

Leasing is renting a resource needed by the business. The resource can be bought, if desired, at the end of the lease.

Hire purchase is a type of medium-term credit to buy by instalments after paying a deposit.

Debentures are long-term loans from investors.

18

Sources of finance – external

The type of external finance a business chooses to use depends on how long it wants the money for and what it wants to do.

Short term

Bank overdrafts	Trade credit	Debt factoring
A bank allows a business to spend more than is in its account. It is a cheap way of borrowing because you only pay for the amount borrowed on any day. The limit must always be agreed and it can be risky because a bank can 'call in' the debt if it is worried that it might not get the money back. This often results in the business going under.	*A business can increase the amount of cash it holds by delaying payment of bills. This often has a cost because early payment often means a discount.*	*Most businesses trade on credit so customers have time to pay. If cash is needed more quickly, the debts can be sold to a debt factor. This is another business, which buys the debt at a discount and waits for payment to be made by the original customer.*

Medium term

Leasing or hire purchase	Medium-term bank loans
Many businesses lease equipment because it avoids tying up cash which they can use for other things. It often comes with a service agreement so they know it will be looked after. There is usually the option to buy at the end of the contract but as technology changes so fast, many firms just replace an old model with a new one. Hire purchase has the same effect but extends payments over a period of time. At the end of the contract the item of equipment belongs to the business.	*Businesses borrow from the bank for a fixed time at an interest rate that may be fixed or flexible. It is more expensive than an overdraft because the loan is for a fixed amount of money.*

Long term

Long-term bank loans	Debentures	Selling shares
Long-term borrowing works in the same way as medium-term borrowing. Banks may be unwilling to lend to small or new businesses unless they feel quite sure that they will get their money back. Business Link, the government agency which helps small and medium-sized businesses, can help to organise guarantees which make it easier for businesses to borrow.	*Debentures are loans made to companies. They are for a fixed period and some can be sold to other investors during that time.*	*All companies sell shares when the business starts. Owning a share means ownership of part of the company. If a business wants to raise further funds, it can issue more shares. A private company will sell shares to people after the agreement of existing shareholders. A public company will sell them to anyone and they will be traded on the Stock Exchange. The Alternative Investment Market deals in the shares of smaller companies. It is part of the Stock Exchange but has less stringent rules.*

Selling shares versus borrowing

Many businesses use a mix of debt and equity, or shares, to fund activities. It can be hard to decide which to use and will depend on whether the owners want to give up some control and whether a business can borrow enough to carry out its plans.

	Advantages	Disadvantages
Sell shares	*You don't have to pay it back*	*Shareholders own part of the company, have a vote and expect a return on their investment*
Borrow	*Ownership of the business doesn't change*	*Interest has to be paid on the debt*

Critical thinking

1 Draw up a table showing the sources of finance that are available to sole traders and partnerships, private limited companies and public limited companies.

2 If a business wants a photocopier, what finance would you suggest it used?

3 What about
  a opening a new shop?   b designing a new product?
  c building a new factory?   d starting to export a company's products?

Public and private ownership

starSTUDY

Working together

Mansfield's town centre was pretty run down and people were going elsewhere to do their shopping. Businesses were closing down and moving out. Something had to be done. The local council, the owners of the 4 Seasons Shopping Centre, Boots, the local college, the police, the market traders and the Chamber of Trade all got together to make a difference.

The local council set about regenerating the town centre. It was pedestrianised and attractive lights, seats and rubbish bins were installed. The whole environment was enhanced. The people of Mansfield returned to do their shopping so new businesses started to move back in.

Why did Nottingham Building Society decide to sponsor the painting of street furniture and installation of litter bins?

1 Which partners in the scheme are public and which are private?
2 List the objectives of each partner.
3 Why does an improved environment help business?
4 How do you think each partner benefits from the regeneration scheme?
5 What are the advantages of the public and private sectors working together?

Public or private?

In Mansfield the public and private sectors have been working together. The organisations have different objectives but gain benefits from their common purpose in the town centre. The objectives of the public sector depend on the party that has been elected to power in national or local elections. The private sector generally aims to make a profit.

The private and public sectors

The **private sector** makes up about half of our economy. It is mostly made up of organisations that aim to make a profit for their owners. It includes all sole traders, partnerships, private and public companies. Charities are also part of the private sector. Their 'profit' or surplus is used for charitable purposes.

The **public sector** makes up the other half of the economy. It is owned or run by the government and local councils. They provide social services, fire and police, education, defence, law, police and transport. A key objective for the public sector is to satisfy the people and businesses that pay taxes to keep them going. If people do not approve of what is

happening, they can change things by voting at the next election.

These services are often provided because the private sector would not supply customers at a price that everyone could afford. Some of the services, like the police and armed forces, would be difficult for the private sector to provide. As businesses generally want to make a profit, social services are unlikely to be provided by the private sector. Schools and hospitals are to be found in the private sectors but the prices charged are often beyond the means of many people.

Remember – don't confuse public limited companies with the public sector.

Royal Mail plc

Royal Mail Group plc

Royal Mail is run by the government but it is a public limited company. It is completely owned by the government, its only shareholder.

Royal Mail provides an essential public service on which local residents, businesses, government and public services all depend. Despite the introduction of e-mail and other electronic messaging, 82 million items are delivered every day – a figure that continues to grow.

It has a legal duty to provide a letter delivery service to every one of the 27 million addresses in the United Kingdom at a uniform price, irrespective of the distance travelled. It must also make at least one collection every day from postboxes.

Post Office®

Ninety-four per cent of people in the UK live within a mile of a Post Office® branch. Twenty-eight million people visit a Post Office® branch every week to use one of the 170 different products and services available. These include financial products, travel services, government information and retail products.

Post Office Ltd owns around 500 Post Office® branches. The others are owned by the people who run them, including franchisees and subpostmasters and mistresses.

Postcomm

Postcomm is a watchdog. Its primary responsibility is to maintain the provision of a universal postal service at a uniform tariff. It has set tough standards of service and monitors them closely. In addition, Postcomm has licensed other companies to compete with Royal Mail.

POSTCOMM

1. Why does the government insist that Royal Mail delivers to every address in the country at a uniform charge?
2. Why would the private sector be unwilling to do this?
3. Who are Royal Mail's competitors?
4. Are there any private sector activities within the Post Office?
5. Why do you think the government thought it necessary to set up Postcomm?

Critical thinking

- I work for Virgin Mobile customer care in the Trowbridge call centre.
- I design shop layouts for Carphone Warehouse.
- I'm a nurse in a private hospital.
- I sell mobile phones for Carphone Warehouse.
- I'm an electrician and help refit shops.
- I'm a postman.
- I'm a geologist with Shell.
- I work in health care in the community.
- I'm a teacher in a comprehensive school in London.
- I work behind the bar in the local pub.
- I work for Wiltshire Council collecting business rates.
- I work behind the bar in the House of Commons.

1. Are these jobs in the private or public sector?
2. How does each person add value to the organisation?
3. Explain why each activity is in the public or private sector. Could the job exist in the other sector? Give an example.

KEY TERMS

Private sector includes all organisations that are owned by individuals or groups. The main objective is to make a profit.

Public sector includes activities undertaken by local and national government.

Magic in Paris

Disneyland Resort Paris opened for business in 1992, five years after reaching an agreement with the Paris authorities to go ahead with the development. The authorities had promised to improve the infrastructure. The area to the east of Paris was largely undeveloped. The resort alone covers an area of 20 sq. km and is about one-fifth the size of Paris.

In 1992 it reached its target of 11 million customers but the business made a loss. The customers simply did not spend enough. The costs were also higher than budgeted. Labour was planned to be 13% of total costs, but in 1992 it reached 24% and in 1993 rose to 40%. The French labour laws made it difficult to employ staff on a part-time, temporary basis so too many staff had to be employed in winter when there were fewer customers. With more money going out in costs than coming in from customers the company found it difficult to pay back the bank loans. Something needed to be done.

The rescue package included reducing costs – this meant cutting the number of administrative staff and coming to new working time arrangements with the six different trade unions that represented the employees. More flexibility came at the cost of a reduction in working hours.

The company also raised money by issuing more shares. Not all budgets were reduced. Customer research and experience of other resorts suggested ways the company could increase added value. Decisions were made to invest in developing new attractions such as Space Mountain and Honey I Shrunk the Kids. Further expenditure in the Fastpass system helped reduce waiting times at the most popular attractions. A recent investment has been the opening of Walt Disney Studios in 2002 making the resort a more desirable 2–3 day short break. Better marketing has helped to increase occupancy levels in hotels.

The story has come good for the company. Its income rose to over €1 billion a year and the company now makes a good profit. Some of this goes out in dividends to shareholders of Euro Disney SCA. This is the company which runs Disneyland Resort Paris. It is the equivalent to a UK public limited company. Some of the profit is kept back to invest in the company.

Some 12,000 well-trained employees are required to look after the 13 million visitors a year. These visitors need food, drink and accommodation and many will buy merchandise made all over the world.

It has also been good news for the community. The public sector authorities kept their side of the bargain and built road and rail links to Paris. The new community has new housing, shops and schools and colleges offering the latest training. France Telecom has invested heavily to improve telecommunications. Hotels outside the Disney complex serve the resort. Some 25,000 jobs have been indirectly created.

Some big-name famous brands have become Euro Disney preferred suppliers. These include Nescafé, McDonald's and Coca-Cola. Other businesses in the local area, big and small, have also benefited from the success of Euro Disney.

Year	1994	1995	1996	1997	1998	1999	2000	2001	2002
Turnover in € million	632	697	757	835	897	920	959	1005	1076
Net operating profit in € million	6	71	110	134	176	166	175	185	176
Net operating margin %	1	10	15	16	20	18	18	18	16

Source: Disneyland® Resort Paris.

The Resort

Two theme parks, 7 hotels, 2 conference centres, 61 restaurants, 52 shops, more than 50 rides and shows...

Source Disneyland® Resort Paris website

The Workforce

'Every day, men and women of all nationalities from all walks of life use their skills to work magic. Disneyland® Resort Paris offers a whole range of skills, contracts and working hours which are very different.'

The company agreement on the 35-hour working week with no reduction in salary went into effect in 1999. Between June 1999 and June 2000, it led to the creation of 608 new jobs at Disneyland Resort Paris.

Hotel Occupancy

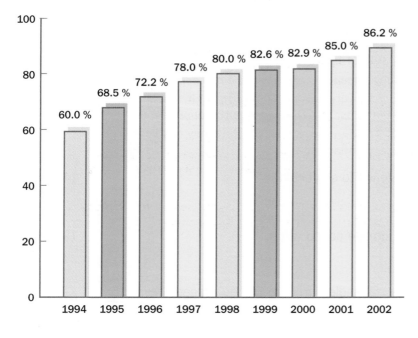

Share ownership

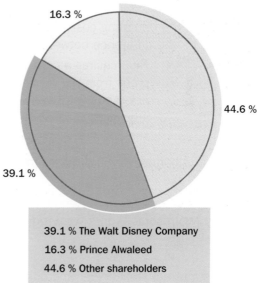

39.1 % The Walt Disney Company
16.3 % Prince Alwaleed
44.6 % Other shareholders

testing–testing

The nature of business – assessment questions

(Note the business trades under Euro Disney, but its brand is Disney Resort Paris)

1 What is a stakeholder? Identify examples of stakeholders from the evidence. **(4 marks)**

 A straightforward opening question. You should provide a clear definition and apply this to the case study. Try to avoid lists.

2 State why would the banks be interested in the performance of Euro Disney? **(2 marks)**

 This requires a straightforward application, but you should try to think of the key term or concept required, which is the stakeholder.

3 Discuss the effects of the rescue package on stakeholders. **(14 marks)**

 This requires you to identify the most appropriate stakeholders and then comment on how they are affected. The two most obvious stakeholders are the banks and the employees who are represented by the unions. However, there will also be effects on shareholders and customers. A good answer may look at the effects both in the short run and the long run and look for supporting evidence from the case study.

4 Explain the term 'added value'. In what ways is Euro Disney attempting to add value in looking after its customers? **(4 marks)**

 A straightforward question. You should provide a clear definition and apply this to the case study. Try to avoid lists.

5 What were the operating costs for the company in 1994 and in 2002? What might account for the difference between these two sets of figures? **(8 marks)**

 This requires a calculation. You will need to take away the net operating profit from the turnover in order to work out the costs. Secondly you are asked to identify why costs might rise. Use the evidence to support your argument, but also think about things you know about that may not be in the evidence, such as the effect of inflation.

6 Why is it important for Euro Disney to pay dividends to shareholders? **(4 marks)**

 (Go to page 8)

7 Identify two resources that were required to increase added value. **(2 marks)**

 (Go to page 6)

8 For one internal stakeholder and one external stakeholder to Euro Disney suggest why it is important to look after their interest. **(6 marks)**

This is not dissimilar to question 2 except you have to choose the stakeholder.

9 To what extent do you think Euro Disney has kept its stakeholders happy? **(14 marks)**

'To what extent' requires an answer looking at a balanced view taking account of both the positive and negative views and then coming to a judgement. You don't need to complete this for all stakeholder groups. A good candidate will provide a link between the stakeholders.

testing–testing

(Note the business trades under Euro Disney, but its brand is Disney Resort Paris)

1 Disney Resort Paris operates in the tertiary sector. Identify the other two sectors of economic activity and provide an example of each that would support the Disney resort. **(4 marks)**

> A straightforward question.

2 State why type of legal structure is Disney Resort Paris?
What responsibilities does this legal structure place on the owners? **(5 marks)**

> (Go to page 15).

3 Evaluate the suitability of this type of legal structure for Euro Disney. **(14 marks)**

> Any evaluation question requires you to give the argument for and against and then suggest which you believe outweighs the other.

4 In what ways has the development of Euro Disney supported small businesses in the area? **(4 marks)**

> A straightforward question. You should provide a clear definition and apply this to the case study. Try to avoid lists.

5 There are many measures that can be used to identify the size of this business.
Suggest two measures most suited to Euro Disney and one least suited.
Give reasons for your choices. **(9 marks)**

> You may need to brainstorm ways of measuring size. Part of this question is about application so you will need to use the evidence to indicate you understand the measures. By selecting measures most appropriate and inappropriate the question is testing your ability to analyse the information you have used. By making a recommendation you are evaluating.

6 Using turnover to measure the size of the company calculate how much the company has grown by between 1994 and 2002. **(4 marks)**

> It is best to put the formula in, as you may earn some marks even if your calculation is wrong. In this case you should divide the change in turnover by the initial turnover and multiply by 100 to get a percentage.

7 What do you understand by the term 'profit'? In which year was the largest operating profit made? **(3 marks)**

> The first part is asking you for simple definitions and the second part is testing your ability to see the link between the two sectors.

8 Analyse four different reasons why Euro Disney needs to raise finance and provide examples of how this may be raised. **(8 marks)**

> The reasons should be separate categories and not just examples of the same category. The context is merely a way of getting you to apply those categories to the evidence. Make sure the finance is appropriate to the short-term, medium-term and long-term loans.

9 What is the difference between the public sector and private sector? In what ways has the public sector contributed to the success of Euro Disney and the region? **(6 marks)**

> The first part is asking you for simple definitions and the second part is testing your ability to see the link between the two sectors.

Important objectives

Specification Content

Corporate objectives; the central nature and role of objectives; different types of objectives and their changing nature; risk, reward and ownership

Helping customers at Carphone Warehouse

starSTUDY

Carphone Warehouse: Aims to Objectives

Our aims:
'We firmly believe that by remaining wholly focused on the customer, while also deepening our relationships with network operators, we will deliver superior returns to shareholders.'

Our objectives:
- To continue to expand our retail presence and gain further market share in our key markets
- To expand our Telecoms Service business through growth of our UK and French operations and the identification of similar opportunities in other countries where we have a significant retail presence
- To develop compelling residential fixed line and corporate mobile offerings for the UK market through integration with Opal Telecom

How?
- If we don't look after the customer, someone else will.
- Nothing is gained by winning an argument but losing a customer.
- Always deliver what we promise. If in doubt, under promise and over deliver.
- Always treat customers as we ourselves would like to be treated.
- The reputation of the whole company is in the hands of each individual.

Source: Carphone Warehouse website

1. What is the focus of Carphone Warehouse's aims?
2. How does the company translate its aims into objectives?
3. How is the business aim put into practice?
4. Why is its commitment to customer service likely to be the way to achieve its aims?
5. How is the business's relationship with its staff likely to influence its success?

Aims → Objectives → Actions

A business usually has to have a clear idea of where it is going if it is to be successful. Carphone Warehouse has been at the forefront of the mobile phone business from the early days. Charles Dunstone, its founder, realised that the mobile phone had great potential for ordinary people at a time when phones were just for big business and the rich. He could, for example, help builders or plumbers stay in touch with their customers. He knew that if this market was to grow, there had to be clear, accessible information and helpful staff who wanted to ensure that each customer got the phone and contract which suited them best. All this took planning. This philosophy has underpinned everything since. It has led to profits and rapid growth.

go to
Find out more about planning on on page 17.

Setting objectives

Businesses have one or more of three broad **objectives**.

- **PROFIT** Without profit, a business won't survive in the long run. The owners of a business need reward for taking a risk. It also provides resources for running and developing the business.

- **GROWTH** Many businesses are in search of growth. It is difficult to stand still because markets change, so most businesses aim to grow. Some small businesses are looking for a quiet life and are content to stay as they are.

- **SURVIVAL** The vast majority of businesses want to survive. It only becomes an objective when they are under threat.

The objectives are turned into a **strategy**, which sets out how the business will achieve its aims and objectives.

The diagram shows the decision-making process. As things rarely stand still, a business is constantly going through the cycle of asking questions about what it is doing in order to achieve its objectives. This may mean changing the strategy if objectives are not being achieved. Communication plays a big part in any business. Ensuring that the staff are onside and understand the objectives and strategy is an essential part of running a successful business. All businesses must plan objectives and strategy carefully so they deliver the aims which have been set.

MAKING DECISIONS

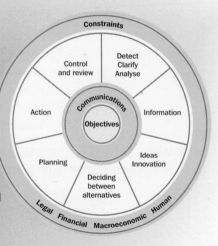

Profit, in simple terms, means that revenue is greater than expenditure. In Business Studies, it is important to distinguish different sorts of profit because any confusion may mean that the wrong decisions are made.

The right sort of profit

GROSS PROFIT is the profit from selling products before any costs of running the business are taken into account.

NET PROFIT is the profit from selling products after the costs of running the business have been taken into account. It can be shown before or after interest and tax.

DISPOSABLE PROFIT is the money that is left to distribute to owners. Sole traders and partners take drawings and shareholders receive dividends.

RETAINED PROFIT is kept by the business to provide funds for development.

Wider objectives

Many businesses now consider a sense of responsibility to the community to be critical to success. Customers tend to expect a high standard from businesses and will reject the products of those that behave badly. Social responsibility and profit can be hard to separate so some consider this to be part of the objective of making a profit.

go to → Find out more on page 80.

WWW

www.carphonewarehouse.co.uk

www.tesco.co.uk

www.sainsburys.co.uk

Charities aim to make a surplus rather than a profit. The surplus is then used to further the activities of the charity. Public sector organisations are expected to break even. They can spend within the limits of the money they receive from the government and any revenue from activities.

Critical thinking

1 Some supermarkets are more successful than others. Compare two that you know and work out what their objectives are. Do you think they are achieving them? Is one more successful than the other? Why?

2 You can find out more about the companies from their websites. Their objectives are often set out in the front section of the Annual Report and Accounts. Have a look.

Next steps

1 What are the objectives of your school or college?

2 How are they put into practice?

3 Do you think they are effective?

KEY TERMS

Objectives are targets which can be measured and therefore help to drive activities.

Strategy shows how objectives will be met.

Objectives in practice

starSTUDY
Carphone Warehouse's strategy circle

REPLACEMENT
Fashion, wear and tear and new technology all lead to phone replacement. The company anticipates that this will continue and develops its staff to support changing technology.

REPAIRS
The company repairs nearly 1 million phones each year. Almost half of these have been bought from other suppliers. Providing an excellent service attracts customers to come back for their next phone.

CONTENT
Developing technology means that customers are in search of content for their phones. The company aims to meet this demand.

ACCESSORIES
Accessories add to the customers' spending especially as new technology has increased the value of individual items. As phones become more sophisticated customers return to customise their phones.

DISTRIBUTION
More, high quality stores in prime locations. Develop web sales and telephone sales across Europe.

RANGE
Maintain wide range at good price. Size of the business gives strong buying power so customers have wide choice and latest phones.

INSURANCE
Maintain quick, efficient service for customers. 90% of claims are honoured so customers return. It adds value to customers and a steady profit stream.

SERVICES
Income stream comes from managing customers for networks and therefore protects the business from the volatile handsets market. It keeps the company in touch with the customer when contracts come to an end so gives access to the replacement market.

Circle diagram:
1. distribution
2. range
3. insurance
4. services
5. accessories
6. content
7. repairs
8. replacement
...for a better mobile life. all round

1 How does each of these elements of the strategy contribute to the company's profits?

2 How do they help the company to grow?

3 What do you think the company should do to make sure that the strategy works?

4 How will the company be able to measure whether it is being successful?

Strategy and success

Most businesses that are in search of success have worked out their strategy. Sometimes success just happens – but not often. It may be a chance event or a change of fashion but without a strategy, it is likely to be short lived. Barbour, a maker of country wear, suddenly became cool but quickly faded from the fashion scene. Burberry followed soon after.

Carphone Warehouse has developed a strategy. It wants to gain market share in the mobile phone market and expand its services both in the UK and elsewhere. Its strategy circle aims to do both.

It is based on attracting and keeping customers and therefore investment in employees is critical to its success.

Well-trained, motivated employees are much more likely to persuade customers to return. Knowing how a strategy will be turned into reality is very important.

The **culture** of the business will affect people's willingness to implement a strategy. Carphone Warehouse wants employees to have fun. It even runs to monthly sessions at the local bar or pub!

From objectives to strategy

A business decides on its objectives and develops a strategy. To make things happen, the departments within the business must plan their contributions and make sure that they all fit together.

Meetings will be held to decide what must happen if the objectives are to be achieved. This may involve:

- research and development to update a product

- packaging design

- market research to test it in the market

- checking that the figures add up

- organising production

- an advertising campaign

- organising distribution.

The marketing department will have made set objectives for the product. They will include the target market, pricing policy and expected sales. The plan will be detailed – even setting targets for sales staff. A business that is product oriented rather than market oriented will produce the product they want to sell rather than looking at what the market wants.

This can be a recipe for disaster, as the products may not sell.

STAYING ON TRACK

It is important that everyone is kept informed. People don't like being kept in the dark and it affects motivation. Communication within the business must be built into the strategy.

Monitoring at every stage must take place if deadlines are to be met and quality is to be maintained. If some products don't reach the market at the right moment, the expected profit will turn into a loss. Who wants Christmas trees in January?

Any strategy needs to be flexible. If the source of raw materials fails, another will have to be found. A plan that relies on distribution by train may have to change if the rail network is disrupted.

The process needs to be under continuous review and future plans will be amended in light of the lessons that have been learnt.

A positive culture

Culture will vary from one business to another. There is not one perfect solution. The attitude of employees will be affected both by the nature of the work and the working environment, but the way people are treated can have the greatest impact.

Changing the culture of an organisation can be difficult. It often underpins everything that goes on. Without a positive culture, strategies are unlikely to succeed because employees are unlikely to persevere when things get difficult. Good leadership and careful management of people are most effective. There are many strategies for motivating people in different circumstances. Find out more on page .

Developing a culture

Critical thinking

Your current objective is to get good grades in your AS studies.

1 Work out your strategy for doing this.

2 Are there any factors that might mean you need to change the strategy?

3 What will the impact be?

4 What sort of culture keeps you working effectively?

Next steps

1 You often talk to people who work in businesses. It may be on a helpline or in person. Try to work out the culture of their organisation. You can often tell from their approach, friendliness, willingness and knowledge to solve your problem. Give them marks out of ten.

2 What persuades you to go back to a business?

KEY TERMS

The culture of a business covers the attitudes, customs and expectations of staff. It affects how they carry out their roles.

A product-oriented business focuses on the product rather than the customer.

A market-oriented business aims to make the product match what the customer wants.

Analysing business

Specification Content

Methods of business analysis; SWOT and its use in diagnosis; how objectives influence corporate behaviour

star**STUDY**

Pizza revival

Pizza Express was the UK's first chain of pizza restaurants. For many years it had a great reputation for producing high quality pizzas, just like the Italians make. Suddenly it found itself in difficulties and needed to work out what to do next.

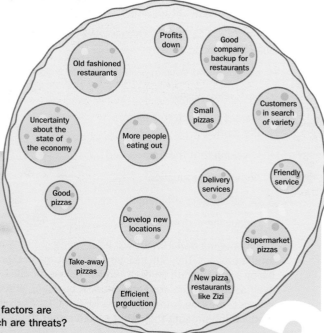

Profits down · Good company backup for restaurants · Old fashioned restaurants · Uncertainty about the state of the economy · Small pizzas · Customers in search of variety · More people eating out · Delivery services · Friendly service · Good pizzas · Develop new locations · Supermarket pizzas · Take-away pizzas · Efficient production · New pizza restaurants like Zizi

1 Divide the factors into those which come from inside the business and those which come from outside.

2 Which of the 'inside' factors are strengths and which are weaknesses?

3 Which of the 'outside' factors are opportunities and which are threats?

4 Can you think of any more factors to add to each of these categories?

5 What do you think Pizza Express's objectives might be?

6 How does this analysis of a business help it to meet its objectives?

What's going on?

If business objectives are to be achieved, reviewed and updated, there must be a continuous analysis of how things are going. The analysis of Pizza Express shows how a business might go about the process. SWOT analysis looks at the strengths, weaknesses, opportunities and threats that a business has to deal with, or make the most of, if it is to thrive.

The big picture

A formal SWOT analysis is a major task. The analysis of the world beyond the business can be challenging because businesses only give out the information that the law requires in order to keep their competitive advantage. For many businesses, it involves keeping a constant eye on events.

The SWOT analysis should take account of the views of all the stakeholders both inside and outside the business. They may appear in any box because they can be strengths, weaknesses, opportunities or threats. Whatever their contribution to the picture, a business must decide the significance of their role in order to give weight to views. This is the case for any statement in any of the four boxes. Some are more powerful than others and will therefore have a greater effect on the future of the business.

KEY TERMS

SWOT analysis is used to sum up the internal and external factors that affect a business. Strengths and weaknesses are internal. Threats and opportunities are external. It can be used for departments within the business or for the business as a whole. It is the basis for developing or reviewing strategy.

go to →

Find out more about the factors that affect a business on page 69.

SWOT

SWOT analysis is a way of analysing a business's situation from both inside and outside the business. 'Strengths' and 'weaknesses' are about the internal environment of the business. 'Opportunities' and 'threats' concern the external environment.

It is a formula that is often used in the marketing department to decide on a marketing strategy, but it is also used throughout the business to help make decisions about future plans. The chart shows the internal and external factors that should be considered.

Internal factors	External factors
The company's reputation: do people come back for more?	*The economy: are people likely to spend more or less?*
The product: does it match customers' needs?	*Competition: are competitors proving to be a threat?*
The business: is it producing the products efficiently?	*The market: are there any gaps?*
The future: are there new products in the pipeline?	*New developments: can technology help?*
	People: is the changing population opening new opportunities or proving to be a threat?

USING SWOT

When a business is developing or reviewing its strategy, SWOT is a key part of the decision making. It can be carried out in each department of the business as well as for the business as a whole.

The process of working out what is going on internally and externally to the business focuses the attention on the future. It is very easy for businesses to concentrate on the task in hand rather than working out what happens next.

The results are often set out in diagrammatic form. By bringing the information together in this form, it is easier to see the contrasts and similarities within the different boxes.

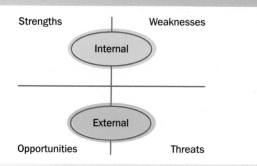

In a large business, SWOT is generally carried out formally as part of strategic development. In a small business it can be carried out without people being aware of the formal process. Just watching what is going on inside and beyond the business means that the person in charge is keeping a finger on the pulse. A competitor may be using a different marketing strategy or a new production technique which has become available that reduces costs and increases quality.

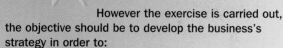

However the exercise is carried out, the objective should be to develop the business's strategy in order to:

- add value more effectively
- develop competitive advantage.

Competitive advantage is a feature that puts a business ahead of its competitors. It may be based on reputation, innovation or the relationship with customers and suppliers.

Critical thinking

1 Why is it important for a business to understand its internal and external position?

2 Carry out a SWOT analysis on your school or college.

3 Carry out a SWOT analysis on Carphone Warehouse or another business that you know.

4 What do you think they should do next?

Next steps

1 Ask someone you know who runs a business, or works in one, to identify its strengths, weaknesses, opportunities and threats.

2 Ask what changes they might make in the light of this information.

Who influences strategy?

Specification Content
How stakeholder objectives, including government macroeconomic objectives, affect the behaviour and decisions of the firm

starSTUDY Pizza Express

A Pizza Express restaurant

1 Who are Pizza Express's stakeholders?

2 What effect can each stakeholder have on the business?

3 What should Pizza Express do to keep its stakeholders happy?

4 How can government actions affect the business?

5 Why is it important to think ahead about changes that might be taking place in future?

Strategic influences

Pizza Express must keep a close eye on its stakeholders when it develops a strategy for the future. If it doesn't take their objectives into account, they may be dissatisfied with any changes and this may damage the business.

All businesses should be watching the objectives of stakeholders if they are to make successful progress. Government policy should also be taken into account because it will probably affect customers' spending powers either positively or negatively.

Critical thinking

1 Work out what gives each stakeholder power.

2 Think of two examples for each stakeholder – one showing a weak position and another showing a powerful position.

KEY TERMS

Pressure groups are groups of people with common interests who try to persuade business, government and others to take their views into account.

Stakeholder objectives and strategy

IN THE KNOW

OWNERS

The objectives of owners depend on the type of ownership. Sole traders, partners and people who run small private companies are looking for a return for their efforts and the risks involved. They may also be looking for growth and security. Strategy will obviously reflect the objectives of the people who run the business as they are the owners.

In larger private companies and public companies owners often do not run the business on a day-to-day basis. They risk their money through buying shares. These shareholders are mainly looking for a return on their investment. Without a good return, they will quickly sell their shares and buy ones in a different company that provides a better reward. Providing a reward for shareholders must therefore be part of the strategy.

CUSTOMERS

Customers buy things from businesses that meet their needs. Businesses want to keep existing customers and attract new ones so they have to take customers' objectives into account. A bad experience drives customers away – if there is an alternative. Many of the products we buy need aftercare and this has to be part of the strategy, although many businesses don't seem very good at it.

Customers can have considerable power, especially when they join together. The Consumers' Association is a **pressure group** that influences the activities of businesses and government. There are laws that determine how businesses behave towards customers.

go to Find out more on page 68.

A business's strategy may incorporate a range of actions which are designed to attract and keep customers in order to achieve other objectives. It might mean opening more stores, setting up an online service or making its customer service work more efficiently.

EMPLOYEES

People often have a variety of objectives when working. Everyone wants to be paid well but other factors are important too. Job satisfaction, training and opportunities are often on the list. An employee who feels well looked after is usually more effective than someone who feels that the employer doesn't really care.

go to Find out about motivating people on pages 164–168.

If a business wants to make the most of its staff, it must know how to motivate them and build this into the strategy. It must also make sure that its actions are within the law.

go to Find out more about employees and the law on page 66.

SUPPLIERS

Suppliers, like any other business, want to make a profit. They are dependent on the businesses, which are their customers, to pay on time. These customers are dependent on them to send supplies as requested. If there are only a few reliable suppliers, they will be in a more powerful situation. If there are many – or they are dealing with very powerful businesses – they will have less power.

Some businesses build a supplier relationship into their strategy. If a supplier feels that there is a close working relationship, he or she are more likely to work hard to send products quickly in a crisis, for example.

LENDERS AND CREDITORS

Businesses often depend on borrowing to keep going. It is therefore wise to make sure that lenders and creditors are considered in the strategy. Becoming a bad risk makes it harder and more expensive to borrow money in future. Creditors will want rapid settlement and won't give any leeway on payment time.

A lender or creditor can close down a business when no payments are received. This may not be the best way of dealing with the situation because the money may never be paid once the business ceases trading. It is often worth trying to negotiate an agreement, but in the end it may be impossible.

THE COMMUNITY

The community often has strong views when businesses want to make changes. A new factory may add to noise and traffic nuisance but on the other hand may provide more jobs. The development of an airport is almost always subject to heavy pressure from the community because of its impact on the community around it.

Many businesses work with the local community to produce schemes which reduce the impact on the neighbours. They also devise inducements to compensate. This might take the form of a new school or leisure centre incorporated into a development scheme.

go to Find out more on page 8.

THE GOVERNMENT

The government always has objectives for the economy. These can affect businesses in all sorts of ways. Higher taxes mean people have less to spend and reduce a company's profits. Reducing unemployment may mean setting up schemes to help businesses train people. The government has organisations that aim to help businesses develop and make the most of government support.

A business needs to be aware of government objectives and strategy if it is to plan effectively. Changes in interest rates and taxes, including national insurance, can have a big effect on businesses, so they need to be alert to what might happen when they develop strategy.

go to Find out more about government strategy to control the economy on pages 42–55.

Amazon delivers

There is a big new warehouse off the M1 at Junction 13 near Milton Keynes and it belongs to Amazon, a private limited company.

Amazon used to be a business which existed entirely on the net. The original concept that Jeff Bezos had was that Amazon would run the website and take the money, but book distributors would do the difficult stuff, namely hold the stock and handle the deliveries. Good thinking, because you have none of the big overheads.

But the strategy has changed. Amazon has recognised that to provide a superb service to customers it is dangerous to rely on others. The warehouse is its new distribution centre.

The belief is that big rewards from e-commerce would be gained by businesses that succeeded in blending bricks-and-mortar expertise with the power of the net. Anyone can put up a website and accept credit cards, but it takes organisational skills to ensure that the goods are delivered on time. In Britain Tesco developed its online shopping business by doing it in-house via its own software and stores; John Lewis moved into cyberspace by acquiring a financially weak but technologically sound e-business called Buy.com.

If you want a simple test of whether a company knows what it is doing online, try this: can you find out what a product or service costs in three clicks or less?

Adapted from an article in the *Observer*, 11 May 2003.

Amazon's mission

Amazon seeks to be the world's most customer-centric company, a place where people can find and discover anything they might want to buy online. We are not a book, music, or toy company; we are a customer company.

'Our mission requires us to innovate constantly while continuing to provide our customers with an unparalleled online shopping experience. We've been able to succeed in these categories by building superior technology and world-class fulfilment capabilities.

'As we grow, we continue to promote small working teams and cross-functional teamwork. This team diversity encourages creativity, an open exchange of ideas across groups, and a respect for the challenges and trade-offs present across our business.

'Our employees also have a stake in the success of the business. They are given the option to buy shares to promote a sense of ownership.'

Source: Amazon website

The Royal Mail

The Royal Mail, a public sector organisation, has cut its annual losses to £611 million after its first improvement in trading performance for five years.

'We're largely still being pretty inefficient but this is the first time in five years the numbers have gone in the right direction,' chairman Allan Leighton told BBC Radio 4's *Today* programme. 'I'm pretty confident we'll be profitable this year.'

The Royal Mail is already one year into a three-year renewal programme designed to turn the company round.

Nearly 17,000 jobs have already gone and more than 30,000 will have been lost by 2005. The Royal Mail also proposes to close 3,000 sub-post offices by 2005.

The number of days lost through strikes last year fell by 90%, making it the Royal Mail's best year for industrial relations in a decade. Postal workers have stopped the rot, claims the chairman.

The Royal Mail has targets to reduce the number of road journeys, experiment more with electric vans and use more gas as a fuel. When bikes are renewed the old ones are reconditioned and given to charities linked with Africa. Post and passenger service buses are seen as an important lifeline to rural communities.

Source: BBC Radio 4, 22 May 2003.

assessment questions

1 a Provide two pieces of evidence that suggest Amazon is a market-oriented business. **(2 marks)**

  b Is the Royal Mail market or product oriented? Explain why. **(2 marks)**

  > *help!* It is useful to provide a brief definition and then say why you think some evidence in the case study supports this. For the second part, if the organisation is making a loss what does this suggest about it meeting customer needs?

2 Giving an example using Amazon, what is an aim? **(2 marks)**

  > *help!* Straightforward definition and application to the case study. Amazon's aim should be stated in one sentence.

3 What objectives did the Royal Mail set itself? **(4 marks)**

  > *help!* Objectives need targets that can be measured. Look for some data that has improved. The data is usually a symptom that something is wrong, getting better or getting worse.

4 Suggest an objective that Amazon might set itself. **(2 marks)**

  > *help!* Use something within the mission as an objective and then try to translate this into a target.

5 What is a strategy? How did strategy change in each organisation? **(6 marks)**

  > *help!* Straightforward definition and application to the case study.

6 Construct a simple SWOT analysis for each organisation. **(8 marks)**

  > *help!* The phrase 'simple SWOT' implies that you need only recognise one relevant example of each element.

7 Contrast the culture differences between the two organisations. What recommendations would you make for the Royal Mail in order to improve its culture? **(14 marks)**

  > *help!* Go to page 27–28 and apply the ideas.

8 What is meant by 'social responsibility'? To what extent is the Royal Mail meeting the social objectives of its customers and its owners? **(14 marks)**

  > *help!* A clear definition is worth 2 marks so the bulk of your answer asks you to recognise some social objectives from the evidence that the Royal Mail claims to be meeting, but also look for evidence to suggest it is not always a positive picture. Try to conclude as to why the customer as a stakeholder will not always be satisfied.

The changing market

starSTUDY

> We rented a house in the south of France for our holidays this year. Travelling with Ryanair and hiring a car worked out about the same price as the ferry, stop over hotels, petrol and motorway tolls. We were there in a few hours – not days.

> We booked our weekend break in Prague over the Internet. The fares are so low these days.

easyJet.com
the web's favourite airline

RYANAIR
THE LOW FARES AIRLINE

EasyJet, a low-cost airline, carried 39% more passengers in March 2002 than it did a year previously.

The combined market for easyJet and Ryanair for short haul flights in March 2002 reached £2.28 million. It surpassed British Airways' £2.17 million.

BA has reacted by lowering prices and has started to eliminate unprofitable routes.

1 Which of the three businesses, Ryanair, easyJet and BA, has the biggest share of the short haul market?
2 Why do you think demand for tickets with Ryanair and easyJet is increasing?
3 Why is BA trying to cut costs?
4 Why might people increase or decrease the number of flights they take?
5 What do you think would happen if people cut back on the number of flights they wanted to take?

What's going on?

Markets don't stay still. People want different things and businesses produce different things. Prices and costs change so markets are dynamic.

- High prices encourage existing businesses to supply more and new businesses to enter the market, but high prices discourage customers from buying.

- Customers will want to buy more if the price is lower, but there is not so much profit to be made for the business supplying the goods or services. It seems that low prices discourage businesses from providing goods and services.

Critical thinking

1 If BA could not reduce prices significantly for its European market what would happen to the business? How would this affect its stakeholders?

2 Choose a business you know and work out what is happening to prices. Are they staying the same, going up or going down? Explain why. A phone shop would be a good example.

Specification Content

The interaction of demand and supply, market equilibrium and the effect of excesses

KEY TERMS

Supply curve shows the relationship between the price and the quantity supplied.

Demand curve shows the relationship between the price and the quantity demanded.

Market clearing means that supply exactly matches demand. In reality this is difficult to achieve.

Equilibrium is the point that the market clears. It is said to be in equilibrium because there is no need for prices or output to change.

Excess demand means that the demand for a good or service outstrips the supply.

Excess supply means that too much is being supplied in the market.

Dynamic demand: dynamic supply

The supply curve shows how much businesses are prepared to put on the market at different prices. It slopes upwards from left to right because low prices discourage businesses from supplying the goods and services, while high prices make them want to supply more.

The demand curve shows how much people want to buy at different prices. It slopes down from left to right because at low prices customers want to buy more but at high prices customers buy less.

JUST RIGHT

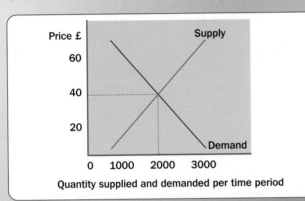

Quantity supplied and demanded per time period

Where the two curves cross, businesses want to sell 2000 items at £40 each. Customers are willing to buy 2000 items at £40 each. This is known as the equilibrium – the market is in balance.

But how does it work? How do businesses know what to charge and how much to supply? The answer is that they don't always get it right.

PRICE TOO HIGH

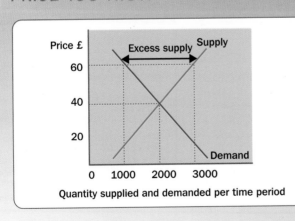

Quantity supplied and demanded per time period

At a price of £60 people only want to buy 1000 items but businesses want to supply 3000. The symptoms for a business would be a build-up in stocks or underused capacity. An airline, for example, would have empty seats.

A business may react in two different ways.

* Producing less. The airline might cut out some flights.
* Cutting prices. If prices are reduced, people usually buy more. If the price is cut to £40, the market clears because producers are happy to sell 2000 items and customers want to buy 2000 items.

PRICE TOO LOW

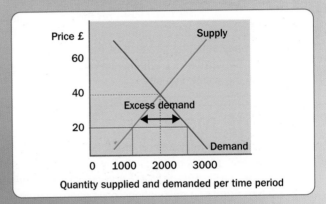

Quantity supplied and demanded per time period

If the price is £20 customers want to buy 3000 items but businesses only want to sell 1000. Demand outpaces supply. Stocks quickly run out and many customers are left disappointed.

Airlines haven't enough seats in the aircraft. The suppliers have again misjudged the market. They have two alternatives:

* Supply more. This is not always easy in the short run. For example, the number of extra flights an airline business can put on is dependent on having spare planes and staff.
* Raise prices. At £40 demand matches the supply and the market once again clears.

1 Low cost airlines can pass on savings they make in lower fares to customers. Explain how this leads to a bigger market for this type of air travel.

2 Theory suggests that excess demand will not exist for long. Why is this?

3 BA decided to cut back on flights. Why?

4 What would happen if BA could not significantly lower costs?

Next steps

Look at the shops in your area.
When and why do they have sales?

Where's the market going?

Specification Content

How do changes in demand and changes in supply affect the allocation of resources?

star**STUDY**

Flying less

Passenger numbers on North Atlantic routes were down only 7.7% last month on the previous year, compared with a 31.3% plunge in October. Air travel was already suffering because of the global downturn but the September 11 attacks delivered a devastating blow to the airline industry.

Flying more

In 2002, 5.6 million short break holidays were taken. In 1997, 11.7% of all holidays were short breaks compared with 15% in 2002 and growth will continue. Eastern European destinations have seen a surge in demand. Prague, for instance, saw a 121% increase in popularity before the floods in August 2002.

Source: ABTA.

The web accounts for 94% of Ryanair's bookings.

Plans

- easyJet aims to operate 300 aircraft.
- Ryanair plans to buy 150 new aircraft in the next 8 years.
- BA, a long haul specialist, plans to cut its fleet by 49 aircraft to 305 by Summer 2003.

UK spending power

There has been a rise in our disposable incomes. Between 1995 and 2002 they rose by over 20%.

1 Use the data to explain which parts of the air travel markets were

a growing?

b declining?

2 What happens to the number of people and planes in each business as things change?

3 How do you think airlines plan ahead?

Critical thinking

1 Why were customers more prepared to book online?

2 Why would Internet booking reduce costs?

3 Identify the factors which have led to an increase in supply and an increase in demand. Draw demand and supply diagrams to show what has happened.

4 What options are available to a business that faces a decline in demand for its products or services in the short run and the long run? How could you show this using supply and demand curves?

5 How do you think the growth of short haul flights has affected the demand for travel by the Channel Tunnel and the ferries? Use the Internet to research the changes in these markets.

6 Why would it be useful for businesses to keep track of changes in demand and changes in people's income?

7 What has influenced the investment decisions of mobile phone companies, cigarette companies and sports equipment?

KEY TERMS

Short run is the time period when businesses cannot easily react to market changes.

Shift in supply refers to the movement of the supply curve.

Shift in demand refers to the movement of the demand curve.

Business entrepreneurship means having an eye for business opportunities and taking a risk in order to achieve them.

Markets on the move

Markets can be very dynamic. Demand can change and supply can change. However change comes about, the price will change as a result. There will be shifts in demand and shifts in supply.

WHEN COSTS CHANGE

When costs are cut businesses are prepared to supply more and people want to buy more as the price falls. In this case the price falls to £20. Businesses want to supply 3000 items and demand rises to 3000 items so the market is in equilibrium again.

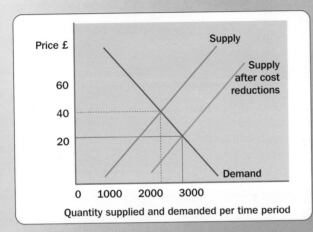

Quantity supplied and demanded per time period

When costs rise businesses will supply less and people will want to buy less at the higher price. If the price rises to £60 businesses only want to sell 1000 items and demand falls to 1000 so the market is in equilibrium again.

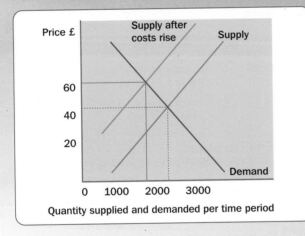

Quantity supplied and demanded per time period

WHEN DEMAND CHANGES

People change their buying habits for all sorts of reasons:

- they earn more or less
- fashions change
- population changes
- advertising
- changes in the law
- the price or supply of other products changes.

When people want to buy more, the demand curve shifts to the right. As business costs will rise if more is to be produced in the short run, the end result is an increase in price. The price rises to £60 and 3000 items are sold.

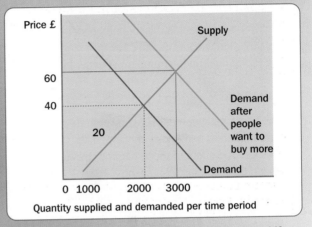

Quantity supplied and demanded per time period

When people want to buy less, the demand curve shifts to the left and prices fall because business costs are reduced. The price falls to £20 and 1000 items are sold.

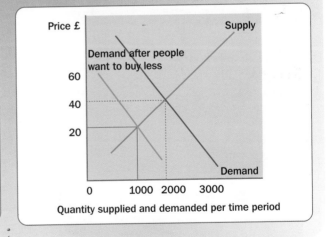

Quantity supplied and demanded per time period

Next steps

1 The air travel industry is a rapidly changing market where consumer trends and business entrepreneurship help shape the direction of the market. Some markets are relatively stable but others are constantly changing. Choose six businesses and rank them according to how stable or volatile they are.

2 Changes in your local shopping centre reflect changing markets. What changes have taken place in your shopping centre lately and why do you think these changes have taken place? Look up mobile phone shops and cafés in your local Yellow Pages from a current edition and compare this with one from a few years back.

Competitive decisions

Specification Content
The effect of competition

starSTUDY
Competition down the road

The millennium was not good for Dan yr Ogof Show Caves in south Wales. One of its major competitors, Big Pit Mining Museum, dropped its admission charges to nothing after the National Assembly for Wales passed legislation to provide free admission to the publicly owned museums. Visitor numbers are down 55% with schools in particular switching to Big Pit for their underground experience. In contrast Big Pit has seen an increase of 70% in its customers.

The business has been damaged by both a change in market and a loss of competitive advantage. The effect of these hammer blows has seen its customer base slump.

1 Why have customers deserted the Show Caves?
2 What effect is this likely to have on the business?
3 What options are open to this business?
4 What businesses may be badly affected by the Show Caves' declining customers?

starSTUDY
Competition in the air

Radio advert: 'Try our new chauffeur link service to Bristol Airport and take the strain out of your travel arrangements.'

easyJet		
Year to end September	Revenue (£m)	Profit (£m)
1998	77.0	5.9
1999	139.8	1.3
2000	263.7	22.1
2001	356.9	40.1

Source: easyJet

easyJet	Routes	Aircraft
1995	2 from Luton to Glasgow and Edinburgh	2
2003	105 routes between 38 European destinations	67 with an order to buy 120 more

1 What does the data suggest about the European short haul business?
2 Why might this have happened?
3 Do you think the business will continue to grow? Why?
4 What do the changing profit levels suggest about easyJet?
5 How will competitors be reacting to this market?
6 What other business might be affected by this growth
  a positively
  b negatively?

KEY TERMS

Substitutes are alternative products for consumers. Businesses offering close substitutes are in competition for customers.

Complementary goods are related products so when demand for one increases so does the demand for the other.

Market signals

PROFITS AND LOSSES act as signals to businesses about how well the market is performing. Businesses and investors must react to changes in the market and therefore changes in the level of profits and losses.

If a business believes its market will grow it will need to plan ahead and invest in capital such as buildings and equipment. It must also employ and train staff. The business will try to work out what profits the investment might bring. Profit is a necessary part of the business and a growth in profits provides an indicator to investors and to other businesses that this might be a good market to invest in. The profits after tax are split between rewarding investors and making further investments in the business.

These other businesses may well be competitors offering close substitutes and are trying to get in on the act and earn themselves good profits, or they may be in a complementary business such as car hire and air travel. It is complementary in that when demand for one grows or declines so will the other.

Losses or a decline in profits might be a result of a declining market. Such information informs the business that future investments might not bring about the desired returns and would be too risky. It may be better for owners to move their investment elsewhere.

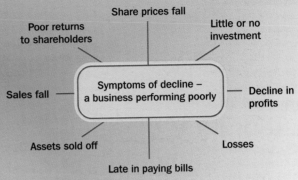

Poor returns to shareholders — Share prices fall — Little or no investment

Sales fall — **Symptoms of decline – a business performing poorly** — Decline in profits

Assets sold off — Late in paying bills — Losses

Picking up the signals

easyJet became a plc in 2000 in order to help it raise finance to invest in its expansion plans. Part of the finance will come from the growing profits and it could also borrow from banks. Much of the finance has been used to buy new planes and some to invest in developing its e-commerce facilities. Some was used for training and recruitment. When easyJet opens a new route other businesses, such as car hire, taxi services and local hotels, will see a growth in the demand in their markets. Not all businesses are growing, however, and many struggle to keep going. For example, Dan yr Ogof has problems covering its £100,000 a year maintenance costs. In an effort to survive it has reduced costs such as cleaning and repairs. One of the two show caves has closed and 20 employees have been made redundant.

Critical thinking

Dan Yr Ogof Show Caves is a business on the edge. Its plight can be represented diagrammatically (see the graph). There has been an inward shift in demand, while the graph of Big Pit, a close substitute, shows that the lowering of prices has increased its customers. It has only been able to achieve this by receiving a government grant. There is some good news for Dan yr Ogof. A grant from the Countryside Council for Wales will allow schools to visit the caves free of charge.

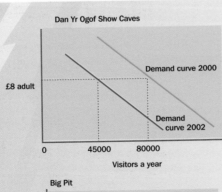

Dan Yr Ogof Show Caves

£8 adult

Demand curve 2000

Demand curve 2002

0   45000   80000

Visitors a year

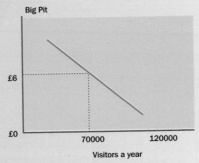

Big Pit

£6

£0

70000   120000

Visitors a year

1 What has happened to the turnover of Show Caves between 2000 and 2002?

2 Why can't the business afford to ignore what has happened?

3 What has happened to the number of visitors at Big Pit?

4 How might the grant to Big Pit be distorting the market?

5 What happens when a business that offers a close substitute lowers its prices?

6 List some examples of complementary goods or services.

What are interest rates?

Specification Content

Interest rates: their use and purpose

star**STUDY** Headlines

Local business builds new factory

The cost of borrowing money is at a 39-year low

Rise in interest rates hits small businesses

New lending falls as interest rates rise

Credit card borrowing reached £10 billion

If we all worked for 1 year and saved everything we would just about pay off our debts

1 Why do people and businesses borrow money?

2 What happens to borrowing when interest rates rise and fall?

3 How can low interest rates help business?

4 Why can businesses and people find themselves in difficulties when interest rates rise?

Why borrow?

If families or businesses haven't enough income to match their expenditure they may consider borrowing. It can be sensible to borrow money if you know you can pay it back. Individuals may expect to be paid more as their career improves. Borrowing allows individuals to buy expensive items such as cars before they have saved up enough money. Many families borrow to buy a house and pay this back over 25 years. A business may need to buy computer equipment and software in order to set up e-commerce and in turn gain more customers.

IN THE KNOW

What are interest rates?

Interest rates are the cost of borrowing. A 4% interest rate means you have to pay £40 a year to borrow £1000. This is the charge a lender makes to people and businesses that borrow money.

- **If interest rates fall** then so does the cost of borrowing. This makes borrowers happy because repayments are lower. Lenders suffer because their money earns less.

- **If interest rates rise** so does the cost of borrowing. This makes lenders happy because their money earns more. Borrowers suffer because their repayments increase.

LENDER OR BORROWER?

Businesses that provide financial service, such as banks, insurance and pension companies, link lenders and borrowers.

- People and businesses that save money with these institutions are paid interest.

- People and businesses that borrow money pay interest at a higher rate.

The financial institutions hope to cover their costs and return a profit. The interest offered is also dependent on the amount of money involved as well as the risk of default.

starSTUDY
Setting the rate

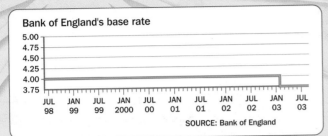

Bank of England's base rate

	JUL 98	JAN 99	JUL 99	JAN 2000	JUL 00	JAN 01	JUL 01	JAN 02	JUL 02	JAN 03	JUL 03

5.00
4.75
4.50
4.25
4.00
3.75

SOURCE: Bank of England

Each month the Bank of England's Monetary Policy Committee (MPC) has the task of deciding whether to increase, decrease or keep the base rate the same. It looks very carefully at what is going on in the economy now and what is expected to happen in future before it sets the interest rate for the following month.

It looks at various indicators to see how the economy is performing. These include changes in industry, trade and consumer confidence, which is measured by working out how much we spend in the high street. If this is falling, the MPC may decide to reduce the interest rate, as it believes the economy is slowing down. A fall in interest encourages borrowing and makes it cheaper for businesses to raise finance to invest. An increase in consumer spending helps the economy grow and if it is growing we feel confident about our jobs and our futures, so we borrow more to buy things we want now.

If consumer spending is growing fast, the Bank might raise interest rates. This raises the cost of borrowing and helps reduce consumer spending. Too much consumer spending is risky as people may find it hard to repay. The MPC aims to keep things on an even keel.

If we adopted the euro as our currency then the European Bank would set the interest rate for all the countries of the eurozone.

1 What might persuade the MPC to cut or increase base rates?
2 If the MPC
   a raises base rate
   b cuts base rate,
   what effect might this have on people and businesses?
3 Find out what has happened in recent months to the base rate which is set by the MPC. Why do you think these changes have taken place?

The Monetary Policy Committee and inflation

IN THE KNOW

The MPC has to keep inflation under control – as well as keeping an eye on the general well-being of the economy. It does this by changing base rates.

Inflation means that there is a sustained rise in prices. It is caused by:

- people and businesses wanting to buy more than is available
- a shortage of products that people and businesses want to buy.

Whether there is too much demand or not enough supply, the effect is the same – prices go up.

The MPC is given inflation targets by the government. Some inflation is considered inevitable but if it appears to be rising above the target, the MPC will increase interest rates. If it is falling below the target, the MPC will cut interest rates.

When the MPC has set the interest rate each month, banks and other institutions where people save and borrow money look carefully at the interest rates they set for customers. They all make a profit from the difference between their rate to savers and borrowers. The market is competitive as people want good interest rates for their savings but low rates when they borrow. Borrowers will also be charged different rates according to the degree of risk and the length of the loan.

go to → *Find out more on pages 54–55.*

Find out more about inflation and controlling the economy on page .

KEY TERMS

Interest rates are the cost or charge for borrowing money or the reward for lending money.

Base rate is the interest rate charged by the Bank of England when lending money to banks when they are short of cash. It is used as a guide for other lenders.

Inflation is the sustained rise in average prices.

Critical thinking

Come up with ideas about how changes in interest rates affect business. Why do you think businesses like stability?

Next steps

1 Find out about banks' interest rates for borrowing money and saving money.

2 How does the length of time and the amount of money affect the rates?

3 Why do you think this is?

How do interest rates affect businesses?

Specification Content

Interest rates: the impact of change on the firm and its market

star**STUDY**

Interest rates at all time low

Businesses throughout the UK welcomed the continuing low level of interest rates. Keeping business costs low is critical if businesses are to stay competitive. Anxiety is still high for businesses which trade in international markets because rates are lower still in Europe and the US.

KEY TERMS

A budget is a financial plan about income and expenditure.

Imports are products bought from other countries.

Exports are products sold to other countries.

1 Why do businesses welcome low interest rates?
2 Why are businesses anxious because interest rates in other countries are lower?
3 How does the MPC come to a decision about the interest rate to set each month?
4 How does a rise in interest rates affect customers?
5 Why is it hard to justify new investment when interest rates are relatively high?
6 What sort of businesses are most likely to be hit by high interest rates?

Not another rise!

The MPC raised interest rates by another half per cent yesterday. Many business leaders squealed with pain as they saw their costs rising yet again. They fear that customers will disappear as the cost of running a home increases. New investment becomes increasingly difficult to justify as potential costs rise.

Outside and inside the business

Businesses can be very sensitive to interest rate changes because they affect their financial situation. Careful planning will have created a budget, which a business aims to stick to. Changes in interest rates can upset plans in a variety of ways.

Customers are also affected because many borrow money, which becomes more expensive to repay. Others depend on savings so their spending power can rise or fall depending on the rate of interest.

How interest rates affect businesses

INTEREST RATES UP

Existing borrowing gets more expensive → costs rise → profits fall or sales must rise

Customers' borrowing gets more expensive → customers have less to spend on other things

Borrowing for investment gets more expensive → new projects must make more profit to cover costs

Customers with savings earn more interest → customers have more to spend

INTEREST RATES DOWN

Existing borrowing gets cheaper → costs fall → more profit

Customers' borrowing get cheaper → customers have more to spend on other things

Borrowing for investment gets cheaper → more projects become viable as level of profit needed to cover costs falls

Customers' savings give lower returns → customers have less to spend

Knock-on effects

Businesses generally don't like high interest rates because they increase costs, reduce consumers' spending power and make investment for growth more expensive.

INVESTMENT

A business will calculate the estimated return from a project and see if this exceeds the interest it receives from its savings or the interest charged if it borrows the money. It will also try to estimate likely changes in future rates. Any rise in the interest rate increases business costs and will make some projects less viable. A fall in the interest rate will increase the likelihood of businesses undertaking investment.

CHASING DEBTORS – DELAYING PAYMENTS

If costs are rising because interest rates are high a business will chase debtors more quickly to keep cash coming in more quickly. It may also try to delay payments to others in order to stop cash flowing out.

RAISING PRICES

If costs rise, businesses often want to pass the rise on to the customers by putting up the price. Their ability to do this will depend on demand and supply. If their competitors don't raise prices, it will be difficult as customers will go elsewhere. If the product is a luxury or has substitutes, customers again will be lost if the price rises. If it is something that people really can't do without and there is no alternative, people will have to pay up – whatever the price is.

COMPETITIVENESS

If interest rates in other countries are lower, it will be difficult to export to those countries. It may also make trading conditions difficult generally because imports will be cheaper than home produced purchases.

Critical thinking

1 If we joined the euro we would have to accept an interest rate set by the European Bank. How might this affect businesses and consumers if the rate at which we joined was lower than the rate set by the Monetary Policy Committee?

2 What will be the likely effect of a reduction in interest rates on
   a short haul holidays abroad
   b house purchases
   c our purchases of vegetables?

3 Which types of businesses would be affected by this change in demand for short haul holidays abroad and houses? How might these businesses react if they believed that future interest rates were unlikely to rise?

Next steps

A monthly survey of retailers suggests sales are slowing down.

A purchasing managers' survey has found business confidence in the services sector at its lowest level for a year.

Amicus union warned that tens of thousands of jobs are at risk unless the interest rate is lowered.

There were 43,500 business failures in Britain in 2002, a 7.2% increase on 2001 and the highest level for eight years.

The Nationwide Building Society says house prices rose by an annual rate of 25.5%, the highest for 13 years.

Both the US and the European Central Bank have already made interest rate cuts to support their flagging economies.

1 What would business want to happen to interest rates in each of these situations? Explain why.

2 What do you think the MPC should do? Explain why.

3 Economies are forever changing and so will the pressure to change interest rates. You should track interest rate changes in the next few months by listening to Radio 4 or 5 and by searching articles on *http://money.guardian.co.uk/interestrates* and *http://news.bbc.co.uk/1/hi/business* and search the term 'interest rate'.

4 If you have contacts with a local business find out how significant interest rate changes are for that business.

What are exchange rates?

starSTUDY
Web trade: Discarray

Justin Kyriakides set up a business that sells innovative, decorative CD storage. He worked hard to launch it on the market, finding the web combined with articles in magazines a successful strategy.

He soon found that he had orders from countries including Finland, the USA and Ireland, as well as the UK. He had always priced in pounds but now he had to think about selling Discarray in other currencies.

The website makes it easy as customers can choose the currency they want. He just has to work out what the price should be in each currency.

As the value of the pound changes against other currencies, he has to make sure he always has the right price. If he's behind the times, he might lose out because he would be selling at a lower price than he planned – or perhaps the price might look very expensive in another currency.

1 Selling Discarray overseas has both advantages and disadvantages. How many can you think of?

2 His sales to the USA will be in dollars. His sales to Ireland will be in euros. Find out how many dollars and euros you get for a pound. www.bbc.co.uk will help you.

3 Why does he have to be sure that he has the latest information about the value of the pound in other currencies?

4 How would the business be affected if it used resources imported from abroad?

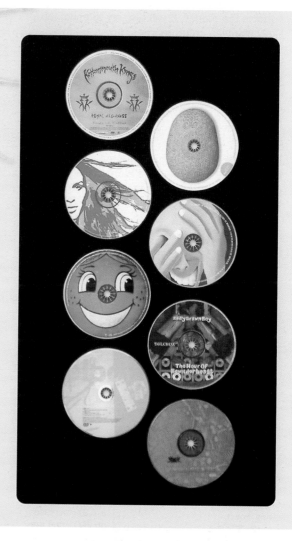

Changing currencies

Justin needs to translate the price of his products into other currencies if he is to sell abroad. He needs to know exactly what the **exchange rate** is in order to set the price for his product. The exchange rate is the price you pay if you want to buy one currency with another. The information is readily available from banks and the media.

KEY TERMS

The **exchange rate** gives the value of one currency expressed in terms of another. For example, the value of the pound (£) in euros (€).

Eurozone includes all the countries that use the euro.

What are exchange rates?

When you buy a meal in France the restaurant would want to be paid in euros (€), the currency used in France. This is the currency of euro-zone members of the European Union, so you would also pay in euros if you bought goods and services in other European countries such as Italy and Germany.

To pay for the meal and buy other products and services in France you will need to exchange your pounds for euros. You would go to a bank or other organisation that changes money, and buy euros with your pounds. Instead of buying a product or service you are buying a currency. Paying for a currency means it has a value. Just as the euros have a value in pounds so pounds have a value in euros. If an individual or a business wants to buy pounds from a bank they need to pay in another currency such as euros, dollars or yen. The exchange rate is the price of that currency expressed in another currency.

WHY DO EXCHANGE RATES CHANGE?

When the demand or supply for a product changes, the price changes. When the supply of new houses does not keep pace with growing demand, house prices rise. On the other hand if we demand fewer houses then prices will fall. Exchange rates work in exactly the same way.

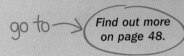

go to → Find out more on page 48.

WHY DOES THE SUPPLY OF POUNDS INCREASE?

Going on a holiday in France is an import. We are buying a French holiday in the same way as we may buy a French car. Both are imports. Both need to be paid for in euros so we have to sell pounds to exchange for euros.

If many people want holidays and cars from France then they will want to sell pounds to buy euros. The number of pounds on the market will rise. If the number of euros stays the same, the value of the pound will fall.

In the example in Figure 1, the supply of pounds shifts from S1 to S2 and the price or value of pounds falls from €1.5 to €1.4.

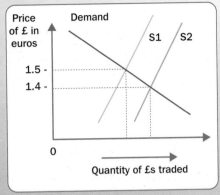

Figure 1. The effect of an increase in imports

If imports fall, people need fewer pounds to pay for them. The number being put on the market will fall so the value of the pound will rise.

WHY DOES THE DEMAND FOR POUNDS INCREASE?

Trade isn't only one way. People from France come to the UK for holidays. They also buy our music. These are both counted as exports. They will have to pay for their purchases in pounds. They will need to buy pounds with their euros. This would increase the demand for pounds on the exchange market. Figure 2 shows what happens when the demand curve shifts from D1 to D2 leading to a rise or appreciation in the value of pounds against the euro.

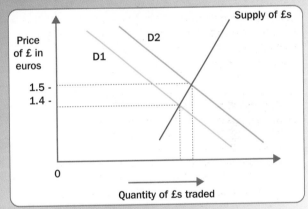

Figure 2. An increase in exports

A decline in exports would lead to fewer pounds being demanded and a fall in the exchange rate.

Critical thinking

1 Would you prefer to
a buy from
b sell to

the USA or the **eurozone** in the period you have been monitoring exchange rates? Explain why.

Next steps

Track the pound against the euro and the dollar for a period of two weeks by looking in newspapers or on the web.

Exchange rates and business

Specification Content

Exchange rates: the impact of changes on the firm and its market

starSTUDY

Rising pound: failing pottery

Joan Beagle, the Managing Director of Archer's Pottery, announced the decision to sell its pottery in Belgium. Exports to Belgium quickly grew to 20% of sales. Plans were set to increase this and budgets calculated. However, less than two years later exports had dwindled to near nothing. The reason was a 17% rise in the value of the pound against the euro. This made the pottery too expensive for Belgian consumers. 'We cut our prices a little, but could not afford to lower them further.'

Rising euro hits economy

A rapid rise in the value of the euro against the dollar could have damaging consequences for Europe's economy, the German banking federation has warned.

The euro was trading at above $1.07 on Wednesday morning, its highest level for more than three years.

The single currency has risen almost 25% against the dollar from its low of 86 cents just over a year ago.

A strong euro dents the competitiveness of companies exporting from the eurozone, making their products comparatively more expensive.

Source: BBCi 2003.

1 Why couldn't Joan keep prices in Belgium the same?
2 What effect did this have on her business?
3 Archer's Pottery is one of many UK companies that export to the eurozone. What effect is this change going to have on them?
4 What effect would the change be likely to have on the UK economy?
5 The value of the euro had risen by 25% against the dollar. What effect would this have on the price of exports from Germany, and other members of the eurozone, to countries outside the zone?
6 What effect is this likely to have on sales of their products beyond the zone?
7 What effect is this likely to have on the economies of these countries?
8 What would an exporter have to consider before changing prices?

Changing rates

The movement of exchange rates means that businesses throughout the world must keep their eyes on the ball. They all have to watch the price of their currency in places that they trade with. Changes can have both positive and negative effects on a business's budget. Resources they buy from other countries may become cheaper, so costs fall. They may also become more expensive, so costs rise. Just the same can happen with export markets. If your products become more expensive, other countries will not want to buy them. If they become cheaper, sales will probably rise.

KEY TERMS

Transactions costs are the cost of exchanging currencies.

Hedging is minimising the risk of currency rate fluctuations by buying currency now for delivery at a future date.

Next steps

1 Investigate a business you know and find out how much it imports and how much it exports and who to.

2 Find out what effects exchange rate changes have on its business decisions.

Exchange rate costs

The effects of exchange rates on business are:

- **Transactions costs.** Every time a business changes one currency into another, the bank charges a fee. The process makes every transaction more expensive.

- Exchange rate risk. Currency values change against each other. If a business has planned its cost and pricing on the basis of the exchange rate at the beginning of the year, changing rates can affect the plans.

WHAT HAPPENS WHEN THE POUND RISES AGAINST THE EURO?

↑ Imports become cheaper because UK businesses will need to pay for the goods and services in euros. Pounds will buy more euros than before.

↓ Exports become more expensive since UK businesses need to be paid in pounds. Euros will buy fewer pounds than before.

HOW DOES IT WORK?

- A UK business exports to Ireland. Its products are priced at £20.00.

- Exchange rate: £1.00 = €1.40. €1.00 = £0.71.

- The Irish business pays €28.00.

- The value of the pound rises to €1.70, so €1.00 = £0.59.

- The Irish business now pays €34.00. It might look elsewhere for its supplies.

1 Calculate what happens to the price in pounds that a UK business would pay to import from Ireland given the same rise in the value of the pound. Assume each item is sold at €5 by the Irish business.

WHAT HAPPENS WHEN THE POUND FALLS AGAINST THE EURO?

↑ Imports become more expensive because UK businesses will have to pay for the goods and services in euros. Pounds will buy fewer euros than before.

↓ Exports become cheaper since UK businesses need to be paid in pounds. Euros will buy more pounds than before.

HOW DOES IT WORK?

- A German business supplies components to a UK business at €3.40.

- The exchange rate is €1.70 to £1.00.

- The UK business pays £2.00 for each component.

The value of the pound falls to €1.50 making each component cost £2.67 so the UK business will need to exchange £0.67 more for each component. The increase of £0.67 may force it to find suppliers in the UK.

1 Calculate what happens to the price in euros that a German business would pay the exporting UK business given the same fall in the value of the pound. Assume each item is sold at £10.00 by the UK business.

Why join the euro?

Twelve members of the EU have joined the euro – a common currency that they all use. The UK decided to stay out, but may decide to join in the future.

Is there an alternative way to protecting against currency changes?

Businesses which already deal in foreign currencies often 'hedge their bets'.

They may agree to buy foreign currency at a future date but at the rate fixed today.

Why join the euro?	
Stability	Businesses know that costs and prices will not be affected by exchange rate changes within the eurozone. Fluctuations will continue beyond the zone.
No transaction costs on trade within the eurozone	Cuts costs on trade within eurozone.
Pricing in euros makes market more competitive	More competition for business but provides larger market. Good for consumers.

Why not?	
Economic control from European Bank	Interest rates are used to control the economy. If control comes from Europe, the rate that is set may not be right for the UK. It may be hard to control inflation and unemployment.
Euro strength/weakness	If the euro is strong, trade with the rest of the world can be challenging because our products become expensive. Interest rates could not be used independently to adjust the UK economy to encourage competitiveness.

What is tax?

starSTUDY

People and businesses pay tax

Paid by individuals	Paid by individuals and businesses	Paid by businesses

Income tax – a percentage of income

Council tax on the value of your home

Inheritance tax on money passed on at death

Value added tax (VAT) – a percentage of most purchases, apart from food

Excise duties on fuel, alcohol and tobacco

National Insurance – a percentage of an individual's income

Corporation tax – paid on a company's profits

Business rates relate to the property used by a business

Import duties are paid on things brought into the country. The amount varies according to the product and country of origin.

Headlines

'UK taxes could be set for big increases in coming years'

'Other cities keeping a close eye on how congestion charges in London are working'

'Taxes in the UK are equivalent to around £7000 for every man, woman or child in the UK'

How much tax is raised?

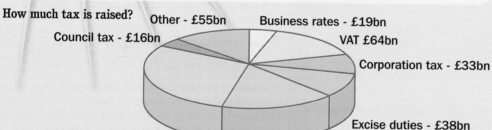

- Other - £55bn
- Council tax - £16bn
- Business rates - £19bn
- VAT £64bn
- Corporation tax - £33bn
- Excise duties - £38bn
- Income tax - £118bn
- National Insurance - £65bn

Source: HM Treasury website

1 Rank the taxes in order of importance for raising revenue. Note that the total figures tend to rise each year but the proportions stay much the same.

2 Explain the first two headlines.

3 Clearly not everyone pays £7000 tax. Make a list of the sources of tax and whom it affects. Who will pay more and who will pay less?

4 Find out from the Treasury website, www.hm-treasury.gov.uk

  a how much is being raised from each type of tax this year

  b the percentages paid for income tax, national insurance, VAT and corporation tax.

Taxes

CENTRAL GOVERNMENT TAXES

INDIVIDUALS: The main direct tax paid by individuals is income tax. It is a tax on income from working and saving. It is a direct tax as it is deducted straight from our earnings. Unless you are self-employed, it is paid directly from the pay cheque and is therefore known as a direct tax.

We also pay tax on our spending. Value Added Tax is added onto the price of most of the things we buy apart from items such as food and children's clothes. We also pay excise duties on alcohol, tobacco and car fuel. These are known as indirect taxes.

BUSINESS: Businesses pay corporation tax on the profits earned. They also pay VAT on all their purchases as well as collecting it for the government. This is seen as an extra cost by businesses. Businesses along with employees pay National Insurance. This is a tax on workers, which is often

thought to pay for healthcare, pensions and benefits. In fact, it just goes into the same kitty with all the other taxes.

OTHER TAXES: There are also taxes on individual items such as television licences, plane trips and buying and running cars.

LOCAL TAXES

Local government sets and raises taxes mainly through the business rates and council tax.

BUSINESS RATES are related to the value of the annual rent that the property would receive if let on the open market at a certain date. They are reviewed every five years. Therefore a shop in the centre of a town would have a higher business rate than one in a suburb.

COUNCIL TAX is on all domestic property. The higher the value, the higher the tax.

Why taxation?

The government has three main objectives when it adjusts taxation:

1 To raise revenue in order to be able to pay for all the services the public expects. The chart shows the range of government expenditure.

2 To control the economy. If it takes more in taxation, we have less to spend on other things so demand falls. If it cuts taxation, we have more to spend.

Find out more on page 52. ← go to

3 To change our habits. Raising the price of cigarettes by increasing tax aims to cut the number of smokers. A congestion charge aims to cut the number of people who drive in city centres.

Where does the money go?

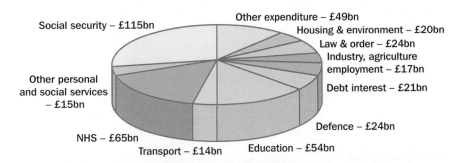

Social security – £115bn
Other expenditure – £49bn
Housing & environment – £20bn
Law & order – £24bn
Industry, agriculture employment – £17bn
Debt interest – £21bn
Defence – £24bn
Other personal and social services – £15bn
NHS – £65bn
Transport – £14bn
Education – £54bn

Who decides?

Every year the government sets out its plan for the UK economy and produces a budget designed to deliver this plan. The Chancellor of the Exchequer, who runs the Treasury, is responsible for the budget.

The plans will be determined by the state of the economy and the government's objectives. Some governments use the budget to redistribute income so people have a fairer deal.

Taxes can be used to redistribute income when they are applied progressively. A progressive tax means that people who earn more pay a higher proportion of their income. With income tax this is achieved through having a tax-free allowance followed by different bands of income being taxed at different rates.

Evading taxes

No one likes paying tax. Tax evasion is a problem because it is not fair on others. People and businesses which are honest pay more than they would otherwise in order to maintain public spending. The government has recruited a 400-strong team of fraud investigators for a major blitz on the hidden economy.

'Every year billions of pounds are lost to the informal, or hidden economy. People conceal their income or the record of what they have sold in order to evade income tax and VAT. Others defraud the social security system by claiming benefit for being unemployed when they are in work. Many employers are committing or colluding in a range of different offences at the same time. Honest taxpayers have to pick up the bill.'

Source: The HM Treasury

Critical thinking

What would happen to our economy if we decided to get rid of all taxes? Sketch out your thoughts in a spider diagram and then compare your ideas with a friend.

 www

www.hm-treasury.gov.uk

www.inlandrevenue.gov.uk

http://www.uktax.demon.co.uk/

http://www.hmce.gov.uk/

http://www.bbc.co.uk

Next steps

Look back at the last budget on the Treasury and BBC's websites and find out what happened. What do you think the government was trying to achieve?

KEY TERMS

A direct tax is a tax on incomes.

An indirect tax is a tax on spending.

Tax and business

starSTUDY
Tax connections
Budget extracts

- Increase the duty on alcopops

- VAT increased by 1%

- Tax incentives to encourage business to invest in energy-saving technologies

- Level at which businesses start paying tax is raised

- New tax credit to boost research and development by large firms

- One per cent extra on National Insurance contributions to be paid by employers and employees

1 Which of these measures might change people's buying habits? How?
2 Which of these measures might change business activity? How?
3 Which of these measures aim to promote enterprise in business? How?
4 Which of the measures would businesses not like? Why?
5 Which have other objectives? Explain.
6 Which of these taxes are direct taxes and which are indirect taxes?

The Confederation of British Industry (CBI) – The employers' association

- Warned the government that high taxes are holding back British companies.

- Published a survey showing that the green tax on energy use, or Climate Change Levy (CCL), penalises the hard-pressed manufacturing sector and is driving jobs abroad.

1 Why might high taxes 'hold back' UK businesses?
2 Why might the CCL drive businesses abroad?

'22.1 billion cigarettes were seized by Customs and Excise'

'Limit raised for Cross-Channel cigarette shoppers. 800 ↑ 3,200'

'20% of the cigarette market in the UK is illegal'

'Tobacco smuggling alone cost taxpayers £3.8 billion last year'

Source: HM Customs and Excise

1 What evidence suggests our duties are much higher than in France?
2 Who are the losers from smuggling? How?

European harmony

The EU wants to harmonise VAT rates and excise duties so that businesses across Europe can compete more fairly. For example, British road hauliers pay much more for their diesel fuel than their competitors in other European countries. Excise duty on alcohol is still out of line with Europe.

Critical thinking

1 Decide how businesses might actually win from the following tax changes:
a Congestion charges.
b Increased income tax to pay for higher state pensions.
c Increased duty on car fuel to support a road building programme.
d Increase in council tax to provide more classroom assistants.

2 Why do British brewers want duties to be harmonised across the European Union?

3 'As a citizen of the EU surely I can choose to shop where I want for my own personal goods within the EU.' What are the arguments for and against this statement?

4 Taxes are a good thing. Discuss the statement from the point of view of the customer and business.

Taxation and customers

Raising taxes means that people have less to spend, so businesses tend to be wary of governments which increase taxes.

- An increase in income tax or National Insurance cuts income, so people cut consumption.

An increase in income tax or National Insurance will reduce people's disposable incomes. They will have less money to spend on goods and services, which is not good for businesses. If the structure of tax is changed, things may be different. If low earners are left with more money, spending may increase in total because they use a higher proportion of their income for everyday things.

- An increase in VAT will raise prices so people cut consumption.

Businesses can either pass the indirect tax increase on as higher prices to customers or accept lower profit margins. Sometimes they can't pass all the costs onto the customer. For instance, if the government raised VAT then the increased prices of products and services will reduce the people's real incomes. In other words, they won't be able to buy so much with their pounds. Unless they are prepared to borrow they will buy fewer goods and services. Businesses then have to react to lower demand. Stocks increase, so production will be cut back and businesses may be forced to lower prices to get rid of unwanted stocks.

Any increase in indirect taxation like VAT does not redistribute income, as it is a tax on spending. It won't lead to a fairer Britain because lower earners tend to spend a higher proportion of their incomes than higher earners.

- Taxes on specific products can change buying habits.

Excise duties on car fuel, alcohol and tobacco are designed to influence buying habits and bring in revenue. Increasing excise duties on these products will reduce consumption, but the amount depends on alternatives.

Other indirect taxes include tariffs or import duties. Such tariffs discourage customers from buying the imports and encourage them to buy home-produced products. However, businesses may still need to import components which are subject to duties. Tariffs are set by the European Union (EU) on a range of goods and services imported from non-EU countries. The UK government cannot go alone and change these.

Taxation and businesses

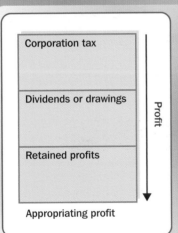

| Corporation tax |
| Dividends or drawings |
| Retained profits |

Profit

Appropriating profit

A decrease in corporation tax will leave a bigger slice of the profits in the business. Companies can choose to give higher dividends to their shareholders or retain more within the business for future investment. Either way a decrease in corporation tax should be an incentive for businesses to invest while an increase would be a disincentive.

An increase in National Insurance will be a cost to businesses as they pay part of this. A decrease would benefit them, as their costs would fall and workers would have more disposable income to spend.

Next steps

Find out more about how tax affects businesses by using a combination of key terms such as 'business tax, UK, CBI, tax evasion, tobacco, smuggling' into news sites like the BBC and the Guardian. You can also find information from the websites listed below.

WWW

www.hm-treasury.gov.uk

www.inlandrevenue.gov.uk

http://www.uktax.demon.co.uk/

http://www.hmce.gov.uk/

http://www.bbc.co.uk/

http://www.guardian.co.uk/

Winners and losers

It may sound as if any increase in tax will be detrimental to businesses, but remember that the tax is being raised in order to be spent by the government. Some of the money may be spent in ways that help business either directly or by providing business opportunities. Transport, health and education are all important to business and cost the government money.

KEY TERMS

Real incomes is where incomes have been adjusted to take out the effect of price increases.

Disposable income is the amount people are left with after tax and other deductions and the addition of tax credit.

What is the business cycle?

Specification Content

The business cycle and changes in the level of economic activity

starSTUDY
Booms and slumps

Businesses continue to expand but unemployment is low and land is not vacant. Businesses must pay higher wages to attract staff from other businesses. Rents for properties go up.

The increase in costs is passed onto the consumer in higher prices. The products and services are less competitive because it is cheaper to buy from abroad.

Businesses invest in new equipment and buildings to meet high demand. They employ more people. Consumers spend more even if it means borrowing more.

People become worried about their future. They may be concerned about the risk of losing their jobs so they cut back on some of their spending, borrow less and save more.

The boom gets going when consumers and businesses have confidence in the future.

The demand for UK goods and services drops. Businesses cut production and employ fewer people. As unemployment rises, consumer spending and confidence falls further.

Many businesses become more cautious and suspend their plans to buy new equipment and the recession deepens to a slump.

1 What effect does 'having confidence in the future' have on consumers and businesses?

2 Why do businesses invest in new equipment and buildings?

3 Why does this investment help the economy to grow?

4 Why do prices go up?

5 Why does it become hard to sell the products?

6 Why do people spend less? What effect does this have on business?

7 If businesses reduce investment, how does this affect consumers?

8 What will happen to prices in a period when investment falls?

KEY TERMS

Business cycle shows the patterns of growth and decline in the economy. It creates fluctuations in demand for many products.

Boom occurs when output is growing very fast.

Recession happens when output is growing more slowly after a period of rapid growth.

Slump occurs when output actually falls over a six-month period.

Next steps

Economic indicators vary from country to country and from region to region.

1 Find out the current inflation rates in the UK, some EU countries and in the USA. What has been happening over the last five years? Also find out their rates of economic growth and the interest rates.

2 The rate of unemployment can differ widely between countries too. Check what is happening in your selection of countries.

3 House price changes can be used to indicate inflationary pressure in regions. Visit www.nationwide.co.uk/hpi/quarterly/prices.htm to find which areas of the UK are experiencing the highest house price rises and which the lowest. Explain your findings.

4 Find out how unemployment and wage levels vary across the country using www.nationalstatistics.gov.uk

The business cycle

Economies generally grow but not on a steady path. Sometimes they grow fast, other times they grow more slowly or even shrink. This path is known as the business cycle.

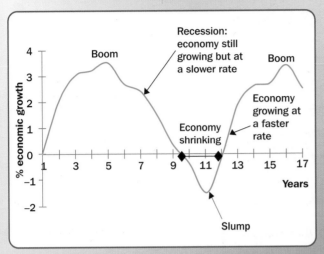

The period of rapid growth is called a boom and the part of the cycle when businesses reduce their output is called a recession. If total output actually falls, a slump has set in. The government tries to even out the peaks and troughs of the business cycle to make the economy more stable. They try to stop inflation and unemployment rising because of the negative effects on people, businesses and the economy in an international context.

WHAT ARE THE SIGNS?

A growing economy will make a country and its citizens better off. Governments need to know how well the economy is performing and the trends for the future. Some indicators are clearly visible. Is there a lot of construction going on or are more buildings left empty when businesses close down? Other information can come from surveys. Are people spending more or less than they used to? Are they more or less worried about losing their job? Data is collected all the time as the government and other organisations try to predict the future. The formal economy is measured by working out what has been produced in one year. This is known as Gross Domestic Product (GDP).

WHY FEAR INFLATION?

Inflation is caused by:

> People having too much to spend. House prices, for example, rise fast when there are more buyers than sellers.

> Costs rising. If oil prices rise, costs rise for all businesses that use oil and petrol.

Businesses don't like inflation because it increases costs. They may be able to pass this on by increasing prices but they may have to cut their profit margins and absorb the increase if customers are not prepared to pay more.

Costs may rise for all sorts of reasons. Wages or materials may rise. Admin costs will also rise if there is constant change because shops will have to change prices and forms. Computer systems will have to be updated.

Businesses in one country can also lose out if inflation in other countries is at a lower rate. The price rises make our products and services more expensive to buy. Rising prices in the UK will make holidays here cost more and these will become less attractive. More of us will go abroad for our holidays and fewer foreigners will want to come here for their holidays.

WHAT'S WRONG WITH UNEMPLOYMENT?

When economies are in recession or slump, unemployment generally rises. If businesses cut production, they often make people redundant. Unemployment causes many social problems and costs the economy money because taxes are used to pay benefits to those who can't find work.

Businesses do not like periods of high unemployment because if people don't have jobs, their spending power is cut and demand falls. This makes selling products more difficult and businesses may find it hard to make a profit. Wages in some parts of the country may fall, making production cheaper but the fall in demand may offset this.

Critical thinking

1 What evidence of the business cycle can you see in your local area? Evaluate the effects of these changes on people and businesses. How do the changes contribute to the growth or recession in the economy of the country as a whole?

2 The reactions of businesses when the economy starts to see slower economic growth can contribute to a recession. Why might this happen? In what ways can business confidence be a self-fulfilling prophecy? Can governments talk up the economy in a recession?

3 The project to build Terminal 5 at Heathrow airport will create a shortage of building workers in the south-east for other projects. How will the new terminal contribute to economic growth? What problems and benefits will the new terminal cause for businesses in the south-east?

Interconnected business

starSTUDY
International connections

Japanese economy booms

Euro rises steeply

Dramatic rise in oil prices

Fear of war hits trade

Inflation faster in UK

Unemployment rises fast in France and Germany

1 What effect will these changes have on either the country concerned or the world economy?

2 What effect will these changes have on the UK economy?

3 Why will businesses that are not involved in trade be affected by changes in other countries?

4 What changes in the local, national and international economy might affect a hairdresser, a computer retailer or a car manufacturer?

5 What might businesses do to protect themselves from potentially damaging changes in the UK or elsewhere?

Specification Content

Changes in level of economic activity at local, national and international level

KEY TERMS

Business failure data measures the number of businesses that go into liquidation every quarter. These can be added to give annual figures.

Discretionary spending is the spending we make after all our contracted outgoings have been met and after all purchases for basic needs.

 www

http://www.cbi.org.uk/home.html

http://www.insolvency.gov.uk/

Business links

Businesses can't insulate themselves completely from changes taking place in other parts of the world. Every country has its business cycle and they do not all move together so while one country might be booming another may be in recession. Countries with large economies can affect others because a recession will mean less demand and therefore people will buy fewer imports. Equally, a booming economy will mean more demand and more imports.

There is a close link between the business cycle and business failure as the graph shows. As the rate of economic growth slows, more businesses fail. More British companies went under in 2002, for example, than in any year since the recession of the early 1990s.

1 Describe and explain the relationship between business failures and the business cycle.

2 Why can businesses fail even when the economy is growing?

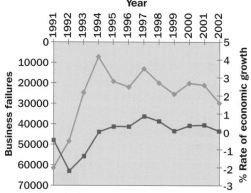

Business cycle and business failures

Year	Number of business failures	% Rate of economic growth
1991	47777	-2
1992	62767	-0.5
1993	55733	2.2
1994	43688	4.2
1995	41303	2.8
1996	41107	2.5
1997	36368	3.5
1998	40847	2.7
1999	43365	2.1
2000	40847	2.7
2001	40539	2.6
2002	43458	1.6

Legend: Number of business failures; % Rate of economic growth

Who survives?

WHO SURVIVES?

Not all businesses are affected in the same way from the ups and downs of a trade cycle. Some can ride out the storm easily. The demand for their products and services is hardly affected but for others a downturn in economic growth rates makes life very difficult. Some of these businesses are on the margins of survival. A small change in demand may just tip the balance and hard won profits turn into losses. A build up of stocks combined with lower sales revenue also causes cash flow problems. Banks are reluctant to lend and the receivers can be called in.

Businesses that continue to perform well in a recession would include those providing for contracted outgoings such as mortgage and insurance companies and those providing basic or necessary products and services such as food and petrol. These are things we continue to need and must buy. In fact some businesses, such as white goods repairs, actually benefit from a recession.

Discretionary spending takes place when all necessities have been paid for. In an economic downturn the amount of discretionary spending falls because more people are out of work, or have lower incomes from less overtime. They are also more worried about their jobs, so may save more. Businesses that produce goods and services, which are paid for from discretionary spending, will suffer in an economic downturn but thrive when there is increasing growth.

The pattern can be uneven both geographically and according to the type of business. Some areas of the country are affected more than others. Variations also occur between countries. Some will grow more quickly in a period of growth and others will be more affected by a recession than others. There can also be a difference within towns.

Surviving the cycle

The data on business failures suggests that many businesses find it difficult to cope with downturns in the business cycle. These are often small businesses supplying large companies which either reduce their orders, force down prices or use their power to delay vital payments. This puts pressure on profits and also more businesses find it difficult to raise cash to pay creditors.

Many businesses are geared up to ride the ups and downs of the business cycle. They may have a flexible workforce so are able to employ a greater number of

In a recession

- Diversify and spread risks
- Look for greater cost cutting measures. For example they might cut training and replace equipment less frequently
- Reduce risk-taking investment
- Reduce prices and profit margins
- Release workers and cut production
- Cut overtime

In growth

- Put up prices and increase profit margins
- Increase investment
- Increase overtime
- Introduce another shift
- Increase research and development

temporary workers in growth and then release them in decline. Another tactic is to employ people for a specific project so they are on short-term contracts.

Critical thinking

The booming Trowbridge-based company, Apetito, is recruiting more staff. Apetito is the largest supplier of frozen ready meals to vulnerable groups in the country, supplying 55% of the meals-on-wheels market. The number of vulnerable people increases year on year since we are an ageing population. These people have to eat and it becomes the local authority responsibility to make sure they get this basic need.

1 Explain why Apetito is safe in recession.

2 Identify four businesses that are recession-proof and explain why.

3 Identify four businesses that are vulnerable to recession and explain why. What might they do to become more recession proof?

Next steps

1 Find out how a business you know reacts to the business cycle.

2 Use the Internet to search for up-to-date information about our economy and business performance.

testing–testing

External influences – the market

Cinema proves pundits wrong

The resurgence of the cinema business during the past decade or so has been astounding. For years doom and gloom pundits had written off cinema as a mass entertainment industry. Television and later home videos were the nails that would finally close the coffin of this once all-powerful media. The dark days of the 1970s and early 1980s witnessed countless once much-loved local cinemas across the country converted into bingo halls or just simply left to rot. UK cinema audiences hit their lowest point in 1984 when 54 million visits were made.

How things have moved on. Events have changed and the 1990s saw a resurgence in the film industry. Improved marketing combined with better films shown in new comfortable multiplex cinemas began to attract back customers.

Today sees work start on Bath's first multiplex cinema complex as the city – rather belatedly – jumps on the back of an entertainment revolution.

Many fear that Bath's existing cinemas will not survive for long when the Odeon multiplex opens in around 18 months' time. One small independent cinema will focus even more on specialist films in an effort to survive.

Source: Bath Chronicle, Cinema admissions

Cinema admissions and screens

	Admissions	Screens
1980	*101 million*	*1562*
1984	*54 million*	*1450*
1990	*91 million*	*1715*
2000	*142.5 million*	*2700*
2001	*155.91 million*	*3164*
2002	*176.91 million*	*3258*

Source: British Film Council

Disposable income

Between 1995 and 2001 disposable income rose by 20%.

easyCinema

easyCinema has chosen Milton Keynes for its first cinema. Booking early means you pay less. Booking off peak also means lower ticket prices. You must buy online as there is no box office at the cinema. It's a no frills service.

Source: easyCinema

1 What evidence is there that demand to see films has changed? **(4 marks)**

 Look for data in the evidence in the form of numbers, graphs or text. Remember demand can fall as well as rise. Think about whether the market is a volatile one.

2 a How has demand changed? **(2 marks)**

  b Suggest possible causes of this change. **(6 marks)**

 Part (a) wants you to point out if the change has been in one direction or if it has switched. You should use some of the data to illustrate the change either by quoting directly or preferably by providing a percentage change. Part (b) wants you to link the evidence to some of the standard reasons for people changing their buying habits.

3 Demonstrate the change in demand using a diagram between 1980 and 2000. **(3 marks)**

 You will need to be able to construct a simple diagram showing the shifts in demand curve. It is easier if you keep the price the same and then you can use actual admission figures on the x-axis. Your diagram must have a written explanation.

4 How might the cinema industry react to the trends in the short run and in the long run? **(8 marks)**

 You must consider both the decline in demand and the increase in demand to see films. Remember that businesses react differently in the short run from in the long run.

5 Demonstrate the change in supply using a diagram **(3 marks)**

 A change in supply is referring to the long-run position. You will need to plot three different supply curves to show the shifts in them. As with question 3 it will be easier if you keep the price the same and then you can use the actual number of cinema screens on the x-axis. Your diagram must have an explanation.

6 To what extent is there a danger of over supply in the market? **(10 marks)**

help! You should consider reasons why there might be an oversupply. There could be a short-term explanation, but also consider the long-term factors. Risk takers can get it wrong for a number of reasons. The introduction of a new player in the market with a different strategy might also be significant.

7 a How is easyCinema attempting to gain a competitive advantage? **(4 marks)**

  b What effect will easyCinema have on the competition should it be successful and open cinemas throughout the UK? **(8 marks)**

help! Part (a) wants an explanation of what 'competitive advantage' might be and for you to apply this to the strategy adopted by easyCinema. Part (b) wants you to consider the negative effects on the other cinemas, but also how they may react.

testing–testing

Conversions

Terry manages and owns shares in W H Bence Ltd. The business converts vans and lorries into mobile libraries, exhibition units and any other vehicle the customer wants. Terry's business is sensitive to the business cycle and other external influences, because the firm depends on other companies' and local authorities' spending plans. When money is tight these organisations cut back on their orders to W H Bence. The opposite happens during times of economic growth.

A couple of years ago the order book was full for the next three months. Orders were coming in thick and fast and Terry was turning away customers. He even introduced additional shift work, as deadlines could not be met with overtime alone. To recruit workers Terry needed to attract them from other businesses by offering higher wages. He was able to pass the increased costs onto his customers. After all, he had a full order book.

But times have changed. The economy is slowing down and some forecasters believe we will soon be entering a recession. The government increased national insurance rates to both employees and employers. These higher costs have affected all businesses. Many of Terry's customers have to find savings in order to manage their budgets. Some have cancelled their orders and others are asking for the bare minimum to be done on conversions. It is bad news for Terry, his business and his workforce. Orders have nearly dried up and he has already made several of his employees redundant. Less cash is coming in and he still has the same overheads. At least the cost of borrowing has fallen with lower interest rates, but the bank won't support him forever.

With all these pressures Terry still has to devote more time to finding new orders. This means looking into European markets to export his products. He has been on several trips to France and Germany, both countries that are part of the eurozone. The value of the pound has been falling against the euro, which means the exchange rate gives him a price advantage over his foreign competitors, especially since he buys most of his materials from UK-based businesses and so has few imported components. However, buyers would have transaction costs to consider in exchanging euros for pounds. He doesn't like all the paper work involved in trading with the EU but he feels that he has to look for new markets.

Corporation Tax take falls

As profit levels fall, on average, the Inland Revenue is recording a reduction in revenue from Corporation Tax

National Insurance rise hits all

The increase in National Insurance, announced in the budget, has hit pay packets. Both employers and employees are

assessment questions

1 What is meant by the terms business cycle, recession and boom? **(6 marks)**

> *help!* Straightforward question asking for definitions, but do try to relate the three terms together.

2 What decisions did Terry make during a period of economic growth?
How might such decisions affect the inflation rate if adopted by most businesses? **(6 marks)**

> *help!* Use the evidence to state the decisions he made and then you must comment on the connection between these decisions and changes in inflation levels.

3 a National Insurance is a direct tax. Define direct tax and provide another example of it. **(2 marks)**

   b Explain the effect of a decrease in direct tax on disposable incomes. **(4 marks)**

> *help!* Part (a) is straightforward. Part (b) requires you to make the connection between direct taxation and disposable incomes

4 What is an indirect tax? Give two examples? **(3 marks)**

> *help!* Straightforward

5 a In what ways might an increase in National Insurance affect both businesses and the economy? **(4 marks)**

   b Suggest how this might affect the UK's competitiveness against other countries. **(4 marks)**

> *help!* Part (a) wants you to make the connection between tax increases and costs and therefore inflation. Use the answer to Part (a) to support your Part (b) argument.

6 Why might the government choose to increase National Insurance tax at the same time as the economy is slowing down? **(4 marks)**

> *help!* You should comment on the effect that increasing National Insurance has on people's disposable incomes and their spending. Say why this accelerates the slowdown in the economy. There must be a reason for the government doing this. Think of the need to balance its budget.

7 Evaluate Terry's strategy of looking for new markets in Europe. **(10 marks)**

> *help!* Evaluations ask you to look at arguments for and against as well as short and long term. Explain the need to look in the eurozone and then comment on the advantages of the declining value of the pound in the short run. Suggest some difficulties that Terry may face and then make a comment about exchange rates moving in both directions.

8 Explain how an increase in the UK exchange rate might affect UK businesses? **(6 marks)**

> *help!* Comment on the rising value of the pound on both importing and exporting businesses. Think about the worry of currency fluctuations and how this can be resolved. Does this present opportunities in the domestic market?

9 Analyse the effect changes in interest rates will have on Terry's business? **(9 marks)**

> *help!* You need to consider both rises and falls in interest rates and whether this has a positive or negative impact on Terry. Can Terry's businesses easily cope with interest rate changes? Are others subject to the same difficulties?

Technology: threat or opportunity?

Specification Content

Technological change: opportunities and threats of technology upon the firm of new products and production methods

starSTUDY

A virtual business

Virgin Mobile is a technology business. It sells technology and it runs on technology. It doesn't make phones and it doesn't run a network. It sells phones that run on the T-Mobile network.

The business runs from a call centre in Trowbridge, Wiltshire which employs 1200 people. It has 2.6 million customers who are sold products and looked after from Trowbridge. Virgin Mobile's objective is to grow. Customer care is Virgin Mobile's key strategy for adding value so the systems have to guarantee that every customer is contented. The Customer Service Agents (CSA) have to be well trained, motivated and monitored and technology can help.

The company has a huge management information system which monitors the

- quality of the call
- CSA performance
- reaction time in dealing with a call.

The Real Time Management system juggles the workload. When things get hectic, multi-skilled employees are brought into the front line. When all is quiet, CSAs are taken off duty for training.

Monitoring is carried out by another system that enables calls to be selected randomly. The aim is to improve staff retention and motivation by financial rewards for good performance. This in turn serves to improve the quality of the service as well as identifying training needs. This all saves team leaders' time.

Vision is Virgin Mobile's intranet. It provides staff with information about orders and payments. It also has e-learning material for staff to use at quiet times.

The Knowledge is an expert diagnostic system that helps CSAs to meet customer needs to best effect by picking out key words and giving alternative solutions. The agent can then choose the one that fits the bill.

Despite all the technology, Virgin Mobile tries not to forget the people. It is hard to recruit in Trowbridge, so trained people are valuable. The rate of turnover was very high but is now coming down as the company develops strategies for keeping people involved and happy.

1 How does Virgin Mobile use technology to achieve its objectives?
2 How does it use technology to save money?
3 How can it use technology to motivate its staff?
4 What would happen to Virgin Mobile if it got left behind in the technology stakes?

Keeping ahead of the game

Businesses have always had to watch how technology changes. It just seems to change more quickly today than it did a hundred years ago. There is often a fear that technological change leads to unemployment – and in specific industries this is often the case. Introducing a laser operated cutting machine in a clothing factory will probably put people out of work but it may also mean that the clothes are cheaper, therefore people can buy a greater variety of products – so demand and employment increase in other areas.

Technology has resulted in falling prices for many products. Electrical goods of all sorts are relatively much cheaper than a generation ago so we all have more of them. Technology has therefore helped businesses grow and has improved our standard of living. Things we now take for granted, such as washing machines and battery operated radios, were luxuries fifty years ago. Microwave ovens had not even been invented.

Some businesses thrive on doing things in the traditional way but most need to watch developments if they are to keep their place in the market.

Opportunities and threats

IN THE KNOW

OPPORTUNITIES

- **To make business more efficient**

Technology is often used to cut costs or raise quality. Both developments can make a business more competitive. Cutting costs may lead to falling prices and higher sales so both the business and customers win.

Technology can raise quality because a computer which is well programmed does make not mistakes. It is very difficult for a human being to be perfect every time. Quality has become a critical factor for most businesses because customers expect high standards. Cars now break down less frequently because they are built with much more sophisticated systems.

- **To create exciting, new products for customers**

Businesses that develop new products can achieve an advantage over others. It may not last long because others are always trying to catch up. Many work hard to stay ahead of the game. It is important to

be able to recognise potential success. The Sony Walkman nearly never made it to the market place because the company's directors could not imagine that people would want to take music wherever they went!

THREATS

The main threat is that other businesses will get there first. Another is that your business will simply cease to exist because people don't want your products anymore. The final typewriter factory shut down because even the most stuck-in-the-mud typist had finally started to use a computer!

A threat to one stakeholder can be an opportunity for others. Cheap, easy communications, which led to the introduction of the call centre for businesses to access its customers, has changed dimension as call centres are now shifting to India and other places with a cheaper, skilled workforce. This means cost and prices stay low but there is less employment in the UK.

Critical thinking

Broadband comes to Marlborough

The Chamber of Commerce in Marlborough is organising a public meeting to discuss the advantages of broadband. The objective is to discuss ways in which businesses can turn the fast, cheap internet connection to advantage. It is also hoped that the availability of broadband will help to attract businesses to the town.

1 What sorts of businesses might be attracted to Marlborough by the arrival of broadband?

2 How might existing businesses turn it to advantage?

3 What effects might the development of such businesses have on the town?

How might it affect places nearby which do not have broadband?

Next steps

What sorts of businesses are there in your area which use technology to good effect? Use Yellow Pages to see what's there.

People patterns

Specification Content
Social and cultural demographic changes, consumer and employee patterns and influences of other stakeholders

starSTUDY

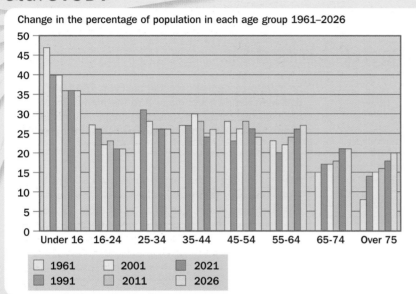

Change in the percentage of population in each age group 1961–2026

Legend:
- 1961
- 1991
- 2001
- 2011
- 2021
- 2026

1 Describe the trend in each age group over the period.

2 What changes do you think have and will take place in the pattern of the products that people want to buy because of these changes?

3 What changes are there in the age structure of the workforce over the period?

4 What effect will the changing balance of dependants have on people's spending power during their working lives?

5 What effect will it have on people who have retired?

6 How does the changing age profile of the population affect the services that governments need to provide?

Source: Social Trends 2003, HMSO.

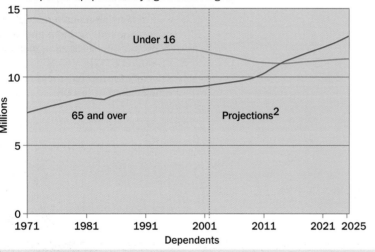

Dependent population: by age United Kingdom

Under 16

65 and over

Projections[2]

Source: Social Trends 2003, HMSO.

Getting older

Businesses are affected in a variety of ways by the size and shape of the population. The bar chart shows that we have an ageing population because the birth rate is falling and people are living longer. This affects both the products that are in demand and the people who are available for work. It also affects what the government needs to provide.

Demographic change also includes the ethnic balance of the population, which results in changes in demand and in the business sector.

www

www.statistics.gov.uk

KEY TERMS

Demographic change means the changes that are taking place in the population.

Changing demand

As people want to buy products that appeal to their age group, the demand for some products will increase and others will fall. There will be less demand for 18–30 style holidays and more for cruises with Saga – unless other things change too.

• Tastes change over time so older people expect to have a different lifestyle from their parents – thus, they may not want to go on cruises.

• Younger people are more affluent than they used to be, so demand for 18–30 style holidays may continue to increase even when there are fewer young people.

• Advertising aims to affect our choices. Cruises are advertised as holidays for a wider age range. There are lots of adverts for holidays for young people.

Demand for both types of holidays might therefore increase.

• The law can sometimes affect demand. If a law were introduced which limited the amount of money you could take out of the country, the demand for all holidays abroad would fall.

• Chance factors can be responsible for changes. The weather is a prime example. A hurricane can reduce demand for all types of holidays in some parts of the world.

1 Make a list of other examples for each of these factors which influence demand. Sketch a diagram showing what happens to demand for each example. What effect does change have on price?

Population change and the world of work

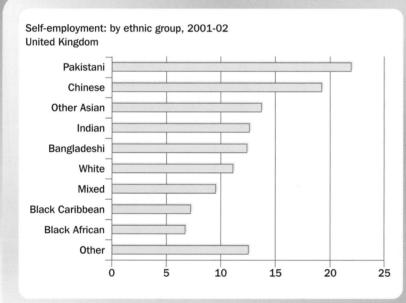

Self-employment: by ethnic group, 2001-02
United Kingdom

Source: Social Trends 2003, HMSO.

As the population grows older, there will initially be a larger proportion of people in the working population, but after a while this effect will diminish. As fewer babies are born and people live longer, the size of the working population will shrink. There will be fewer people earning incomes to support their dependants.

A different ethnic mix can also result in a different attitude to employment. The bar chart shows that some ethnic groups are more likely to be self-employed than others. The structure of employment can therefore shift over time as the ethnic composition of the population changes.

Other stakeholders

Stakeholders can affect demand in all sorts of ways. Pressure groups are key examples because they generally want to cut or increase demand for a product. The anti-smoking lobby has successfully campaigned against tobacco advertising and their availability. Low alcohol beers are now a standard line in every supermarket partly in response to drink-driving campaigners.

Critical thinking

You are planning to set up a business which you intend to be successful. Decide what your business will do, using the factors that influence demand to help you.

Next steps

Chose six businesses in you local area and work out how their sales are affected by changes in demand.

Employment rights and wrongs

Specification Content

The purpose and impact of legislation upon the firm regarding its employment policies

star**STUDY**

Man sacked after 11 years with no complaints

A man sacked unfairly after 26 years' service said his reputation has been restored after an employment tribunal awarded him maximum compensation.

Malcolm Clark was awarded £58,300 after the tribunal ruled he had been dismissed unfairly by Moores Furniture Group Limited.

The company, which sells kitchen and bathroom units to bulk buyers, claimed that Mr Clark was not up to his job, despite having been regional sales manager for 11 years without any complaints from his bosses.

Collar and tie ruling thrown out

Matthew Thompson was celebrating last night after winning his case for sexual discrimination. He had challenged a ruling by Stockport Jobcentre that men had to wear collars and ties while women could wear T-shirts.

The tribunal ruled that he was being treated less favourably because the requirement to wear a tie was gender based.

Asian employee wins case

Amit Bhadhuri was overlooked for the post of racial harassment co-ordinator. Despite the fact that he speaks three languages apart from English and met all the criteria for the job, it was offered to someone else. The employer claimed that he had not performed well when interviewed but the notes taken at the time did not reflect this.

The job should have been an internal appointment but was given to a white woman from outside the organisation. The tribunal ruled that this was a serious case of discrimination.

1. What was the cause of discrimination in each of these cases?
2. Why is it important for businesses to keep records such as interview notes?
3. Why are people paid compensation if their ex-employer is found to have broken the law?
4. Why is it important to have laws about fair employment?

Who holds the power?

Employees usually hold a weaker position than their employers, so laws are in place to protect them. Laws are passed by parliament, having gone through many stages to ensure that they are well conceived and agreed by the majority. In this field, laws are civil rather than criminal so people who feel that their rights have been infringed will take a case to a court, known as a tribunal, rather than being dealt with by the police.

Employees, business and the law

The law protects people who work, or are seeking work, in a range of ways. The laws apply to everyone who works, whether it is in a business or government organisation.

- Organisations must not discriminate between people because of their sex, religion, ethnic origin or disability. From recruitment to promotion, all decisions must be seen to be even-handed. It is important to keep records so that there is evidence to show how decisions have been made.

- Organisations must not dismiss people unfairly. There have to be very clear reasons why people are dismissed and formal processes must be carried out. If things are changing, they will be entitled to training rather than dismissal. If the job has really come to an end, the person can be made redundant. An employee can take the employer to an Employment Tribunal if they consider the decision to be unfair. The Tribunal will come to a conclusion about whether the employer's action was fair and the process was carried out properly. If the employer is found to have broken the rules, the ex-employee will be granted compensation.

- Organisations must provide a safe and healthy working environment. There are standards laid down for many aspects of the working environment. They range from the safe use of computers to protection on machinery and fire risks. Visitors must be protected too.

go to → *Find out more about the law on page 160.*

Most larger organisations employ human resource managers to ensure that the systems are in place to deal with recruitment, selection and other aspects of responsibility to employees. Part of the job involves checking that the legal requirements are met and keeping records to show that everything has been carried out correctly.

go to → *Find out more about human resource management on page 154.*

You don't need to know the names and details of the laws. What is important is why they are there and how they affect people, businesses and other organisations.

Employees have responsibilities too

The law is there to protect people in employment because they are usually in a weaker position but, as employees, they also have responsibilities. Their legal responsibility is based on the contract they sign when they start a job. This will specify their working hours, holidays and what they are expected to do.

The criminal law also applies of course. People should not steal, damage property, hurt people or break any of the other laws that affect everyday life.

go to → *Find out more about peoples ethical responsibility on page 78.*

Next steps

Local newspapers are a good source of information about businesses and the law. Have a look at a local newspaper's website and search for Employment Tribunal to find out what's been going on locally.

Critical thinking

1 Employment law can add to the cost of a business. Explain how. Why do you think people are more likely to work effectively if they feel that they are being fairly treated?

2 Change can be challenging for a business and its staff. Draw up a spider diagram showing the issues that might arise if a business wants to put in a new, automated system of production on a new site. How might this affect the staff?

KEY TERMS

Compensation is paid to people when a business has broken employment law.

Contract – a legal agreement between people. An employment contract will lay down the rights and responsibilities of employee and employer.

Discrimination occurs when people are not given equal opportunities. Such action breaks the law if it is on grounds of sex, religion, ethnic origin or disability.

Employment Tribunals are set up to decide whether employers have acted illegally towards employees.

Redundancy occurs when the work a person does is no longer required.

The law, customers and other stakeholders

PART 1: BUSINESSES, THEIR OBJECTIVES AND THE ENVIRONMENT

starSTUDY

£20,000 Pirate CDs seized in market raid

Four men were arrested after trading standards officers raided Walton Street market in Hull. Computers and copying devices plus thousands of master disks were subsequently removed from houses in the city.

The real value of the CDs, in terms of losses to the music industry, was approaching £1 million.

The trading standards department said they frequently received complaints from local retailers who were suffering because of the activities of these pirates and customers who have bought these low quality recordings.

Prison for crooked car dealer

Gordon Booth, a car dealer from Bexhill-on-Sea, was sent to prison for three months after being found guilty of five trading standards offences.

He had turned back the clock so it showed a false mileage and pretended to be a private seller rather than a business. A customer had returned a car on discovering that the clock had been turned back, but Mr Booth sold it to someone else who had no idea that it had a false mileage.

A spokesperson for Sussex County Council said, 'Our Trading Standards Officers will continue to focus on the rogue element of the motor trade and bring to book those who set out intentionally to mislead the public.'

Source: adapted from www.eastsussexcc.gov.uk

Honesty is the best policy

A complaint by a customer was upheld by the Advertising Standards Authority (ASA) when Dell made the following claim about one of its computers: 'Everything about it is bigger except the price – over £120 off – was £1,121'.

There was no evidence to show that the price had really been cut.

The ASA has a voluntary code for advertisers, which is generally respected. When criticisms are made, companies take notice and change their ways.

1 How were customers hurt by each of these offences?

2 How were other businesses hurt by the offences?

3 Why is it important to challenge businesses that try to take advantage of customers?

4 Why do you think that organisations abide by the rulings of the Advertising Standards Authority?

Specification Content

The purpose and impact of legislation upon the firm regarding its productive organisation and marketing

Protecting the customer

Customers hope they will receive the product they think they are buying. When they see an advert, they expect it to reflect the product that is on offer. This is not always the case. Customers are usually in a weaker position than the companies they are buying from unless there is a lot of competition. Even then – if a product doesn't match the claims, it can be hard to get redress despite companies' offers of customer service. The law is there to protect people.

Looking after the shareholders

IN THE KNOW

People who invest money in a business also need protection. Every year a public company must produce an annual return and accounts. This report sets out the financial situation of the company and gives an account of the key events of the preceding year. A company must also hold an Annual General Meeting which the shareholders are invited to attend. At the meeting, they can challenge directors of the business if they are not happy about events. Companies have to give shareholders details of directors' pay and conditions. When this came into force, shareholders expressed concern about rewards that they felt were excessive and directors had to explain their actions.

Customers and the law

IN THE KNOW

The law tries to prevent businesses and other organisations from misleading and endangering customers and other businesses.

- Cars that are inaccurately described may turn out to be death traps.

- People can be tempted to buy one company's product rather than another's because of inaccurate advertising claims.

- 'Fake' products may be poor quality and damage genuine competitors.

The law therefore expects products to be:

- as they are claimed

- safe.

A range of laws covers these aspects of consumer protection. They are enforced by Trading Standards Offices, who work for local authorities. They inspect catering premises and other outlets as well as responding to complaints from unhappy customers.

The main effect on business is to increase costs. New legislation on safety, for example, means a tighter specification and more inspection of products. Safety is obviously of paramount importance but sometimes businesses feel that the requirements are excessive.

BUSINESS POWER

Customers are very dependent on the businesses that supply their utilities such as water and power. Although there is now competition between these businesses, the government has set up bodies to oversee the industries.

Ofwat and Ofcom control the water and communications businesses. Profits are limited in the hope that customers will not be exploited. Competition itself can have this effect but these bodies offer additional protection.

Parliamentary power

Parliament passes laws to protect people and businesses from the power of others. Much of this is now influenced by European law as the European Union seeks to bring legal harmony across Europe.

However, the Treasury each year sets rates of taxation in the budget and decides on government spending. This affects business in a variety of ways.

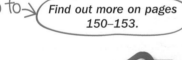

go to → Find out more on pages 150–153.

PEST, PESTg, PESTLE or STEEPLE?

Businesses often want to know what's going on around them and how these factors will affect them. You'll find more information about these factors in the remaining pages of this part of the book. These acronyms may help you to remember the range of influences:

- Political
- Economic
- Social
- Technological
- Environmental – or green
- Legal
- Ecological

KEY TERMS

PEST analysis helps a business to look at some of the external factors that affect it. It stands for political, economic, social and technological. A 'G' can be added for green issues – the environment.

www

www.asa.org.uk

Critical thinking

1 The government banned all advertising of tobacco. Draw up two spider diagrams showing the winners and losers from this decision.

2 Why are shareholders concerned about company directors receiving large reward packages? What effect does it have on the business?

Next steps

1 Have a look at the website of your local trading standards office. You will find it on the local council's website. How does it aim to protect consumers? Is there evidence of recent prosecutions? If so, what are they about?

2 Carry out a web search to find out how businesses are viewing the European Union. What issues are at the top of the agenda? Are there different views? What do you think? Why?

Government – a consumer and provider

Specification Content

The state as a consumer and provider

starSTUDY

Capita plc – government business

Capita plc is a big business with a turnover of about £1 billion and profits of over £100 million. It runs government activities and provides services for the private sector. About half its business comes from the government. Here are some examples of the work it does.

Criminal Records Bureau

Organisations often want to know if people they are recruiting have criminal records. People who work as teachers and in childcare have to be checked. The CRB carries out these checks. Capita runs it.

Local e-government website

The website uses information, practical tools and best practice recommendations to help local councils make e-government a reality in their communities. Capita set up and runs the website.

London's Congestion Charge

Capita sets and manages the customer services infrastructure. This includes multi-contact customer service centres for payment by telephone, web and IVR (interactive voice recognition), the back office processes and the retail network where payments

can be made, such as shops, kiosks and petrol stations.

Council Tax in Brent, London

The London Borough of Brent selected Capita to organise and collect the Council Tax and Business Rates as well as providing IT support.

Enforcement service

Capita's transport team advise on where to set up cameras and controlled zones, install the communications infrastructure, introduce and operate transport schemes, manage the back office processing operation and the penalty enforcement process.

1 What do these activities have in common?
2 Why do you think the government wants businesses to run them?
3 How would you select a business to run such activities? Why?
4 Look back at page 51 where you will find a chart showing government spending. Use this information to make a list of the things that governments must buy.

Running government business

Big business

The government spends over £400 billion every year, which makes it the country's biggest consumer by far. This is about 40% of all the country's spending.

Business is affected both directly and indirectly, depending on how the money is spent.

• Contracts with businesses to provide products and services keep companies like Capita busy. The work will increase turnover and, hopefully, profits. To make sure that the government is getting value for money, every contract is put out to **tender** so companies have to put a document together showing how they will organise the work and what it will cost.

The government then chooses the one it thinks will work most effectively.

• Benefits for people who need help increases their spending power, so demand for products rises.

• Paying people who work for the government increases spending power and the money is recycled to business.

When people's spending power is increased, the money is often used to buy more consumer products, including services, so business as a whole benefits. People who work for the government provide all sorts of services that we need but they do not add directly to the country's output and wealth.

Providing services

Businesses need the **infrastructure** that government provides if they are to work effectively. They need, for example:

- an educated workforce

- a healthy workforce

- transport networks to move resources and products around the country

- a law-abiding population.

All these things are the result of government spending. The pie chart on page 51 shows how much is spent on each of these services.

How the government spends our taxes

IN THE KNOW

Governments spend a high proportion of the country's total spending. The objective is to support people and the economy. In doing so, it provides the infrastructure that businesses need and opportunities for them.

As a customer, the government has to buy a wide range of products for schools, hospitals and its other services. The customer will be a local authority or hospital trust but the money will come via the government from the taxpayer.

The government also 'buys' roads and other major items of infrastructure such as schools and hospitals. Major construction companies will tender for the work in competition with each other. This is such big business that companies have been set up to gather information on new opportunities so that suppliers know what is available. The Tendermatch website is just one example.

As a provider, the government uses its revenue to ensure that people and businesses have the support that they need. This comes in the form of benefits, pensions, education and healthcare etc. The decisions about what is provided and the level of provision are political and will depend on the attitudes of the government of the day.

How does education help business?

Critical thinking

Work out how a business would be affected by a poorly educated or unhealthy workforce. How would its costs be increased?

KEY TERMS

Infrastructure includes all the investment in communications, transport and local services, which helps people and businesses to live and work effectively.

Tenders are put out by organisations for work to be done. Bidders put together a document explaining how they will carry out the work and the costs involved.

 **www**

www.cbi.org.uk

www.tendermatch.co.uk

Next steps

1 Find out how congestion affects business. Try the website of the Confederation of British Industry and the government department responsible for transport. What is the government trying to do about it? How successful are its schemes?

2 Have a look at the Tendermatch website to find out the range of tenders that are on offer at the moment. What are tenders looking for?

3 Find out about another business that wins government contracts. Try Group4 or Jarvis. What services does the business offer? Try a newspaper search to see if there is any comment on its activities.

Government: supports and constraints

starSTUDY
A root and branch make-over

Christine Newman runs Civic Trees, which provides both trees and advice about them. She even supplies trees for films and television. The business seemed to be doing well. It had 24 staff and its turnover was growing, but on closer inspection it was making a loss. Christine turned to her local Business Link to help her solve the problem.

The adviser looked at the business and gave advice. He then worked with her to put it into practice. He suggested that she:

- looked at the value that was being added instead of turnover and profit

Civic Trees on location

- cost more carefully when she gave quotes to customers.

Once she had got this right she should look for more customers to build the business.

Within a year Christine's profits were up three-fold while turnover fell. This meant that in the past some of their projects had earned no profit.

1 How does Christine's business add value?
2 What sort of costs does a business like this have to cover?
3 How can a business have an increasing turnover but be losing money?
4 What costs do you think Christine forgot when giving quotes for new business?
5 Why is it easier for an adviser to identify the problems than someone who works in the business all the time?
6 Why was this advice important to the local area as well as the business itself?

A helping hand

The government provides assistance to businesses of all shapes and sizes. Christine turned to her local Business Link, a nationwide service that offers guidance and some grants to small and medium-sized businesses.

The nature of the help generally depends on the part of the country where the business is located.

In wealthy areas, guidance and some small grants are available. In areas of high unemployment more help is possible. On some occasions big businesses are given help to prevent them going under and creating more unemployment.

State support

The government provides help in a variety of ways for small and medium-sized businesses. This may mean:

- grants for innovation which cover the costs of hiring an expert to advise

- venture capital for starting businesses in disadvantaged areas

- providing guarantees for businesses with insufficient capital for a bank loan through the Small Firms Loan Guarantee Scheme

- tax relief on new investments.

The type of support available changes over time and according to location. The Department of Trade and Industry website gives the latest information. The EU limits the help that a government can give so that businesses in one country are not given an unfair advantage over others.

Brewing power?

Interbrew, a Belgium brewing company, bought the brewing part of Bass plc. It had already acquired Whitbread's brewing business and now had a market share of up to 38% of UK beer production and distribution. The merger was referred to the Competition Commission, a government agency that investigates the effect of mergers and takeovers. Its objective is to maintain a level of competition that prevents any business becoming too powerful.

After looking carefully at the effect on customers and other businesses, Interbrew was told that it would have to sell Bass.

1 Why do you think Interbrew wanted to buy Bass?

2 What effect do you think it would have had on customers and competitors?

3 What effect do you think the existence of the Competition Commission has on businesses which are thinking of taking over or merging with another business?

IN THE KNOW

Too much power?

Should Granada merge with Carlton? Should newspapers in one area all belong to the same company? Should Safeway be taken over by one of the other major supermarkets groups? Should Blockbuster take over Apollo? Should shopkeepers be allowed to put Mars ice creams in a fridge provided by Walls?

These are all issues that are dealt with by the Competition Commission, a government body which investigates mergers and takeovers. If one business controls too much of the market for a particular product, it can have an adverse effect on both competitors and customers. It may mean that the price of the product increases or competitors' products don't get a look in, so choice is restricted.

The Commission takes all these things into account and comes to a conclusion which is 'in the public interest'. Sometimes, just being referred to the Commission means that a business thinks again. When Blockbuster wanted to take over Apollo, it withdrew when it realised that the plan had been challenged.

The Competition Act, the law that is the basis of the Commission's decisions, relates to European law. In an attempt to have a 'level playing field' for businesses in Europe, laws are the same across the EU.

Critical thinking

1 Find out about a recent decision made by the Competition Commission. Explain why the decision was made.

2 Why might one business think of the Competition Commission as a constraint while another is pleased that it exists?

3 Find out about the assistance that businesses in your area might be offered by the government by looking at the small business support area of the Department for Trade and Industry website. Compare it with help offered in another part of the country. Explain reasons for the differences.

Next steps

Find out if a business near you has had any help from Business Link. Was it helpful in solving a problem?

WWW

www.dti.gov.uk

www.competition-commission.org.uk

KEY TERMS

Mergers occur when two businesses join together.

Takeovers occur when one business buys another. It may or may not be amicable.

Competition Commission is a government agency that aims to maintain competition between businesses in order to protect the consumer and other businesses.

Business and the environment

Specification Content

Environmental influences on business

starSTUDY

Chemicals kill 100,000 fish

An estimated 100,000 fish were killed after insecticide got into drains on an industrial site close to a river.

The pollution spread over a 13-mile stretch of the River Slea in Lincolnshire, devastating fish stocks. Grown trout, dace, perch, pike, roach, tench and eels were killed. 'It is one of the most serious river pollution incidents in Lincolnshire in living memory', said an officer of the government-run Environment Agency.

'What makes this case particularly sad is that it could have been easily avoided had the procedures for the storage and movement of dangerous chemicals been followed properly.'

The agency confirmed a prosecution was being considered. 'We will continue to do what we can to bring this stretch of river back to life.'

Source: adapted from *Yorkshire Post*, 24 February 2003.

1 What effect did business have on the environment?
2 What costs were incurred by this event?
3 Who pays for these costs?
4 How does the government try to prevent such incidents?

Damaging the environment

Business can damage the environment both deliberately and by accident. Whether it is in the town or country, there are plenty of opportunities for pollution. These often incur social cost because society picks up the bill rather than the people who have caused the pollution.

Critical thinking

A change of power

Drax power station is looking ahead because it will lose its supply of coal when the Selby coalfield closes. Coal will then come from Kellingley coalfield. The problem is that Selby's coal was low in sulphur but Kellingley's has a higher sulphur content. The power station has all the equipment to remove sulphur from its effluent at a level that works for its existing supplies – but won't be adequate for the higher sulphur coal. It has requested to be allowed to raise the level of sulphur in the gases that come from its chimneys.

If it is permitted to do so, it will be able to go on using British coal. If not, it will have to turn to imported coal with a lower sulphur content.

The people of Selby are not happy.

Protesters want people to support their case. The business wants to make the change. Write a leaflet for each side justifying its point of view.

Next steps

Look at some big businesses' websites to find out how they work with the environment. Pick an issue and carry out a search to see if other people have other views about the issue. What do you think?

 www

www.unilever.com

www.bp.com

www.riotinto.com

What sort of pollution?

WATER POLLUTION happens in both rivers and the sea.

- Agriculture causes run off from chemicals that are put on the land so rivers fill up with nitrates that get into our water supplies.

- Businesses quite frequently have accidents, which result in river pollution.

- Rubbish is dumped at sea as a means of getting rid of waste.

- Accidents at sea lead to oil pollution along coasts.

AIR POLLUTION is caused by individuals and businesses.

Whenever we drive cars and trucks, we cause pollution. Businesses cause pollution from certain processes. There are permitted levels for many processes that are monitored by the Environment Agency.

NOISE POLLUTION is caused by both production and service industries.

- A pub or club may keep local residents awake at night.

- An airport, road or railway can disturb people's lives around the clock.

- Businesses can cause noise, but there are regulations to limit nuisance.

WASTE is processed in vast quantities by people and businesses.

Just look at the packaging from your shopping. Most goes into the dustbin and has to be disposed of. Business produces waste as well. There are businesses across the country that collect and dispose of oil and fat because it can't be put down drains. There are also waste products that have to be dealt with in special ways so they don't harm people. This ranges from hospital waste to nuclear waste. Sometimes waste is produced because systems are inefficient or do not use modern technology to minimise the impact.

There are few satisfactory ways of disposing of waste. Incineration and landfill both cause environmental problems. The most satisfactory solution is to reduce it at source. This may add to costs for the business but saves costs for society.

PHYSICAL DAMAGE is caused by the needs of businesses and people.

Everything we mine or quarry leads to environmental damage, whether we can see it or not. A quarry may have a visual impact but a mine can lead to problems later when land starts to subside. It also creates spoil heaps that are hard to disguise.

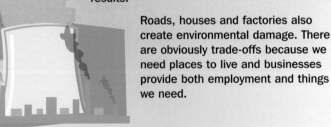

Agriculture changes the landscape in order to produce food cheaply and efficiently to meet market requirements. Questions are being asked about the social costs of producing cheap food because of the environmental damage that results.

Roads, houses and factories also create environmental damage. There are obviously trade-offs because we need places to live and businesses provide both employment and things we need.

Trade-offs

Most activities cause side effects. The extent of the damage will vary and judgements have to be made about the need for a solution. An outright ban on activities may have more costs than setting sensible limits, so the costs and benefits have to be weighed up. Building a new road will have costs to the environment but may save residents in the town from noise and pollution from existing traffic. There is clearly a trade-off. Different people will have different views on the issue. A Public Enquiry is often set up by the government to make decisions on sensitive issues. It will listen to evidence from all parties before coming to a conclusion.

KEY TERMS

Social costs are the total costs of making products. They are calculated by adding up the costs to the business and the costs that are paid by other people and the government.

Environmental controls and business

starSTUDY
Keeping the fish swimming

Specification Content

Managing social costs

Nothing that has yet been done has succeeded in controlling the decline of fish in the North Sea. The European Union laid out its plans for putting things right by revising the measures already in place. It would

- Cut permitted fishing levels by 30–60% according to fish stocks based on scientific evidence
- Set long-term limits
- Limit the capacity of national fleets
- Remove support for purchase of new boats
- Increase funding to help fishermen find alternative employment
- Increase funding for scrapping boats
- Fight illegal fishing
- Involve stakeholders by setting up Regional Advisory Councils.

Source: adapted from www.europa.eu Press releases

But ...

'The most worrying proposal is the cutting of the number of days a vessel could be at sea. Few enterprises could survive cutting 10% of their activity – let alone 50% ... but if it creates a level playing field we're happy with it.'

(Barrie Deas, Chief Executive, National Federation of Fishermen's Organisations)

'We welcome the setting up of Regional Advisory Councils to implement the policy because they will involve trawlermen.'

(John Linstead, Chief Executive, Grimsby Fish Producers' organisation)

'Can nobody see it's due to other causes? They should be addressing oilrig pollution, power station pollution, industrial fishing, seals, aggregate dredging and seismic surveying. There's no one looking at this and everyone's blaming the fishermen. If they cut the fleet by 40% for the whole of Europe the benefit to fish stocks will not be seen.'

(John Linstead, Chief Executive, Grimsby Fish Producers' organisation)

1 Why does the EU consider it necessary to revise the rules affecting the fishing industry?
2 What would happen to the fishing industry and consumers if no measures were taken?
3 How does it plan to encourage less fishing?
4 Why are fishermen unhappy about the plans?
5 Why is the involvement of trawlermen welcomed?
6 Why is it necessary to take action across Europe instead of country by country?
7 How would you deal with John Linstead's comments?
8 Look at the information on the next page and decide which types of measures are being used to control fishing.

Making changes

The fishing industry is just one area of enterprise that is affected by environmental controls. Despite it being generally accepted that something needs to be done, many businesses dislike the interference in their activities. It is particularly hard when dealing with traditional industries in parts of the country where there is little alternative employment. To minimise the impact, most plans include compensation or assistance to make the changes.

Cutting social costs

IN THE KNOW

Reducing social costs often needs legislation because both people and businesses are unwilling to change their habits without a degree of compulsion. Legislation can take a variety of forms. The method needs to be carefully selected so that it works in each situation.

SETTING LIMITS on the use of replaceable resources means using them wisely so they replace themselves. Fishing is a prime example.

BANS ON ACTIVITY may be effective but only work if they can be monitored. Banning traffic from town centres is easy but banning air pollution is more difficult.

COMPENSATION can be paid to people whose livelihood will be affected by change in order to encourage them to participate willingly. This may come in the form of grants and subsidies. A factory might, for example, be given a subsidy to install equipment on its chimneys to remove pollutants.

PERMITS allow a business to pollute to a certain level. If it chooses to cut pollution below the required level, it can sell its permits to other businesses that don't want to cut their levels – but are prepared to buy another company's allowance.

TAXATION can be used to differentiate between products that the government does not want people to buy. This is used to persuade people to use cars that produce less pollution. Cars using liquid petroleum gas (LPG), for example, are exempt from London's congestion charge.

RECYCLING waste can be an effective method of reducing environmental damage. In some countries it is a legal requirement for households. They are provided with containers for different types of waste so they can be disposed of or recycled most effectively.

Putting on the pressure

Legislation isn't always necessary. Pressure groups have effectively persuaded businesses to change their behaviour by letting customers know about damaging activities. Shell, for example, found that customers were boycotting their petrol stations because of their activities in Nigeria. Many businesses now work hand in hand with pressure groups like Friends of the Earth in order to manage their activities without causing criticism.

The fishermen in the Star Study are pleased to be consulted on the plans and their implementation. People are often more willing to participate if they feel that their voice is being heard. It also provides a forum for listening and understanding other people's point of view.

Critical thinking

Changing views

Wind farms have long been banned in National Parks – but things may be changing. The desire for sustainable energy means that compromises might be made. The trade-off between clean power and a visual intrusion in a place of outstanding national beauty is shifting and may lead to a change of view.

Persuasion

The Department of Trade and Industry (DTI) announced its proposals for the provision of capital grants for the development of offshore wind and energy supplies in the UK. The DTI's aim is that the capital grants will fund a number of demonstration projects to help reduce both the costs and risks involved in such developments, and to maximise the contribution to the Government's targets for renewable electricity supply within the UK.

These two examples show how the government's attitude to sustainable energy is changing.

1 Why is there a need to 'help reduce the costs and risks' in the development of sustainable energy?

2 How is the government going about it and why?

3 Why do businesses often need encouragement to be environmentally friendly?

Next steps

1 What evidence is there in your local community of business working to protect the environment?

2 Why do you think they are involved?

KEY TERMS

Sustainable energy is produced by using renewable resources.

What are business ethics?

starSTUDY

Yeo Valley stands by its values

'Our aim remains to produce high quality, value for money organic products and we promise that as the range and availability of organic raw materials improves, we'll keep on innovating and producing new products to give our customers more and more choice.'

Yeo Valley combines its organic and environmental ethos with a strong business objective. It didn't find it easy to move into organic products because there is still an inadequate supply of the milk and fruit it needs for large-scale production. Tesco and Sainsbury's will not stock your products if you cannot guarantee a reliable supply. To overcome the problem, Yeo Valley devised a way of encouraging farmers to convert to organic production.

Not only did it set a price for the milk that guaranteed a profit for the farmers, it also bought the milk that wasn't organic to sell to other people. This strategy ensured that it had enough organic milk and demonstrated its commitment to an ethical relationship with its suppliers.

Its ethical agenda is to be found in other aspects of the business too. Packaging aims to be as recyclable as possible, lorries go out with full loads to avoid wasting fuel, water is conserved wherever possible and employees are encouraged to cycle to work.

1 What ethical principles does Yeo Valley demonstrate?

2 How do these values help the business?

3 How do you think a strong ethical ethos affects the attitude of the staff?

4 What do you think would happen to the business if it were discovered to have been breaking its own rules?

5 Write an ethical statement for Yeo Valley which comments on the relationship with each of its stakeholders.

Specification Content

Moral and ethical: recognition of possible conflict in addressing different perspectives

There's a place where the grass really is greener.

Ethics and business

Many big businesses now have **ethical statements** that set out the relationship of the business with stakeholders. Some people suggest that they are just a cynical way of making the business look good, but once a business has made a statement of this sort, the media and pressure groups tend to be quick to identify and publicise any contraventions.

Businesses started to develop such codes in the 1990s after a series of corporate disasters that led to environmental damage and financial disaster. To begin with, having an ethical code or statement was something special. It gave a business a unique selling point, which made it stand out from the crowd.

An ethical approach needs to be embedded in the business. If it is just a superficial statement that is never put into practice, the company will soon be caught out by the media or pressure groups. The Institute of Business Ethics helps organisations of all sorts to develop a code that involves everyone.

Making ethics work

THE INSTITUTE OF BUSINESS ETHICS' FORMULA FOR AN ETHICAL STATEMENT

It should include:

THE PURPOSE AND VALUES OF THE BUSINESS. The products which are being provided – financial objectives and the business's role in society as the company sees it.

EMPLOYEES. How the business values employees: working conditions, recruitment, development and training, rewards, health, safety and security, equal opportunities, retirement, redundancy, discrimination and harassment. Use of company assets by employees.

CUSTOMER RELATIONS. The importance of customer satisfaction and good faith in all agreements, quality, fair pricing and after-sales service.

SHAREHOLDERS OR OTHER PROVIDERS OF MONEY. The protection of investment made in the company and proper 'return' on money lent. A commitment to accurate reporting of achievements and prospects.

SUPPLIERS. Prompt settling of bills. Co-operation to achieve quality and efficiency. No bribery or excess hospitality accepted or given.

SOCIETY OR THE WIDER COMMUNITY. Compliance with the spirit of the law as well as the letter. The company's obligations to protect and preserve the environment. The involvement of the company and its employees in local affairs. The corporate policy on giving to education and charities.

IMPLEMENTATION. How the code is issued, used and reviewed. Ways of obtaining advice. Training programme for staff.

More than just the law

The law of most countries lays down how many of these relationships should be handled. Business ethics takes things a step further. Businesses can often make decisions that are within the law but don't treat stakeholders ethically. There is nothing to prevent a business having short-term contracts with suppliers but an ethical approach might mean taking a longer-term view, as Yeo Valley does.

The number of businesses that have developed ethical statements has increased rapidly through the last decade. This change gives a clue to the perception of such statements within business because they cost money to develop.

Critical thinking

Draw up a spider diagram showing why a business might develop an ethical code. How might it affect the relationship with its stakeholders?

Next steps

1 Have a look at some big companies' websites to find out about their ethical codes.

2 What similarities can you find?

KEY TERMS

Business ethics are a code of behaviour that is morally correct.

An ethical statement or code is a business's view of the way it behaves. It explains how ethical decisions are made throughout the organisation.

WWW

Institute of Business Ethics: www.ibe.org.uk

Ethics and/or profit?

Specification Content

Moral and ethical: recognition of possible conflict in addressing different perspectives

starSTUDY

A tough decision

Core values of the Corus Group

Corus Group's 'Core Values' detail company beliefs, which both current and future policies are built upon, enabling all employees to work towards the common goal of maintaining our position as a global leading metals provider.

Objectives

Corus aims to be recognised as a leading global metals provider with a strong technological base and an outstanding level of service. To achieve this requires the combined efforts and professionalism of all our employees.

Corus seeks to be an excellent employer:

• Through a commitment to creating a stimulating work environment and enhancing employability.

• By seeking to provide competitive remuneration.

• By creating opportunities for employees to develop their skills.

• By providing an open and fair working environment.

The Group places the highest value on:

• The health, safety and welfare of all employees.

• Teamwork, based on mutual trust and respect.

• Personal commitment and individual involvement.

• Integrity and reliability in all circumstances.

In Corus, respect for all stakeholders and open communication are leading business principles.

Corus and the individual

Management will encourage employees to buy into Corus Group's common purpose and responsible business practices.

All employees must be assured of clear and open access to management to discuss matters of personal concern as well as those of wider interest to the Group.

Steelworkers face uncertain future as Corus admits job losses are inevitable

THOUSANDS of Welsh steelworkers face an uncertain future, as up to 3,000 jobs at British plants are threatened in the wake of Corus's failed rescue bid.

The knock-on impact has plunged the company, which is £1bn in debt, into heightened uncertainty after it admitted earlier this week that redundancies and plant closures were inevitable.

Last night speculation was rife that the cash crisis would trigger the end of steel production at the Redcar works in Teesside, which employs 3,000 – sparing Corus's major plants at Port Talbot and Scunthorpe, with 4,000 workers each.

But sources revealed there was also disquiet that Llanwern could close completely with the loss of 1,400 jobs.

Source: adapted from The Western Mail, 14 March 2003.

1 What message is Corus's 'Core Values' giving about working for the company?

2 Why is Corus in difficulties?

3 How is this affecting its commitment to its core values?

4 Which stakeholders appear to be most important?

5 If Corus did not take tough decisions, how might the future of the business be affected?

6 What effect would this have on remaining stakeholders?

Who comes first?

When a business sets out its ethical agenda, it shows how it aims to work with its stakeholders. When everything is rosy, this works well. When the environment becomes more challenging, it becomes harder to treat everyone as equally and openly as the code suggests.

A business that is in difficulties may want to keep its plans to close a plant under cover until the last moment, despite consultation with employees being part of its ethical statement. Its commitment to its shareholders, and employees who will be retained, might come before the employees who will lose their jobs in order to protect its future.

Testing the code

IN THE KNOW

Businesses make their codes available to the public, so they must think that they help. There is, however, a cynical view that they are simply an attempt to show the business in a good light and, therefore are, really part of the marketing strategy.

It can also be difficult to embed a code if employees are wedded to a traditional shareholder perspective. Persuading people that an ethical code can actually make a business more effective can take a long time.

Some parts of a code are easier to comply with and demonstrate to be working than others. If a business is making environmental claims, it is reasonably easy to show that they are being upheld. It may be more difficult to demonstrate that bribes are not being paid to officials, a common practice in many less developed economies, as it is in the interest of both parties to keep quiet.

The real test of an ethical code occurs when a business has to make tough decisions. When weighing up the long-run impact on the business, it can be difficult to give all stakeholders equivalent status, especially when a business's survival is at stake.

Win–win?

A business's prime responsibility has to be to its shareholders. If potential investors were in any doubt about this, they would be unlikely to buy shares in the company.

There is, however, a body of evidence suggesting that businesses that have an ethical code are more successful than those that don't. The research, carried out by the Institute of Business Ethics, looked at a range of businesses with and without explicit codes of ethics and compared financial indicators. It found that ones with a code tended to be more successful. This suggests that there is a positive but not definitive relationship. It might mean that a business with a code is well run.

It may also mean that:

- good employees are attracted to an ethical business and stay with it
- suppliers will make more effort for a business that treats them well
- banks will lend more cheaply to a well-run profitable business
- customers prefer to buy products from a business that behaves ethically.

There is obviously a close relationship between behaving ethically and having a stakeholder culture.

Critical thinking

1. What is the difference between obeying the law and behaving ethically?
2. Why is it sometimes difficult for a business to keep to its code?
3. Why is there a close relationship between behaving ethically and a stakeholder culture?
4. Can a business be expected to keep its ethical code when its future is under threat? Explain your answer.

Next steps

1. Search for stories about businesses that are in difficulties.
2. Does the business have an ethical code?
3. Is it keeping it?
4. If not, which aspects are being broken?
5. Why do you think this is happening?

testing–testing

Technology and the law – assessment

Case study A: Changing population, technology and consumer laws

Picking up the bill

We are living longer and this will mean an increase in demand for healthcare, pensions, housing and community care. At the same time, birth rates across Europe are falling. Consequently there will be fewer younger people to drive the economy and pay taxes to meet the costs of the growing welfare and social bills.

The government will have to pay the running costs of these services, including all the suppliers, many of whom are in the private sector.

Source: adapted from Eurostat 2000.

A changing pattern

Under 16s	12.1m in 2000	11m by 2011
Average age	38.8 in 2000	42.6 by 2025
Over 80s	2.4m in 2000	4.9m by 2040

Making e-commerce work

The E-Commerce Directive sets strict rules for UK businesses that advertise or sell goods either via a website, mobile phone or through e-mail. These firms will now have to offer key features on their sites such as contact information, a swift acknowledgement of orders, and the chance for customers to amend an order. The laws are good news for consumers, but they will add to the costs of businesses as they prepare for the change.

Goodnessdirect.co.uk is an online shop selling over 2000 health products from foods to health supplements. There's lots of product information and you can even e-mail an expert. The site meets the European Directive. You can cancel goods after receiving them and there are clear contact addresses. The business operates out of Daventry and uses broadband in order to speed up its service.

The government has committed itself to make the UK the best place for broadband among the seven major developed countries by 2005. As a very significant provider of services, the government has promised to fully embrace the technology in all its departments. However, putting government services online could cost up to 20% of civil service jobs over the next ten years and will also change the way many civil servants work.

The UK has seen a staggering growth in broadband, due largely to falling prices, fierce marketing campaigns and new ways to install the technology. The government is encouraging all of the UK to use the new technology, but we have a long way to go.

The Wentworth Wooden Jigsaw Company sends its products all over the world, and increasingly needs to download pictures and artwork to use in creating puzzles. It operates in a rural part of Wiltshire that does not have access to broadband. Without the fast computer facility, the company's future in its rural location is threatened, together with the jobs of its 18 staff. It has unsuccessfully campaigned to have broadband installed locally over the last two years.

The companies providing fast computer access say it costs a lot of money to convert telephone exchanges and there must be enough demand to make this viable. BT expects 90% of the country to have access to broadband by mid 2005.

Source: BBCi

1 What impact will the change in demography have on
   a the government   **(4 marks)**
   b the NHS   **(4 marks)**
   c NHS suppliers?   **(4 marks)**

   help! Remember that changes in demography will affect both the demand for products and services as well as the nature of the potential employees.

2 How might the government meet increasing spending on health services?   **(6 marks)**

   help! Think about two options available, such as increasing taxation or introducing charging or handing it all over to the private sector. Cuts in other areas are another possibility.
   Make a brief comment on the consequences.

3 The E-Commerce Directive is one of many laws that support the consumer. Why might some businesses welcome laws like these while others see them as yet another burden?   **(8 marks)**

   help! This question is about encouraging good practice, making an even playing field for businesses and understanding why we need laws to protect the consumer.

4 How might the government minimise the redundancies that will come about through its proposed change in the provision of online services?   **(8 marks)**

   help! The question is asking you to recognise that governments often want to keep unemployment down and you should look at two options available to the government.

5 Why does the government wish UK businesses to embrace this technology?
   Why is it important for it to lead by example?   **(6 marks)**

   help! This requires you to think about how using this infrastructure will help to reduce business costs, increase efficiency and competitiveness.
   The government is a major supplier of services and will help boost demand for broadband.

6 Analyse how the government might support small rural businesses that do not have access to broadband?   **(9 marks)**

   help! How can it encourage BT to increase availability to broadband or can it help businesses themselves?

testing–testing

Technology and the law – assessment

Case study B: Employment laws

Women now benefit from better maternity leave rights. Women are now entitled to 26 weeks off, regardless of how long they have worked for their employer. Under the new system the first six weeks of maternity leave is paid at 90% of average earnings, and for the remaining 20 weeks it is £100 a week, or 90% of average weekly earnings if this is less. It has got better for fathers as well. They can now take two weeks' paid paternity leave. There is even more good news for working parents. Mothers and fathers of children aged under six will be legally allowed to request flexible working.

Source BBCi

A senior examiner, who claimed he was sacked for complaining about the grading of exam papers, has failed in his bid to take the case to an industrial tribunal. The tribunal, in Norwich, agreed with Edexcel that Mr Mead was a contract worker, not a salaried employee, so had no legal right to claim unfair dismissal.

When Fineline Cymru, a swimwear factory, went bust the 35 workers, mainly women, claimed they were left without redundancy pay and back wages. Just two weeks after closing the factory, owner John Potter reopened the swimwear factory and began trading under the name Cherub UK.

Lawyers for the GMB union, which represents the former workers, are going to an employment tribunal to claim compensation against the former owner. 'When Fineline closed and Mr Potter opened Cherub UK, all of the contracts of employment should have been transferred over to the new firm,' a spokesperson from the GMB argued.

assessment questions – Case study B

1 Explain why the government wants to improve working parents' rights? Outline two reasons. **(4 marks)**

 help! Go to page 66.

2 Evaluate the effects of the new working parents' rights on a small business and a large company. **(10 marks)**

 help! A small business employing a small workforce may not be able to spread these costs as well as a larger business.

3 What is an employment tribunal? **(2 marks)**

 help! Go to page 67.

4 What is meant by an employment contract? What are the arguments for and against the swimwear workers' case? **(8 marks)**

help! Go to page 67. Apply the reasons for having a contract to the workers' case and the business.

Case study C: The government as a consumer, provider and constrainer

One of Scotland's biggest road building projects, estimated to be worth around £120 million, is being put out to tender by the Scottish Executive.

Plans to restore a ferry link between Scotland and Northern Ireland appear to have drawn a step closer following news that the route will be put out to tender. The service could only be reinstated with an annual subsidy of £1 million, which would initially be contracted for five years.

Local radio group GWR's attempted merger with rival station Galaxy 101 has been overruled by the Competition Commission, which said the tie-up was against the public interest. The commission ruled that the acquisition could reduce local radio advertising competition in the Bristol and Bath, and Taunton and Yeovil areas. The commission also said Swindon-based GWR should be forced to reduce its existing holding in the Galaxy station. Swindon-based GWR has decided to sell all its shares to the majority shareholder in Galaxy.

assessment questions – Case study C

1 What is a tender?　**(2 marks)**

 Go to pages 70–71.

2 Outline two reasons why the taxpayer should subsidise a private sector business such as a ferry service?　**(4 marks)**

 Think about what a subsidy does to costs and comment on what the market would provide if no subsidy were present. Also, a subsidy means the taxpayer is bearing some of the costs.

3. a State one difference between a merger and a takeover?　**(2 marks)**

   b Analyse the factors the Competition Commission might take into account to help it form a judgement about mergers or takeovers?　**(9 marks)**

 This requires you to bring in arguments for and against mergers. Try to back this up with evidence from the case study.

testing–testing

The EU and the environment – assessment

Case study D: Environmental, moral and ethical influences

The EU and the environment

The European Parliament has voted for proposed EU-wide laws to make the polluter pay for environmental damage. Environmental groups are hailing the vote as a major success. But business leaders say that if the draft directive becomes law the survival of many European companies is at stake.

Companies will be obliged to take out full insurance cover, or give guarantees that they can pay for the cost of environmental clean-ups.

The vote is a clear signal that companies dealing with toxic materials, or which carry risks for the environment, must expect in future to work under tougher conditions.

The EU has been spurred into action by the public feeling aroused by incidents in recent years. These include:

- the devastating oil spills from the Erica and Prestige tankers off the coasts of France and Spain
- the cyanide pollution in the Tisza river in Hungary and Romania in 2000

- the widespread pollution from the Donana metal mine in south-west Spain in 1998.

Often local taxpayers have to pay the main cost of the clean-up from oil, chemical or mining accidents rather than those responsible.

Source: BBC 14 May 2003

Latest figures show that reservations for the summer season in south-western France are in sharp decline following the Prestige oil disaster and the ensuing pollution. Bookings are on average down by 50% compared with those made last year Oyster producers have seen their sales drop by almost 40% during the Christmas period, while fish prices have plummeted by between 20% and 40% – even though their products remain unaffected by the oil pollution.

Aquitaine coastal tourism

1.5 billion euros 27,000 permanent jobs 45,000 seasonal jobs

Source: BBC March 2003

Business and the environment

The environment and Shell …

Shell is a very large global petrochemical company. The company's website provides an insight to its views on a range of sensitive issues such as:

- human rights
- politically sensitive areas
- new energy
- biodiversity
- globalisation
- climate change
- water use
- product stewardship.

'We have a responsibility to stick by business principles based on honesty, integrity and respect for people. We must make a constant effort to live by them. For example, Shell operates in countries where bribery and corruption is endemic. Shell will not tolerate this and employees will be sacked if they are found to be involved in it.'

'Must work with sensitive stakeholders e.g. inform interest groups before going into new areas'.

Shell believes that being sustainable:

- encourages innovation, e.g. cleaner fuel
- attracts and motivates best staff
- reduces project risk
- opens new markets.

'It's a matter of enlightened self-interest,' claims Shell's CEO Malcolm Brinded. 'Being transparent within annual reports and published environmental audits help us gain and maintain trust.'

Shell has promised to reveal which 210 of its 1100 petrol stations have mobile phone masts hidden inside the forecourt price signs. The oil company, which has a deal with T-mobile, said the transmitters were safe but campaigners have expressed concerns.

… and T mobile

T-mobile spokeswoman Gill Kerr told BBC News Online the antennae ensured 'that about 46 million people with a mobile in the UK get the best possible service'.

But Mast Sanity, a pressure group, said operators were 'making a mockery' of the planning process. 'They promised faithfully they would consult with residents before they put these masts up.'

Source: BBC October 2002

… and Unilever

'Supplier relationships – practices of suppliers must be in line with our own,' say Unilever, makers of detergents, soaps, perfumes and the like.

1 What is meant by social costs? Provide an example of social costs from the evidence and one of your own. **(4 marks)**

> help! Straightforward

2 Outline two of the social costs associated with the Prestige oil tanker disaster. **(4 marks)**

> help! Try to incorporate data into your answer.

3 a How is the EU intending to manage social costs? **(2 marks)**

   b What impact will this have on businesses? **(2 marks)**

   c Describe three other options open to governments or local authorities to manage social costs. **(6 marks)**

> help! The first and second parts want you to recognise that it is a law that will force businesses to pay for their actions. The third part asks you to describe three alternative methods of cutting social costs. These can be attached to other contexts; e.g. fishing.

4 What is the purpose of pressure groups? **(2 marks)**

> help! Go to page 33.

5 Discuss the motives a company like Shell have for trying to minimise the social costs of its activities? **(4 marks)**

> help! You should comment on the need for big businesses to be aware of environmental and ethical issues that affect them and the law. You might write within a PEST framework.

6 Evaluate the costs and benefits of being a social and ethical business. **(14 marks)**

> help! By asking you to evaluate you must comment on the advantages and disadvantages. You can use your own example or Shell. Try to weigh up your arguments. Would this be appropriate for all businesses?

7 What would happen if the government increased the restrictions of erecting mobile phone masts? **(4 marks)**

> help! Consider why the government would take this action and then explore the effect on the businesses involved. You need to recognise there will be a trade-off. How might the businesses react to the restriction?

8 What does Unilever mean by 'the practices of suppliers must be in line with our own'? **(6 marks)**

> help! This implies that suppliers as stakeholders must be in on the act too. Think why this might be important for Unilever.

End of Part 1 assessment

What to do first when opening your exam paper

There isn't one right way of reading a case study, but it does help to highlight key terms and also try to relate to the concept or issue the examiner might want you to draw out from the sentence.

You may not have to use what you have highlighted and thought about because the questions simply may not require it. However, going through this process will help your thinking and sharpen your mind so that you are more likely to be able to draw in the relevant concepts and ideas behind each question.

You should also highlight the key terms in the questions and also any command words. The command words are those that tell you what to do, such as 'outline', 'assess' or 'evaluate'. Assess and evaluate type questions can earn you more marks because they demand higher order skills from candidates.

Paper 1: Businesses, their objectives and environment

- Time allowed 1 hour
- A total of 45 marks available
- Answer all questions

Note: comments in red *are made the authors.*

Jam at James's

James Porter was made redundant, aged 35, in March 2002 and decided with his redundancy payment to start his own business. Playing guitar was something that had been his hobby since his teenage years and he had often wondered whether he would ever have the nerve to start up a music shop specialising in guitars and amplifiers.

He knew from experience that the town lacked a specialist music shop and all of the musicians he talked to were very enthusiastic (possible market niche). As a result of this encouragement he made a rough estimate of customer numbers, then he considered the factors likely to affect his ability to supply products to his customers. Finally he decided it would be worth taking the risk (part of a simple SWOT?).

James knew that it was necessary to draw up a business plan and also to set clear objectives if he wanted to succeed. He thought that, with luck, he could make sufficient money to retire in about 20 years' time (Personal aims). He saw endless possibilities in the range of equipment that he could eventually offer. He would start as a sole trader, he told himself, but he was sure that the business would grow quickly.

He used the *Business Start Up* pack from his bank as the basis for his plan. He found it quite straightforward and was able to obtain a loan of £25,000. This loan, along with his redundancy money (owner's capital), provided sufficient finance to buy the fixtures (fixed assets) and stock for the new shop. Jam at James's opened for business in a rented unit at the start of May 2002. He had two part-time casual 'employees' (who were musician friends of his) to help out, who he paid 'cash-in-hand'.

As his friends had predicted, there was a great deal of interest in the new shop – at least to start with. James kept a rough record of the number of visitors to the shop each month by keeping a tally on a sheet of paper (Table 1) whenever he remembered. By mid-October he was wondering whether he might expand his business by renting the unit next door. This had been a fish and chip shop that had closed the previous year. Perhaps it could be used as a rehearsal area for bands (added value). He thought it would cost about £4000 to convert (How could this be financed?).

However, by early February 2003 these ideas had been completely disregarded. James's trade had slowed considerably and the future did not look as promising as it had only a few months ago (variance). He now had only one person helping him out in the shop – and that was only for a few hours a day. Running a business in practice was not as easy as it had seemed on paper, he thought sadly. At first when trade slowed down he had simply used the time to practise on his guitar but he now had to admit to himself, the lack of anything to do during the day was making his life rather boring. He wondered whether, taking the good months with the bad, he had actually made a success of his first year's trading.

Month	Number of people entering shop per month
May 2002	690
June	725
July	761
August	799
September	839
October	881
November	793
December	714
January	571
February	457
March	366
April 2003 (so far)	107

He was 'his own boss', he reflected, but he certainly had less money to spend than when he was an employee (Monitoring personal objectives).

One morning in early April, James was staring gloomily at some particularly expensive guitars (Stock that is slow to move). He was managing to pay the rent on the unit but was wondering how long he would be able to keep up the interest payments on his loan. He had not liked what he had read in his newspaper that morning (Appendix 1). At that moment someone he had met at a concert a few months ago, and whom he vaguely remembered as being called Andy, walked in.

'Hi Mate,' said Andy. 'It's about time I called in on you. How's it going? Why are you looking so down? I thought you said things were really good.'

James explained why he was feeling worried about the state of the business.

'I may be able to help,' replied Andy. 'I've got a few electric guitar leads, well about two hundred, that you could have cheap.'

James asked how much they would cost and where Andy had got them from.

'I got them. . . er . . . from a mate who got them from. . . um er . . . a factory in Eastern Europe I think it was, that closed down. The quality isn't brilliant and they probably won't last as long as your usual ones but beginners won't notice! You can have them for two quid each and sell 'em for six or seven. That's a big profit for you – although I'll need a decision very soon, oh yeah and payment in cash. Up front. Right away.'

James promised to think it over and asked Andy to call in again the next day. Andy had seemed a bit vague as to exactly where he had got the leads from, but the offer sounded tempting; perhaps it would help him solve his business's problems.

Appendix 1

Shares on the Stock Market fell sharply yesterday after several leading economists warned of the possibility of a slowdown in economic activity. Some economic indicators point to a fall in consumer confidence over the medium term. A government spokesperson was however quite upbeat. 'The data is not conclusive,' she said. 'Some sectors of the economy are undoubtedly having a bit of difficulty but others are booming. It all depends on what you are selling.

Source: Module 1, OCR, June 2003.

Answer all questions.

1 James established his business as a sole trader. State two features of a sole trader. **(2 marks)**

2 Outline two factors likely to affect James's ability to supply products to his customers. **(4 marks)**

3 James opened his business in 2002 and he hoped to 'make sufficient money to retire in about 20 years' time'. Analyse why James's business objectives might change over this period of time. **(9 marks)**

4 Evaluate the possible ways in which James might judge the success of his first year's trading. **(14 marks)**

5 Discuss whether James should buy the electric guitar leads from Andy. **(14 marks)**

6X appeal

Marketing

Accounting and finance

Part 2
Business decisions and business behaviour

What is marketing?

starSTUDY

Jo and Adam designed and made their product and set about selling it. They liked it so much that they were sure that everyone would want to buy it.

1 What had they done wrong?

What can marketing do?

Marketing is an essential part of almost every business. Even a business that claims that it never advertises will need to know about the market for its products, the prices charged by its competitors and how their products are evolving. This is all marketing.

Most businesses are selling in competitive markets so it is important to make sure that:

- the product is right for the customers
- the price compares well with competitors
- the promotion of the product attracts the greatest number of customers
- the place where the products are sold reaches the maximum number of customers.

Know the market

Effective marketing is based on knowing everything there is to know about the market for the products you are selling. The size of the market is essential information. If people's total spend on a product is low, there is no point in investing heavily in it. The key is then to find out everything you can about your competitors and customers. There are lots of questions to ask.

KNOW YOUR COMPETITORS

- What share of the market do your competitors have?
- What is the image of their brands?
- What are their strengths and weaknesses?
- How do they distribute their products to their customers?
- Why do their customers not buy your products?
- Is there anything new going on?

KNOW YOUR CUSTOMERS

- Who are you trying to sell to?
- What do your customers like and dislike?
- What image do they have of your product?
- Are they loyal to your product?

GET THE PRODUCT RIGHT

- Product: its design and functionality
- Price: right for your target market
- Promote the product: with the right image, in the right place, at the right time
- Place the product with the right distribution methods for your customers.

Product or market oriented?

Jo and Adam had got it wrong. They decided what they wanted to make without finding out if anyone wanted to buy it. They were product oriented. This isn't always wrong because some well-known products such as the Sony Walkman have come about in this way. Drug companies also carry out research and development which leads to new products but they often have an eye on the market. More research goes into cures for high profile diseases with lots of sufferers than more obscure ailments.

A market-oriented business will work out what the customer wants and set about providing it. Whether it is a new product or the development of an existing one, matching the customers' wants is more likely to meet with success. Market orientation is not just about the product itself but also the other aspects of the marketing mix. The business needs to know about the price people are prepared to pay, where they see promotional material and activities and how they will set about buying the product. Customer service is an increasingly important aspect of selling a product. Poor after-care can mean that customers don't return. Carphone Warehouse works hard at this. 'Why win an argument if it means losing a customer?' is one of the principles it expects its staff to work by. It expresses the point of view of a market-oriented business in the service sector.

A successful business combines the strengths of both strategies. Few businesses are starting from scratch, so they have assets. Combining knowledge of what the market wants with the strength of these assets is often the best way forward. It is known as asset-led marketing.

Next steps

1 Choose three products that you use frequently and work out:

a the target market

b how the price compares with competitors

c how its promotion differs from its competitors.

Critical thinking

Work out what marketing might be carried out by the following businesses:

1 A beauty therapist who works from home and finds clients by word of mouth.

2 A fizzy drinks company.

3 A person setting up a website development service.

4 A sports car manufacturer.

KEY TERMS

Marketing involves finding out about your competitors and customers so that you get your product right and sell it effectively.

Marketing mix combines the product, its price, promotion and the ways it is distributed – often referred to as 'place'. Together these make up the marketing strategy.

A market-oriented business will focus on the needs of the customer before developing and marketing a product.

A product-oriented business will focus on the creation of a product rather than considering the needs of the market.

Asset-led marketing involves building on the strengths of the business and customer needs.

The target market is the section of the market in which a business aims to sell its product.

Marketing objectives

starSTUDY

J o and Adam have created a product that no-one wants and it is not selling.

Specification Content

Marketing objectives and behaviour as a means of achieving corporate objectives; marketing and overall objectives

1   How has planning gone wrong?

2   What do you think the overall objectives of the business are?

3   What should the marketing department have done to help the business achieve its objectives?

4   What would you suggest it does now?

Business objectives → Marketing objectives

Businesses set objectives for the short and long term. The marketing objectives must aim to help the business achieve these objectives. The marketing department will make the plans for marketing activity but the overall plan will be determined at a very senior level because it has to be woven into the business's mission and objectives. These are likely to include the **market segment**, the area of the world market to be targeted and the **market share** the business wants to achieve.

The market for a product is divided into a number of segments which reflect the tastes of different types of customers. The jeans market has a variety of segments ranging from the high street store's own label to Levi's and big designer names.

The impossible is easy.
Miracles take a little longer

 go to → *Find out more about market segments and market share on pages 96–99.*

Find out more about market segments and market share on pages 96–99.

The plans must be integrated into the business as a whole. There is no point in setting elaborate marketing objectives if the finance department says there isn't enough money to pay for it.

The target should be realistic. Trying to change the image of Marks and Spencer so it becomes the only place to shop for every student is not realistic. People are unlikely to strive to achieve objectives that they know are impossible.

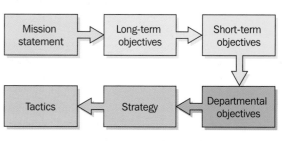

Mission statement → Long-term objectives → Short-term objectives → Departmental objectives → Strategy → Tactics

Critical thinking

1   What objectives do you think the following businesses have?

Starbucks, BP, Tesco, New Look, Carphone Warehouse, Levi, Apple computers, Dell computers.

2   How is the marketing department aiming to meet the objectives?

KEY TERMS

Market segments are distinct parts of the market for a product. A segment may represent customers of different ages, genders, interests etc.

Market share is the percentage of the market held by each supplier.

Marketing targets are short-term goals that are achievable and can be monitored.

Product differentiation means ensuring that your product stands out from the rest.

Matching the objectives

Once the business has set its objectives, the marketing department sets its own objectives to make it all happen. The routes it chooses will depend on the market for the products although any plan will be a combination of different activities.

> Business objective:
> **We want growth!**

> Business objective:
> **Be innovative!**

> Business objective:
> **Continuity matters!**

> Business objective:
> **Make our products different!**

DEVELOP NEW PRODUCTS, BROADEN THE RANGE

New products can be developed from the existing range or can be a completely new idea. The confectionery market has a constant flow of new products. Some become a permanent feature on the supermarket shelves and others disappear. Cadbury's Heroes opened up a different segment for packaged chocolates. Boxed chocolates had been thought of as a present for females. Heroes are acceptable to a much wider market.

The latest computer games console always arrives with great hype. It is the 'must have product' for many young people. Sony and Nintendo work very hard to bring out the most exciting version.

New products come from innovation. Development of products can be innovative but may also provide continuity for both the business and the customer. They should also be distinctive.

IMPROVE DISTRIBUTION

Products won't sell if people can't see them on the shelves. Shops will only stock lines that sell so the marketing department has to work out how to ensure that the company's products are in all the right places. If growth is the aim, placing the products is critical. Some products benefit from a different approach to distribution. Vichy's skin care range is only sold in pharmacies in order to stress its scientific qualities. It limits the potential range of outlets but makes it distinct from others.

PRICE OR QUALITY?

The objectives of a business may mean staying in the same segment, moving into another one or functioning in several.

Some businesses position themselves at the 'low price–high volume' end of the market. Hi-Tec, for example, makes no attempt to sell expensive products. It knows that there are plenty of people who are unwilling to spend £100 on a pair of trainers. Others aim for high price–low volume or if plans work well, high price–high volume.

Increasingly, businesses have lines in different segments. Famous designers, who sell their clothes for thousands of pounds, also run a range through Debenhams. This was an innovative approach for a department store and left Marks and Spencer standing. Ford bought Jaguar to give it access to a top of the range car market. People who are looking for status won't buy a Ford but will buy a Jaguar.

Sometimes businesses cut prices to compete when under threat from competitors. Sainsbury's always meant quality but when challenged by Tesco, resorted to cutting price and lost its standing with the customers because lower prices meant cutting corners.

INCREASE SALES

A business that is going for growth will often have marketing objectives which include increased profits or sales in terms of volume or revenue. The marketing department will have to devise methods of achieving such objectives.

go to → Find out more about marketing activities on page 116.

Find out more about marketing activities on page 116.

Product differentiation is a way to make your products stand out from the rest. People will buy them because they are special, not just because they are cheap.

Setting targets

Encouraging staff to achieve the objectives that have been set can be challenging. Tough objectives can be hard to meet and staff can be disillusioned if they can't see success. Breaking the objective down into **marketing targets** makes it easier. Everyone can see what has been achieved – or not. If targets aren't met, the department must review what has happened and revise the plans. It might decide that more resources should be put into the marketing budget.

Segmenting the market

starSTUDY

Thomson
Young at Heart

Thomson
Winter Sun

Thomson
Florida

Faraway Shores
Safaris, tours and beach holidays

NEW

Portland
HOLIDAYS DIRECT

GREAT CHOICE
SAVE £££s

our lowest prices
guaranteed

Thomson
Cruises

1 Which group of people is
   each brochure aimed at?

2 What are the differences
   between the holidays on
   offer?

3 What are the similarities
   between the holidays?

4 Why is there a different
   brochure for each group?

5 Why do you think holiday
   companies break up the
   market into different
   segments?

6 Can you think of any other
   products that are sold to
   different segments? Why
   do you think businesses
   do this?

Who are the customers?

To target its products effectively, a business must know who buys them. Few
businesses meet the needs of the whole market so it is important to know the
characteristics of the customers. Different target segments will need a different
approach to the marketing mix. An 18–30 holiday will obviously need a different
marketing approach from a holiday for families or older people because the products
are different and the features that sell the holidays are also different. The information
gathered helps to develop a **customer profile**.

They also have things in common. They need flights, hotels, employees and
administration. Selling products which have similarities can lead to lower costs
because flights and hotel rooms can be bought in bulk. A hotel that is full of families
during the school holidays might become an 18–30 venue at other times.

Critical thinking

Newspapers in the UK meet different needs and serve different customers.

Identify the characteristics of each paper and its readers and use this
information to decide on segments to put them in.

Next steps

Investigate market segments in a
business that you know.
What are the products? Who are the
customers? How are the customers
different/the same as those who buy
from other businesses?

KEY TERMS

Customer profile is a breakdown of people who buy a particular product. It will
include age, gender, region, income and social class.

Niche markets are very small segments with specialist products. They may grow
or remain small.

 www

http://www.marketsegment.com shows how a commercial
organisation offers expertise in working out market segments.

Defining the segments

A customer-oriented business must have a clear picture of the segments that it is targeting. They can be defined in a variety of ways.

GEOGRAPHIC

People in different parts of a country – or the world – have different needs and wants. A business must take this into account when it develops products and marketing strategies. Ford cars in Europe are very different from those in the USA. Cheap petrol and low speed limits create different priorities.

On a more local basis, supermarkets around the UK stock different ranges of products to fit the demands of the surrounding community.

• DEMOGRAPHIC

The composition of the population influences the nature of products and the marketing activities used to attract different groups. Businesses will look at age, sex and ethnic background, for example. Data also tells them how spending power relates to different groups within the population so they know how to target these segments.

Social class is often used as a measure because it can reflect the demographic mix. It is, however, important to remember that people are no longer stuck in one category all their lives. Education and employment can move people quickly from one category to another.

Social class

A   Directors and chief executives of large companies

B   Solicitors, accountants and head teachers

C1   Skilled workers, bank staff, teachers

C2   Skilled manual workers, electricians, plumbers

D   Semi skilled and unskilled workers, refuse collectors, warehouse staff

E   Casual workers, state pensioners and students

• PSYCHOGRAPHIC

Lifestyle has become a way of defining market segments. People's attitudes affect what they buy. These attitudes may have come about because of an individual's background, education, income or personality. People who are well educated but not high earners may have attitudes that are different from others who earn the same amount.

The categories are not always easy to define and are constantly changing. Different marketing organisations are always finding new ways to describe these market segments. One consistently used categorisation that reflects attitude divides people into innovators, early adopters, early majority, late majority and sceptics. The strategies that a business uses will vary according to the sector it plans to target and the speed at which it wants to diffuse its product.

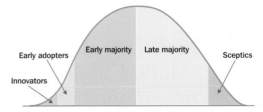

WHY SEGMENT?

Segmentation helps businesses analyse the market they are in and make decisions about where they want to go. It also helps to focus minds on the product itself and how it can best be placed in the market.

Some very big companies have products that span all segments but most will want to be successful in a smaller number. A small business can focus successfully on one segment and get the product right for its customers. It may develop great expertise from specialising.

The different characteristics of customers make business life more difficult. Unlike Henry Ford's early cars – which were all the same and came in black – today's products have to be varied to meet the customers' desires in relation to the price they are prepared to pay.

While focusing on the customers in a segment, a business must not forget that new segments may be developing as customers move on. The niche market, which is a very small segment often containing a new product, is important and can grow into a fully-fledged segment.

SUCCESSFUL SEGMENTATION

Study your competitors

- Work out their objectives and where and why decisions are made.

Study the customers

- Know who buys what.
- Know why they buy what they buy.

Will a segment work?

- Is it big enough to give the return you want?
- Are you asking the right questions about the people in the segment? The questions must relate to the product.
- Are the people in the segment very similar?
- Are they sufficiently distinct from the rest of the market?
- Can you reach the people in the segment?

Target growth

Specification Content

Defining and measuring market share and market growth

starSTUDY

Market share of newspaper sales

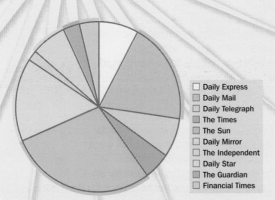

- Daily Express
- Daily Mail
- Daily Telegraph
- The Times
- The Sun
- Daily Mirror
- The Independent
- Daily Star
- The Guardian
- Financial Times

1 List the papers in order of the size of market share.

2 Group the papers into market segments.

3 Choose one of the papers and work out how it might increase its market share.

4 The market for newspapers has generally been falling. Where do you think the competition comes from?

5 Which markets for news do you think have been growing? Why?

6 How might newspapers fight back in order to increase the size of the market?

Growing shares and growing markets

Newspapers are very conscious of their market share and total sales. Much of their revenue comes from advertising and advertisers want to know that they are getting their message to as many people as possible. It is an uphill struggle because the market for newspapers is shrinking. The tabloids compete for scandalous scoops, which raise sales and market share for a period of time.

Market share

Market share is the proportion of a market held by one supplier. It can be measured by volume or sales value. The newspaper figures are by volume because they relate to the number of copies sold rather than the value. Value is calculated by multiplying sales by price.

Marketing objectives often include an increase in market share so it can be regarded as a measure of success. As it measures how well a business or product is doing compared with the competitors, it is a clear indicator of whether the strategy is working.

Having the biggest market share makes a product the **brand leader** and can give a business power over the prices being set and help keep costs low because of economies of scale. Success breeds success because being in prime position means that retailers will take the product, without having to be persuaded with big discounts. A famous name also means that customers are more likely to pick up the product.

www

These two sites have plenty of information about national and regional newspapers.

www.abc.org.uk

www.newspapersoc.org.uk

KEY TERMS

Brand leader is the product with the biggest market share.

Market mapping involves analysing the market to compare the position of a business or product and its competitors.

Market growth

IN THE KNOW

Market growth measures what is happening in the whole market. It can also be measured in terms of volume or sales. Life is much easier for businesses in growing markets but if their individual growth doesn't match or exceed the growth of the market – the strategy isn't working effectively.

The relationship between value and volume is also critical. Rising volume but falling value means that the unit price is falling. This has happened in many computer and electrical markets. Businesses have to run faster to stay in the same place.

Market growth is usually generated from a feeling of economic well being. Higher incomes mean more spending and growing markets. It is hard for individual firms to influence such growth. Other factors that affect it include:

- changing fashions, such as scooters, skateboards, trainers and so on

- social trends, such as more women going to work and therefore buying more convenience food

- innovation, which attracts customers to new products.

Fighting for a share

Businesses watch their market share rigorously and respond quickly if things are moving in the wrong direction. They have more influence over share than growth because the latter is affected by factors beyond their control.

In order to fight for share, a business may change the activities within its marketing mix. Cutting prices, updating the product, different promotion and having products in the right place through improved distribution are all solutions that might be used.

go to → *Find out more about the changes that might be made on pages 112–118.*

Mapping the market

Once all the data has been gathered, a business will create a map of the market which shows the relationship of a product with its competitors. If you want to buy a new personal stereo, you will be faced with lots of choice. A basic model will have a low price. A top of the range model with the latest styling and features will cost much more. The positions of products can be plotted on a market map.

Top price

No style ———|——— Style

Budget price

The labels on the axes will vary according to the product.

Businesses use **market mapping** to decide where they want to go. Burberry, almost by chance, moved from fuddy-duddy/expensive to trendy/expensive but then worked hard to maintain this position by making sure their products were seen on celebrities as well as having a big marketing budget.

A map also shows up any gaps in the market. Finding a niche that can be developed may be a lucrative activity.

Critical thinking

1 What factors affect
   a market share   b market growth?
   Why is it important to distinguish between data on the value and volume of market share and market growth?

2 Map the market for fast food restaurants. Use price on the vertical axis and decide on the feature to use on the horizontal axis.
   a Have any of the restaurants changed their position recently?
   b How can the map help a business to plan its marketing strategy?

Next steps

1 Supermarkets are always fighting for market share. Why is market share more important than market growth in the food business?

2 Find out what changes have taken place in market share recently.

Researching the market

Specification Content

Sources and methods of data collection; primary and secondary

starSTUDY

Gathering data

David Hanson runs CMRC, a market research business in the middle of Croydon. CMRC helps businesses to find out what people think of their products. It uses all sorts of strategies – from focus groups to phone calls. The company specialises in fragrances so it brings people into its offices to smell new products.

Some of the research involves recruiting people from the streets of Croydon to come into the offices to answer some questions about the products.

CMRC carries out primary research for other businesses. It talks to people and therefore brings in first hand information.

Market research can be expensive so many businesses survey their customers and retailers on a regular basis because they have cheap, easy access to them.

1 Why do you think businesses employ CMRC to carry out research for them?

2 Why is the centre of Croydon a good place to carry out research?

3 If you are testing fragrances, what special conditions would you need?

4 What factors would you want to consider when looking at the results of the research?

Critical thinking

A market research company recruits women to test products for them. It sends a product and a short questionnaire about twice a month. What are the advantages and disadvantages of this sort of market research? What factors would you have to consider when looking at the results?

Next steps

1 Have you been involved in any form of market research? What was the product? What was the business trying to find out?

2 Look at some adverts and work out what market research has found out about people's views on the product.

KEY TERMS

Primary research gives a business specific information about how the public views their product.

Secondary research comes from existing information that provides details about the market and other products.

Finding out about the market

PRIMARY RESEARCH

Primary research means asking customers and potential customers questions about your product or a product you plan to bring to the market. It is carried out by market research companies or the business itself. There are a variety of strategies that can be used to find different sorts of information.

QUESTIONNAIRES are

frequently used to find out what people think. The design of a questionnaire is critical to its success. It needs to find out about the respondents as well as their views on the product in order to work out what different people think. The design will differ if the person completes it on their own or with a market researcher. An in-depth interview will use open questions and encourage people to think about how they feel about a product. If the questionnaire is sent through the post, the questions must be short and snappy and easy to answer.Questionnaires are carried out in all sorts of ways.

- Postal/e-mail surveys involve sending out a questionnaire and hoping that people will respond. The rate is often quite low. An inducement might be offered to encourage people to respond. A health club might offer a free visitor's pass. Postal questionnaires seem relatively cheap but the real cost depends on the number of responses.

- Personal interviews give more detailed information but they are expensive because the interviewer has to spend quite a long time with a group or just one individual. The information is often more interesting because the format is less structured and the interviewer can explore areas of interest.

- Telephone surveys fall in the middle. Most are straightforward questions but in some cases interviewers will book a time and be more expansive. The drawback is that people are not always happy about being disturbed by unexpected phone calls which they suspect are trying to sell them something.

- Panel surveys use a team of people whose views are monitored regularly. This has the advantage of showing trends, but it is important to know whether the panel reflects the views of the population. A panel might be asked to test products, reporting on their purchases or record their activities, like the TV programmes they watch – and the adverts they see.

OBSERVATION is used in supermarkets, for

example, to find out how people shop, what they see and what makes them stop. These are all critical pieces of information when trying to design stores, packaging and promotional features.

Experiments are used to compare how changes affect the market. Two similar towns are often chosen so there is a control group, where nothing changes, and one that tests the new product. Market researchers have to be careful in interpreting the data because it is hard to ensure that everything is kept constant.

SECONDARY RESEARCH

Secondary research is also called desk research because that is where it is carried out. An enormous amount of information is collected by all sorts of organisations and is available either free or at a price. The Internet has speeded up this process considerably. The government provides free data about society, the population, industry and the economy. Trade associations gather data for their members and specialist newspapers and magazines also track changes in the market. These cover every aspect of industry from cars to catering.

Specialist reports are also available but the price charged for them is high and prohibitive for many.

Secondary research can provide a useful background for marketing activities but its main drawback is that it is not tailored to the direct interests of a business.

Rules for writing questionnaires

Carrying out primary research is an expensive process so why waste money on a poor questionnaire? You want to know who people are and just what they think. It is important to be able to count up the results.

1 Find out who has answered the questionnaire – age, sex, occupation – but don't become intrusive.

2 Know exactly what you want to find out.

3 Don't ask leading questions.

4 Make sure that the people will understand the question.

5 Ask closed questions in which people put a cross in a box or rank things in order of preference.

6 A few open questions will allow you to find out a little more about what people think.

The questionnaire will vary according to the group that is being tested. The Economist uses its subscription members to carry out surveys and asks quite detailed questions about income. If people are to be questioned on a street corner they may be less willing to answer such questions.

Getting the data right

star**STUDY**

Selecting the sample

MRC specialises in finding out what people think about new fragrances. Some businesses want to know how many people like or dislike different versions of their products. Others want to give people the opportunity to discuss their views in greater depth in order to discover their attitudes to products or potential products. CMRC has to work out the number and sort of people they need to ask in order to find an answer which reflects the views of potential customers.

Specification Content

Reasons for, methods of, and limitations of sampling

1 What advantages and disadvantages do you think there are, from a business's perspective, in finding out
   a how many people like or dislike a new product
   b the attitudes of people to a product?
2 What sort of people would you need to question if you wanted to find out about a sports deodorant, a room freshener, a new perfume and a car freshener?
3 What should a market research business consider when deciding how many people to question about a product?

The right choices

Businesses that carry out market research are looking for evidence to underpin decisions. If things go wrong, the decision-makers can blame someone else – the market researchers! Making sure that the data collected is right for the cause is therefore critical. Counting potential purchasers of a new product or having an in-depth discussion with a few potential customers provides different sorts of information that can contribute to decision making.

The first is **quantitative data**. The second is **qualitative data**.

It is also important that the people who are being asked are representative of the market as a whole. Even if some elderly people can be found at the gym, asking a sample of the over 80s about the design of new trainers would not provide useful information. Choosing the sample – or **sampling** – must also be done with care.

Quantitative or qualitative?

QUANTITATIVE RESEARCH provides numerical information. It is the answers to closed questions, which often have one-word answers. To obtain such information it is important to ask the right people, write good questions and interpret the information.

QUALITATIVE RESEARCH comes from in-depth interviews and group discussions. Because the interviewer, who is often a psychologist, will be free to follow up interesting lines of thought, the responses will give more personal views. Such research may discover how people think, how they are influenced by others or problems that had not been thought of before. It often takes place in people's homes or a comfortable environment where people can be observed.

Sampling

Sampling techniques help market researchers to ask the right people. The first decision is whether to use a random or a non-random sample.

A random sample gives a genuine cross-section of the population. Once someone has been picked at random, from the electoral register for example, it is important to talk to that individual. It gives good data but is expensive because someone has to visit and hope to catch them at home. It can also be done by phone. The researcher works through a list until they have spoken to everyone.

A random sample can be:

- A stratified sample. A company which makes food aimed at children will want to interview mums and children so the people are selected from this group – or strata – of the population.

- A cluster sample. This is used infrequently but aims to find the views of people who live in particular areas. If a business wants to decide on the location for a new club it might decide to carry out a cluster sample in places where there are many young people.

A non-random sample can be:

- A quota sample. This reflects the target market for the product so it chooses people in the appropriate age group and gender. The business that is opening a new club would want to ask young males and females.

- A convenience sample. A market researcher might stand on a busy corner and catch people as they come by. It is a cheap way to carry out a survey but will be biased by the location, time of day and other factors.

HOW BIG?

Size matters, but bigger is more expensive. A sample of 1000 will give great information, which will tell a business more about the target market and therefore give clues about promotional strategies. It might show that a new brand of makeup appeals to the 25–35 age group. This would enable the company to tailor the style of the adverts and where to place them.

Many businesses use much smaller samples because of the cost. A sample of 100 often gives quite enough information to decide on package design or a new taste.

Interpreting the data

The reliability of the data will be determined by the size of the sample and the percentage of people opting for each alternative. A 4% difference between two fragrances in a small sample gives less confidence than 4% on a

large sample. Businesses generally work to a 95% confidence level so they are happy with a result that is right 19 times out of 20. If the results are closer, it will be necessary to take other factors into account – perhaps the packaging that goes with the product.

Critical thinking

Pizza, pasta or ...?

A catering company with an existing pizza restaurant chain is considering developing a new brand. The first thought of the development team was to move into pasta, but is there too much competition in the field? A Spanish tapas restaurant is another possibility. Choosing lots of little dishes that are good for sharing could be popular.

The company wants to know which would be most popular and the demographic pattern of potential users.

A market research company is asked to find the answers.

1 Draw up a questionnaire for them and decide on the best sampling method to use. You will need to be able to explain the rationale behind what you have done.

2 Select and interview ten people according to the sampling method you have chosen. Write a report on how well the questionnaire worked. What would you have changed?

3 Make a presentation about your findings.

KEY TERMS

Quantitative data comes in the form of numbers and can be used to work out statistically valid conclusions.

Qualitative data comes from in-depth interviews and shows attitudes, opinions and judgements.

Sampling involves questioning a proportion of the population. The nature of the sample will depend on the information required.

The life of a product

Specification Content

Product: the role of the product life cycle and portfolio analysis

starSTUDY
Making music

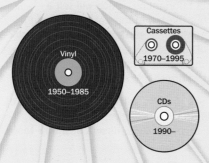

Vinyl
1950–1985

Cassettes
1970–1995

CDs
1990–

Products come and go but music goes on forever. Since people learnt to replicate music, it has been played on all sorts of different machines and stored in as many different ways. As new ways of playing recorded music have entered the market place, their predecessors' lives have been cut short. You can still buy vinyl and cassettes but most buyers opt for CDs.

1 When a new music product is introduced, who does it appeal to?

2 What happens to sales as customers become familiar with the product?

3 What happens to sales when another new music product is introduced to the market place?

4 Draw a graph showing the life of a product in terms of sales.

5 A new product is likely to take much promotion in order to sell and generate revenue. Add a line to your graph, which shows the cash flow it generates.

6 In the light of this pattern, how does a business try to manage the range of products on its books?

IN THE KNOW

The product portfolio

Products at different stages of their life bring in different amounts of revenue, so a business needs a healthy mix to maintain a balance and ensure a secure future.
The product portfolio includes the range of a business's products.

Businesses generally analyse this mix to check on potential future revenue flows. A tool that is often used is the Boston Matrix – so called because it came from the Boston Consulting Group, which sells its advice services to business.

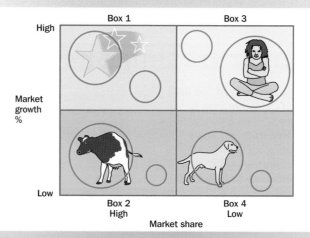

The four boxes of the Boston Matrix help businesses to decide how their products are doing when compared to others. Each circle in the box shows the amount of revenue that a product brings in. A big circle means lots of revenue.

Box 1 High market share/high growth

Stars shine brightly in a product portfolio because they bring lots of revenue, but competitors will want to create a copycat.

Box 2 High market share/low growth

Cash cows are milked to provide money for investment for newer products.

Box 3 Low market share/high growth

Problem children need investment to gain market share.

Box 4 Low market share/low growth

Dogs disappear because they don't bring in much revenue and the market isn't growing.

Every product has a life ...

IN THE KNOW

1 While a product is under development, it is adding costs to the business rather than contributing to profit.

2 In its early stages of introduction costs will still exceed revenue because of promotion costs. This will change as the launch takes root.

3 The growth stage brings an increased market share – or place in a growing market. Profits grow throughout the stage.

4 During maturity sales of the product become more stable.

5 Decline means a fall in profits as customers turn away from the product. The business must do something if it wants the product to continue.

Some products have features which mean that all the businesses in the field move in similar ways. The television, for example, started life in black and white, became colour ... and grew into the television we know today. Others are very personal to a particular business so the product life cycle is less dependent on major technological changes.

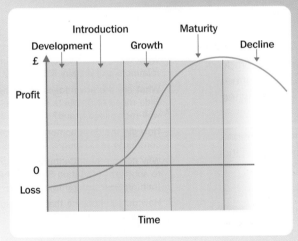

Product life cycle

... BUT A DIFFERENT ONE

Not all products follow exactly this pattern. Some famous flops have hit the market. The C5 was a strange little electric vehicle that was supposed to save city congestion but it did not catch the public imagination and its product life cycle looked very different from the diagram. Some products have very long periods of maturity. Kit Kat has remained almost unchanged for decades. It became chunky but the traditional bar still exists. Nestlé is of course very happy to have products like this in its range.

... OR A LONGER ONE

When a business sees that a product is reaching maturity, it needs to think about what to do next. Making the most of the investment in the product is important, so a plan should be put in place to extend its life.

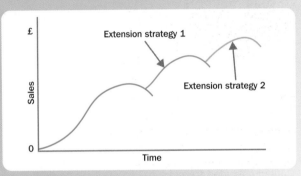

Extending the product life cycle

Businesses try all sorts of ways of extending the life of their products. Sometimes it works and sometimes it doesn't. Coca-Cola decided to give Coke a new flavour but its customers revolted. Classic Coke was quickly reintroduced and the new flavour was forgotten. Cars are updated with little tweaks to their design to give a longer life before an expensive major revamp is necessary.

Success comes down to clever use of the marketing mix. Many products have gone through periods of maturity only to have new life pumped into them by a fresh marketing approach. Lucozade is one of the most famous, having been repositioned as a drink for healthy people instead of being aimed at the sick.

Critical thinking

1 Draw a product life cycle for Kit Kat, skateboards, televisions and Sony Walkman.

2 Select a range of products that you buy and decide whether they are likely to be stars, cash cows, problem children or dogs. What advice would you give the company about future developments?

KEY TERMS

Product life cycle shows the path that many products go through from development to the end of their lives. Many businesses use extension strategies to give products a longer life.

Product portfolio shows the mix of products that a business produces.

Boston Matrix is a way of analysing the products in the portfolio.

Planning marketing

starSTUDY

Creating a purple patch

Specification Content

Formulation of marketing objectives, strategy and plans

Dairy Milk is a brand that is deeply embedded in the minds of people in the UK and beyond, so Cadbury decided to make the most of it. Wispa and Caramel became part of the Dairy Milk family and new products including Mint Chips, Turkish Delight and Crispies were developed to create a purple patch on the confectionery fixture in the shop.

The packaging of the whole range was redesigned to give a more contemporary feel. The swirly Cadbury logo aimed to give the brand name more prominence and was used across the whole portfolio including Cadbury Dream and Bourneville.

The strategy also aimed at broadening the product range so people would choose one of the products to have with their morning coffee. Crispies was specially designed to meet this criteria.

To catch the public's attention, Cadbury's sponsored Coronation Street.

The whole relaunch cost the company £8.2 million, its biggest spend to date.

1. What were Cadbury's objectives in relaunching the Dairy Milk range?
2. What are the advantages of having a wide range of products under one well-recognised brand?
3. How did the development of Crispies contribute to Cadbury's objectives?
4. Why do you think Cadbury's decided to sponsor Coronation Street rather than another programme?
5. How do you imagine that the relaunch of Dairy Milk fits into Cadbury's objectives?
6. What other businesses use the strategy of turning a family of products into one brand?

Why plan?

A business develops its objectives and sets targets. It then has to work out how to achieve these targets. The **marketing plan** is an integral part of the process. Without it, activities would be haphazard and unconsidered. Imagine spending £8.2 million on the relaunch of Dairy Milk without a plan!

Putting the plan together

ANALYSE THE CURRENT SITUATION

The marketing department must look at the market in general, as well as the market for their products, in order to build a picture of the current situation. Secondary research will show what is happening in the market. Primary research will give a more specific picture of the products involved, the market segments and likely target markets. SWOT analysis will help them to work out the strengths, weaknesses, opportunities and threats.

 go to →

page 30 for a reminder on SWOT analysis.

DEVELOP OBJECTIVES AND STRATEGIES

Marketing objectives stem from the business's objectives. If the business aims to develop into new areas of the country, the marketing strategy needs to fit. There are many possibilities including developing new markets, increasing profitability, revamping the image, devising new products or increasing market share.

CREATE A MARKETING PLAN

The plan will be determined by the strategies. It has to use a balance of the marketing mix to best effect. This means weighing up the effectiveness of the product, price, promotion and place or distribution to decide the best combination. The amount that is available to spend will also have a strong influence on the mix.

The plan will include a schedule of actions and events which needs to be clear and readily available for everyone involved. People need to know exactly what their responsibilities are. It helps, for example, to make sure that the public relations staff are putting out messages about exciting changes.

MONITOR OUTCOMES AND REVIEW PLAN

Once the plan is in place, a business can't afford to sit back and assume it will all just work. Sales must be monitored carefully to see if targets are being met. If things are not going smoothly, the plan must be reviewed and changes made to achieve better results.

Getting it right

The evaluation of the marketing plan will be determined by the objectives and strategy that has been put in place. The integration of the strategy into the business as a whole is also very important. There is no point in persuading people to buy a wonderful new product if production simply can't make enough to meet demand. This may give a product short-term notoriety but often leaves customers fed up. It is important not to damage the reputation of the business by being over-ambitious.

The elements of the marketing mix that are used will also contribute to the success or failure of the plan. The product is obviously key to success but the other three must be selected to support the product according to market conditions.

The role of after sales support and customer care is becoming increasingly crucial. They are almost part of the product already because people often need help in using today's gadgetry. A business that puts an exciting new product in the market place but does not look after the customer is likely to fail.

Critical thinking

You are going to run a disco at school or college. Devise a marketing plan for the event. Remember to keep costs in mind. Photocopying an A4 advert, for example, will cost about 4p a sheet. Your marketing costs take a slice of the profits.

Share your plan with others and evaluate your choices and likely outcomes.

Next steps

1 Keep an eye open for new product launches or relaunches.

2 Work out how the marketing mix is being used.

3 Does it seem to be successful?

KEY TERMS

Marketing plan shows the schedule of marketing activity for a product over a period of time. It will show how different elements of the marketing mix contribute to the strategy.

What is a product?

Specification Content

Products

starSTUDY

Stephen's laptop

Stephen needed a laptop to take to clients when they called him in to develop their websites. He went to one of the big name retailers and chose a smart-looking machine with a name he knew to be reliable. He wanted to look professional when he went off to visit his growing client list.

After a couple of months his frustration with the laptop exploded. The battery lasted for about 20 minutes and he was always looking for a socket to plug it in. His clients always seemed to have equipment that worked properly. He just looked inefficient. He rang the manufacturer and was told that the machine had nothing to do with them. The machines had been bought direct from their head office in Hong Kong

and was supported by the big name retailer. He tried contacting them and was told that the laptop would have to go back. But it was only the battery… He needed his laptop to go on working so how could he part with it? After spending hours on the phone, queuing for the helpline, trying to talk to someone who could make decisions, he persuaded them to send a replacement battery. When it arrived it didn't fit!

1. What did Stephen expect when he bought his laptop?
2. Why is aftercare so important with products like this?
3. How did Stephen's costs increase because of the inadequate aftercare on offer?
4. Why should a business think about its products as a 'total experience'?
5. Do you think Stephen will go back to this retailer again?
6. Make a list of the criteria that a business should include in this 'total experience'.

What is a product?

Products are all the things that are sold to customers. Both products and customers vary greatly.

Customers may be:

- individuals in the customer market
- businesses in an industrial market.

Products that are sold to businesses include all the resources that they need such as:

- electrics for the motor industry
- concrete for the building industry
- paper, photocopiers and other office supplies for any business

- services such as cleaning, repairs, insurance or banking.

Products that are sold to customers can be:

- shopping products, such as televisions and fridges, which last a long time and are bought occasionally and need consideration before purchase
- convenience goods which are bought frequently for everyday consumption.

The product doesn't stop at the item or service itself. When Stephen bought his laptop, he expected the warranty that came with it to meet his needs, but it didn't. Many businesses find that customers do not return when customer service and aftercare fall down.

Right product – right market

IN THE KNOW

You are unlikely to see frivolous adverts for insurance. Buyers are looking for security, so want to feel safe in their purchase. Fun might not be ruled out but a customer wants to know that the product is sound – especially when they feel that they do not understand all the small print that goes with it. Such security is an **intangible benefit**. Almost all products offer intangible benefits: cars, trainers, phones and drinks – to give but a few examples. Different cars give different intangible messages. It's easy to guess the nature of the message from looking at a product's styling and advertising.

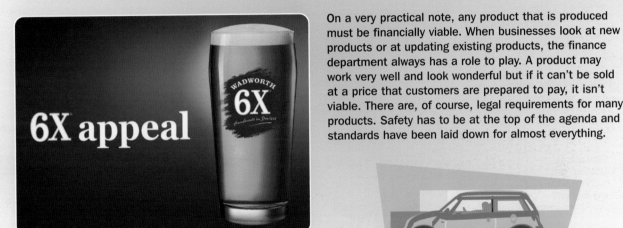

Draught beer has moved into selling with a different sort of intangible appeal!

The **tangible benefits** are more concrete because they can be measured – the washing machine that spins 1200 times a minute rather than 800; the computer that has a bigger hard disk and a faster processor.

To get it right, a business must have a clear picture of the market. It is important to keep a close eye on both customers and competitors.

go to → page 92 to refresh your ideas on knowing the market.

On a very practical note, any product that is produced must be financially viable. When businesses look at new products or at updating existing products, the finance department always has a role to play. A product may work very well and look wonderful but if it can't be sold at a price that customers are prepared to pay, it isn't viable. There are, of course, legal requirements for many products. Safety has to be at the top of the agenda and standards have been laid down for almost everything.

Critical thinking

1 If you are developing a marketing strategy for a product, you need to consider different factors for different products. What factors are important in marketing trainers, a small car, a fridge, an apple, a hairdresser, a garden centre and a theme park?

2 Why is it important to make sure that the product is financially viable? Why not just charge a higher price?

Next steps

1 Look carefully at some adverts and decide on the nature of the tangible and intangible benefit that are determining the advertising strategy.

2 Choose a business that you know and look at its range of products. Work out where each product is in its life cycle and position them in the product portfolio. What makes the products different from each other?

KEY TERMS

Intangible benefits relate to the feel of the product and the image it is trying to give.

Tangible benefits relate to practical aspects of the product.

Developing products

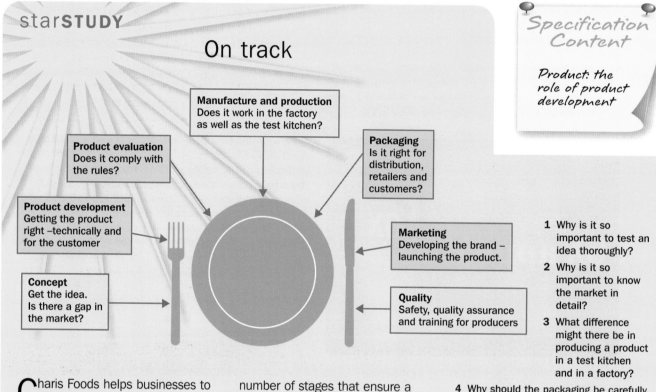

On track

Manufacture and production
Does it work in the factory as well as the test kitchen?

Product evaluation
Does it comply with the rules?

Packaging
Is it right for distribution, retailers and customers?

Product development
Getting the product right –technically and for the customer

Marketing
Developing the brand – launching the product.

Concept
Get the idea. Is there a gap in the market?

Quality
Safety, quality assurance and training for producers

Specification Content

Product: the role of product development

1 Why is it so important to test an idea thoroughly?

2 Why is it so important to know the market in detail?

3 What difference might there be in producing a product in a test kitchen and in a factory?

4 Why should the packaging be carefully evaluated?

5 How might a business use stages of the process to update existing products? Can you think of some examples of products that have been updated or remodelled?

Charis Foods helps businesses to develop new products. It has developed Food Track, a programme designed to guide small and medium-sized enterprises (SMEs) through the process. The development work involves a number of stages that ensure a product meets everyone's needs. A business might also use part of it to develop an existing product. It has been put to work to help companies produce a wide range of new food products or extend the life of others.

Why develop products?

New products almost always attract attention. New cars are reviewed on the television and in newspapers and motoring magazines. New food products often get coverage in a similar way. The launch of a product provides an opportunity for businesses to let the market know what they are doing. It also adds products to a business's portfolio to keep a healthy mix of old and new.

Existing products must not be forgotten. Keeping the product portfolio up to date is important otherwise other businesses will take advantage and a reputation for being behind the times might develop. A steady stream of product development also helps to differentiate one business's products from another. It is, however, important to ensure that the money spent on development is recouped through more sales or the customer's willingness to pay a higher price. As with new products, making modifications to existing ones can elicit media attention.

Innovation also gives a business competitive advantage because customers recognise that it is at the forefront of the market.

Next steps

Choose a range of products and work out how they might be developed in future. Be realistic because lavish expense on change will probably not be recouped if the price can't rise.

KEY TERMS

Small and medium-sized enterprises are independent business, managed by their owners or part-owners and having a small market share.

New product development

FINDING A NICHE for a new product means researching both the market and customers while thinking 'out of the box'. A business must try to identify a product that

- makes the most of new technology

- appeals to customers

- will make a profit

- is not under development in another company.

The decision that a new product can be sold at a realistic price is critical to future development. It is easy to dream up a product that everyone would like but if it costs so much that no one will be prepared to pay the price, it's a non-starter.

DEVELOPMENT OF THE PRODUCT

involves many people in the business:

- Technical people make sure that it works

- Designers make sure it both looks good and functions

- Marketing people check the product against known customer habits

- Finance people keep an eye on costs.

TESTING THE MARKET is important with a new product. The marketing department will try to find an area that is similar to the market they expect to sell into and put the product to the test. This is often combined with local television advertising to draw attention to the new product. While this happens, the market research continues and the findings will offer guidance on the launch of the final product.

LAUNCHING THE PRODUCT once it has proved itself is a major challenge and can cost millions. A careful combination of marketing activities will be used to get the message to the public. Free samples of new food products are often handed out in supermarkets to entice the public to buy. Sachets of shampoo and samples of perfume are frequently to be found in magazines. New cars are often launched at motor shows with much hype and special events are organised for journalists to encourage them to write flattering articles. Drug companies have sometimes come in for criticism for inviting doctors on expenses-paid trips to exotic places to find out about a new drug.

A star, cash cow, dog or problem child?

go to ➔ Review the Boston Matrix on page 104 .

Letting people try the product first often encourages them to buy.

Every business would like to see its new product become a star. Having a large share of a growing market is a very desirable situation. Inevitably, few products achieve this quickly. Some will become problem children because they have taken a small share of a high growth market. Products like this will need further development or different marketing to win more market share, or they will be dropped as a test cause.

A new product is unlikely to become a cash cow quickly because they are usually found in mature markets. A dog would lead to despair. The food industry often has low growth markets, simply because there is a limit on how much we can eat. A new product would aim to have an impact and steal market share from others. A dog would fail to do this.

The Boston Matrix can be put to work like this in order to analyse the position of products in the portfolio of a business. Decisions can then be made about future activities.

Critical thinking

1 Look out for the launch of a new product.

2 How is the product different from others?

3 Work out who the target market is.

4 Does the product appeal to that market? Why?

5 What promotional techniques are being used?

6 How successful do you think the launch is? Explain your answer.

7 Try to find out from the media or the Internet whether is has been successful.

Prices and people

Specification Content

Calculation and interpretation for decision making of price elasticity

starSTUDY

1 What happens to bus company revenue when fares go up? Why?

2 What would happen to revenue if either restaurant put its prices up? Why?

3 Why do makers of electrical products have to think hard before they raise prices?

4 Why does the customer go on buying chewing gum even when the price goes up?

5 Draw up a chart showing

a things that people buy even if the price goes up

b things that people cut back on a bit if the price goes up

c things that people stop buying when the price goes up.

Work out what each category has in common.

6 If you ran a business, which sort of product would you prefer to supply? Why?

7 Many businesses try to make their products a little bit special so that people really want them. What are they trying to do?

IN THE KNOW

Price and demand

If a business wants to put prices up, it helps to know just what will happen to sales and revenue. It might generate more revenue, stay about the same or even fall – so it is worth thinking about.

Price elasticity of demand helps to provide an answer. The formula below gives a figure that shows the outcome.

$$\text{Price elasticity} = \frac{\text{\% change in quantity demanded}}{\text{\% change in price}}$$

If the price goes up by 10% and sales fall by 15%, the formula will look like this:

$$\frac{-15\%}{+10\%} = -1.5$$

This means that a price rise will reduce revenue, therefore it is not a good strategy. Demand for most products is elastic so businesses have to think carefully before putting up the price. If the price of a Solero ice cream goes up, customers will look at the alternatives.

If, on the other hand, a 10% rise led to a 5% fall in sales, the story would be different.

$$\frac{-5\%}{+10\%} = -0.5$$

This means that revenue doesn't fall when the price goes up. It rises. Most business can't do this forever because customers will become more price sensitive as the price rises. Designer labels can put prices up considerably before demand starts to fall but, eventually, even the most fashion conscious person wonders if it is worth it.

Products like gas, electricity and petrol are more price inelastic because they are products which we can't do without. Season tickets for buses and trains fall into the same category. We have to travel to work, come what may.

You will have noticed that all these figures are negative. An elasticity figure is always negative so the minus sign is often ignored.

TO SUM UP ...

Elastic demand
Value of more than 1   Revenue falls when price rises

Inelastic demand
Value between 0 and 1   Revenue rises when price rises

When prices change ...

People's buying habits are influenced by price but they do not react in the same way in all their purchases. The different responses are measured by price elasticity of demand. The examples above show these different responses.

If a business knows how people will react, it can plan its pricing strategy more accurately. Many people in business deny all knowledge of the elasticity for their products but in fact they know just what will happen if they put the price up.

Using price elasticity

IN THE KNOW

Knowing about the price elasticity of your products is clearly invaluable to people running businesses.

SETTING PRICES

Elasticity provides the basic information for decision making. It must be used with other information about the costs and feasibility of changing the scale of production. If a price cut leads to a large increase in demand, can the business cope? McDonald's had a 2 for the price of 1 offer and couldn't meet the demand. The strategy was viewed both as a failure and success. There were some angry customers who couldn't get the cheap burgers but many others stayed and bought something else!

CHANGING THE PATTERN

Elastic demand is not good news for businesses that want to put prices up. Many work hard to try to change people's perceptions or reduce competition in order to make demand more inelastic.

- **Differentiating the product** works by creating a product that is distinct from its competitors. Designer clothing companies do this all the time.

  - **Merging with the rivals** reduces competition so there are fewer substitutes and customers have less choice.

  - **Price fixing** among businesses reduces competition. If airlines decided that they would all charge the same price for a flight to Paris, customers would have to pay up. It is illegal.

Buying habits change with income too

As people earn more, they spend more on some things but less on others. This is known as income elasticity of demand. They don't buy much more milk, but they will buy a more expensive car and long-haul holidays. Demand for some products actually falls. People move from own-brand products to brand names. From a business point of view selling luxury products has great advantages but sales are very sensitive to recessions.

Critical thinking

1 How elastic or inelastic is demand for the products in the Star Study? Explain your answers.

2 Choose a range of products that you know and work out how sensitive they are to price changes. Select one with elastic demand and another with inelastic demand and draw up a spider diagram for each one, showing the factors a business would have to consider before changing the price.

Next steps

Walk round a supermarket or other large store and look at the pricing strategies that are being used. How is price being used to persuade customers to buy? Is it being successful? Why do you think the business is doing it?

KEY TERMS

Price elasticity of demand measures the responsiveness of customers to a change in price.

Income elasticity of demand measures the responsiveness of customers to a change in income.

Setting the price

star**STUDY**

Want to go to Malaga?

Planning to fly to Malaga on a Tuesday in October? There's plenty of choice. It all depends on what you are prepared to pay.

Flight 3711

departs London Stansted at 07:45

web fare **16.49** GBP (phone fare 21.49 GBP)

Flight 3713

departs London Stansted at 11:35

web fare **26.49** GBP (phone fare 31.49 GBP)

Flight 3715

departs London Stansted at 21:15

web fare **21.49** GBP (phone fare 26.49 GBP)

Not including taxes
Fly from Stansted airport. No seat allocation.
Food and drinks available to buy.

BA Economy
Depart London Stansted at 8.25
£139.30 including taxes
Depart London Stansted at 14.45
£139.30 including taxes
Depart London Stansted at 18.30
£139.30 including taxes

Fly from Stansted. Seats allocated before departure. Food and drink provided.

BA Club Class
Depart London Stansted at 8.25
£526.30 including taxes
Depart London Stansted at 14.25
£526.30 including taxes
Depart London Stansted at 19.30
£526.30 including taxes

Fly from Stansted. Wider seats allocated before departure. Better quality food and drink provided.

AIR PARTNER PLC

Air Partners
An executive jet for 6 people from any location, at any time.
£8,000

1 How do these four products vary?

2 Do these variations in price reflect the different costs of providing the service?

3 Are the prices presented in the same way?

4 Why do you think the prices are set at these levels?

5 Look at the information on the rest of these two pages and work out which pricing strategies are being used by each business.

What price?

Businesses set prices with the aim of making as much profit as possible – immediately or in the longer run. An understanding of the elasticity of demand helps because it informs decision makers about the likely effect of a change. Before setting the price, they need to ask:

• **How fierce is the competition?**

If there are many competitors in the market, people will look around for a good deal. On the other hand, the bus company may be able to raise fares because there are no direct competitors. Some businesses will keep the price higher in order to differentiate their brand from others, giving it snob appeal.

• **Will consumers buy if the price is high?**

It all depends on the product and the customer. Those with high incomes might spend £39.95 on an Italian designer orange squeezer, when you can buy a perfectly good one for £4.99.

Snob appeal?

• **Is there much of the product available?**

A shortage is always popular because a business can charge more. When Christmas comes and the favourite toy is in short supply, parents will pay anything to get hold of one! Later on, when supplies are restored to normal, they will be much more careful about looking for a good deal.

KEY TERMS

Discount is a reduction on the price. It is generally expressed as a percentage.

Pricing methods

IN THE KNOW

Businesses use a variety of approaches to pricing. They may be based on cost, competition or customers – the 3Cs.

COST-BASED PRICING

Pricing strategy	How it works	Comments
Cost plus or mark up	Add a certain percentage to costs. e.g. 50% on £50 = £75. This is often done on items bought by retailers from wholesalers.	This is often done by tradition in some industries but isn't very sensitive to market conditions.
Target	A business knows how much return it expects and works out the price of the product to provide it.	The target must be set with market conditions in mind. A business will quickly get into trouble if unrealistic targets are set.
Full cost	A business works out all the costs of producing an item and then adds a profit margin.	It can be hard to allocate all costs exactly when a range of products is being made.
Contribution	Contribution pricing is based on variable costs. If the variable costs are £10, any price above that will make a contribution to the fixed cost of the business. If fixed costs are £50,000 and the price is set at £12, the first 25,000 sales will cover the costs and the 25,001st sale will start making a profit.	The mark up needs to be set in the context of the market. Is demand strong enough to pay the price? A business can compare the effectiveness of a product by looking at the contribution it is making.

go to → Find out more about variable and fixed costs on page 131.

COMPETITION-BASED PRICING

- Price leadership occurs when there is one dominant business that sets the price. Others follow.

- When businesses charge the same price, they are often trying to avoid a price war because this means cutting profit margins.

- Destroyer pricing happens when a business deliberately sets its prices very low to force competitors out of the market. Prices usually rise once the competition has gone.

CONSUMER-BASED PRICING

Perceived value pricing is used to set the price when demand is inelastic. The price reflects the customers' perceptions of the product. Prestige means a high price.

Price discrimination is used when people can be divided into separate markets for a product. Commuters have to travel at a particular time of day, therefore they can be charged a higher price.

Pioneer pricing is used for new products. A business might aim to get in quickly and set a low price. A new gym will often give a discount when it opens in order to attract members. A very trendy gym might decide to charge a premium because it wants to be viewed as elite. This is known as price skimming.

Which strategy?

Many businesses use more than one strategy because they keep an eye on the market and aim to make the most of prevailing conditions. Cost plus pricing is the most frequent method but others are used to make extra profit. A business might give a discount to attract a big customer.

Next steps

Have a look at some businesses in the high street or the web and work out how they are setting their prices.

Critical thinking

1 Which pricing strategy would you use if you set up a new sandwich bar? Why?

2 What effect would a business hope to have if it went for destroyer pricing? Think of an example of this happening.

3 Why is it important to keep an eye on the market?

4 How might a business which offers financial advice aim to develop its pricing strategy?

5 How does price elasticity of demand affect the decision that a business makes on pricing?

Promoting the product

 starSTUDY

What a week of wizardry!

 £1 million spent on a book launch by a publisher

 A character becomes a brand

 Tantalising snips of information leaked from time to time

 £1 million webcast of the author

 £200,000 movie premiere style party

 £100,000 to turn a bookshop into a theme party

 Author has an audience with 4000 readers in the Albert Hall

 Competitions on Blue Peter and MTV

 Book covers for children – another one for adults

 200 products to be found on Amazon

 Media coverage of every step

 200 million copies sold in 47 languages

Read by 1 in 3 adults and innumerable children

What else could it be but Harry Potter? Promotion for J.K. Rowling's books and films has outstripped everything else in the children's entertainment market. The books were released on the stroke of midnight. Children celebrated in bookshops up and down the country. At exactly the same time in New York's Times Square, Potter lookalikes gave away stickers and badges at the same moment as the book cover flashed up on the billboards. Not really surprising for a product that is worth £3 billion a year!

1. Which market segments are Harry Potter books aimed at?

2. Do they sell beyond the intended segments? Why?

3. What is the objective of promotion of this sort?

4. Why is becoming a brand a key to marketing success?

5. How did the marketing strategy achieve even more promotion than the businesses organised?

6. What promotional strategies has the Potter brand used? Why?

Specification Content

Promotion: above and below the line

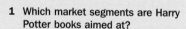

Marketing magic

Harry Potter is a phenomenon. A simple story that turns into a major brand is very unusual. The first book caught the public imagination and then the marketers had a major opportunity and made the most of it. The marketing departments at Bloomsbury, the publishers, and Warner, which makes the films, have used a wide range of promotional activities to make the most of this opportunity.

Promotion

The objective of all promotional techniques is to get a message across to customers and persuade them to buy the product. It should be informative, persuasive or reassuring. Everyone thinks of advertising, which is known as an above the line method, but there are many other strategies as well. They are generally called below the line techniques.

ADVERTISING comes in many different forms and in many different places. It is on television and radio, in the papers and magazines and on hoardings, racing cars and anywhere that there is a little space. Product placement means seeing James Bond drive an Aston Martin or a football star wearing a particular designer's outfits. It is a discreet way of having a product associated with famous names and visible to many.

PERSONAL SELLING also happens in many different ways. It involves direct contact with the customer, so it ranges from selling in a car showroom to knocking on doors or holding marketing parties. Personal selling in general is expensive because of the cost of recruiting, training and motivating staff. Telesales has become increasingly important as it is a cheaper way to get to customers.

DIRECT MARKETING involves using mailshots and catalogues that go straight to the customer.

POINT OF SALE promotion is used where the product is being sold. It can take the form of posters, leaflets, stickers etc.

SALES PROMOTION often involves incentives such as loyalty cards, vouchers for money off your shopping in coming weeks or two for the price of one etc. It also includes getting the branding and packaging right.

PUBLIC RELATIONS tries to put positive messages about a product or a business in the public eye. It uses press releases and contacts to persuade newspapers to write articles about the benefits of a product. It may involve sponsoring an event or competition in order to draw attention to a business or brand name.

How to decide?

There are so many ways of promoting a product that a business might be lost for choice – until it looks at the cost. A thirty-second spot on national, peak time television costs so much that it is only an option for the biggest advertisers. It is, therefore, only an option for big name businesses. Before making decisions, a business must consider the nature of the product, the size of the market and the costs. A mail order company needs to send out a catalogue, put it on the web – or both. The local takeaway might put leaflets through people's doors or perhaps have a short advert at the local cinema. If a product appeals to a specialist market, a specialist magazine or website may be the answer.

The types of promotion that are selected will have been informed by market research. You can often look at adverts and see how they are trying to change people's perceptions. Cruise companies, for example, try to persuade people that their holidays are not just for the elderly.

The marketing department will have been allocated a budget and will have to make choices within its limitations.

Critical thinking

1 Make a note of all the promotional activities that you come across in a day. Why do you think the businesses have chosen each strategy?

2 Who is the target market?

3 Can you spot the messages from market research that have informed the promotion?

4 Do you know of other things that each business does to attract customers? How do you think the mix works?

5 Which business's strategy is most effective? Why? Try to take the amount of money spent into account in your decision.

KEY TERMS

Above the line promotion includes all direct advertising.

Below the line promotion includes all other forms including sales promotion, personal selling etc.

Next steps

You have been asked to promote a new bar/restaurant that is aimed at young people in your area. What would you do?

Placing the product

starSTUDY

Right place – right time

On the day that another Harry Potter book hit the market, 2 million books had to be in the right place at the right time. It was to be found in 6,200 bookshops, supermarkets and even petrol stations in the UK and around the world. Amazon already had 350,000 orders for the book and many orders had been placed on the publisher's website.

After all the hype, failing to meet the deadlines would have been a disaster. The image of disappointed children without their Harry Potter books was not the message that Bloomsbury, the publisher wanted to see. Routes of distribution to retailers, and e-commerce companies were critical, especially in a business that isn't used to working on this scale.

Specification Content

Place: channels of distribution

1 Why do you think the book was available in unusual places like petrol stations?

2 Why was it important to make sure the books were in the right place?

3 Do you think retailers needed to be persuaded to stock the book? Why?

4 What sort of products might a retailer have to be persuaded to stock?

5 All sorts of products are now available through a bigger range of outlets. Give some examples.

6 Why do you think producers
   a welcome this change
   b are less enthusiastic about it?

Right product – right place

Different sorts of products are to be found in different places. Chocolate bars are probably the most widespread product. They are to be found in supermarkets, corner shops, newsagents, petrol stations, vending machines, pubs and many more. A producer of a new chocolate bar, however, might have to work hard to persuade retailers to stock it. Space on the shelves is valuable because a shop depends on rapid stock turnover to keep profit levels up. The best place varies from product to product. Levi, for example, didn't want Tesco to stock its jeans. One reason was that it felt that its image would be tarnished by being associated with Tesco. The second reason was that Tesco wanted to cut the price.

The place where a product is sold is often used to influence the image of the product. When Coca-Cola wanted to relaunch Cherry Coke with a more risqué image, it ran events in clubs across the country.

Harry Potter books don't provide a problem as retailers know that they will sell very quickly, but many products are more of a problem. A retailer will want to know about the promotional activities associated with a product. Will there be television or newspaper advertising? Is there point-of-sale advertising material? Are there any introductory offers on the product?

Getting the product to the retailer also has to be thought about carefully. When shops run out of stocks, customers may buy another product and never come back. Getting it right is critical to keeping and gaining customers.

Channels of distribution

TRADITIONAL ROUTE

 → Wholesaler → Shop →

Wholesalers buy stock from manufacturers and sell them on to shops. This is a helpful process for small shops, which cannot deal with the large quantities at one go. Many small shopkeepers go to cash-and-carry warehouses, which are the equivalent of the traditional wholesaler. The process might even involve an agent who is authorised to sell the product in bulk to wholesalers. The traditional route is also known as a long channel route.

MODERN ROUTE

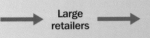 → Large retailers →

Supermarket chains no longer use wholesalers. They buy direct from the producers. The scale of purchase is so great that the supermarkets make deals directly with suppliers. This process is criticised because of the power that these large buyers have over the price. Most producers cannot afford to be ignored by the major supermarket chains, therefore they are prepared to accept lower margins.

Some supermarkets have taken things a stage further. Waitrose, for example, has its own farm which supplies produce direct to the shops.

Food is not the only business that works directly with the suppliers. PC World buys computers direct from the manufacturer. It also has models made specifically for it to give it a cost advantage over other stores.

This is a short channel route.

DIRECT

 → → →

An increasing number of producers sell direct to the customer. The Internet has assisted this process. Harry Potter books can be bought straight from the publisher just like most other books. Some businesses, like Dell computers, have based their whole system on direct selling. The great advantage is that it cuts costs. If a Harry Potter book is sold to a bookshop, the price has to be set so the shop can make a profit on the selling price. The telephone and text messages are also used by direct sales businesses. Cutting costs can mean lower prices, so customers are increasingly tempted to buy direct.

This is a short channel route.

Mushrooms from Waitrose's Leckford Farm on sale in the supermarket

Critical thinking

A business is launching a new model of personal stereo with lots of up-to-the-minute features. Work out where it should want to place the product and how it should persuade shops or other outlets to stock it. Can you think of any other distribution strategies? Explain why you think they would work.

Next steps

1 Have a look at Dell's website, www.dell.co.uk. Find out the price of one of its computers.

2 Have a look in a high street store and compare the price of a computer with a similar specification.

3 How much cheaper is Dell?

4 What are the advantages and disadvantages of buying from Dell and a high street store?

KEY TERMS

Short channel routes include direct and modern channels of distribution. They cut out wholesalers and agents.

Long channel routes are distribution methods that include wholesalers or agents.

testing–testing

Marketing – assessment

Chester Zoo

Chester Zoo is a zoo without bars. You watch the animals by just strolling through the zoo's complex, but it is more comfortable to board the monorail or tour by boat. Highlights are the glass-sided penguin-pool, the Twilight Zone bat cave, the orang-utan breeding centre and the crocodiles in the Tropical Realms.

Chester Zoo is a charity run on firm business lines. The zoo spent £670,000 on advertising and promotion to attract more visitors, raise funds and raise public awareness.
Average spend per visitor continues to rise and last year reached £12.39. This is in addition to the rise in visitor numbers to 1,050,000 for the year. All good news because the extra revenue is essential if the zoo is to achieve its objective of supporting and promoting conservation.

Advertising seen by visitors

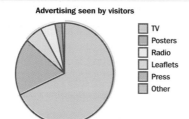

- TV
- Posters
- Radio
- Leaflets
- Press
- Other

Visitors returning to the zoo	
	Re-visits
This year	13%
last year	30%
2-3 years ago	19%
4-5 years ago	13%
6-10 years ago	7%
Over 10 years ago	18%

Age group of visitors	
Age in years	%
0-3	12.5
4-6	7.5
6-7	6
8-10	3
10-12	5
12-15	6
16-19	1
20-24	5
25-34	20
35-54	20
55+	11

54% of visitors have heard or seen advertising about the zoo recently

Overall, how good value would you say the admission charge for here was?
- Extremely good — 10% (results given)
- Very good — 58%
- Fairly good — 30%
- Not very good — 1%
- Not at all — 0%

Visitor numbers to Chester zoo

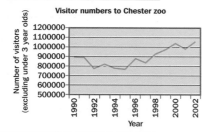

Chester Zoo has five simple and clear marketing objectives:

- To encourage customers to come back.
- To get new visitors.
- To spread the visitors more evenly over the whole season.

- To raise awareness of the zoo's work in conservation.
- To sell more food, drink and souvenirs.

To meet these marketing objectives the zoo must monitor and evaluate its marketing plan.

The marketing department wants to continue developing its nationally recognised brand, explore and trial commercial enterprises and events and develop cost effective promotional techniques.

The zoo believes it offers its customers high standards of care and high quality visitor facilities that cater for all ages. It wants to be sure that its facilities meet the top tourist attraction standards. It won the Zoo of the Year award in 2002, but it needs to be sure it understands what its customers think.

The zoo pays a specialist market research business to make up a questionnaire and analyse the results. Until recently the main method of collecting information was to:

- Undertake yearly visitor surveys carried out by the zoo staff or during the summer months by staff specially employed for the task.
- Read existing published information.
- Encourage all the staff to observe and listen to customers.

Chester Zoo groups the questions into three broad areas.

1. Who are the customers?
   The zoo wants to know their ages, why they decided to visit the zoo, how long they spent there, when they arrived, how they got there and where they came from.

2. Promotion
   How effective are the zoo's promotional activities?

3. Views or opinions of their customers
   This includes likes and dislikes plus how the zoo could be improved.

The marketing team will use the market research information to produce a report or a marketing plan. This will be presented to senior managers from other functional areas who will discuss its implications for their area. For example, the marketing department at the zoo recognised a need to improve catering, but this has an effect on human resources and the finance departments.

From the website:

'Chester Zoo offers a fun and stimulating day out for everyone, no matter what age or ability. As well as our 500 different species of animals and award-winning gardens, we offer first class facilities that ensure your day out really is as enjoyable as possible.

The Zoo is completely wheelchair and pushchair accessible, and all of our toilet facilities have disabled access, as well as plenty of Parent and Baby changing rooms. And parents will be delighted to know that our new *Fun Ark* adventure play area, near the Ark Restaurant, is a great place for children of all ages to let off steam!

There is a wide range of shops, cafes and ice-cream kiosks located around the Zoo; which cater for all tastes and budgets. At our Fountain Shop a fun and professional face-painting service is available during peak periods.

- Bring the family along for a Halloween disco, supper and other creepy happenings. £14.00 per adult   £9.00 per child
- Visit Santa in December
- Corporate and private functions
- Safari evenings when the zoo is closed to the general public, we invite you to bring a private party of 30 people or more for a unique evening's entertainment
- Birthday parties'

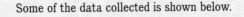
Some of the data collected is shown below.

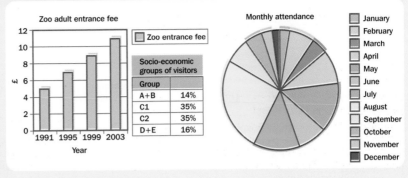

Socio-economic groups of visitors	
Group	
A+B	14%
C1	35%
C2	35%
D+E	16%

assessment questions

1 In what ways does the zoo's marketing objectives help support its overall objectives? **(4 marks)**

 You will need to define the two terms and apply them to Chester Zoo.

2 In what ways is the zoo both customer and product oriented? **(4 marks)**

 This requires you to make the simple link showing how marketing supports the zoo in its main objectives.

3 Discuss two promotional methods that might be suitable for the zoo to use to encourage new customers. What methods might be suitable to encourage repeat customers? **(8 marks)**

 A simple example of above and below the line promotional methods that might be used by the zoo to attract the two types of customers. Try to justify which might be more cost effective.

4 What is market segmentation? How and why might the zoo segment its market? **(4 marks)**

 Straightforward definition followed by two examples using evidence from the case study.

5 Explain one internal and one external factors that have influenced the rate of growth of customers to the zoo. **(6 marks)**

 'Internal' means talking about what the zoo has done to attract more customers and 'external' wants you to write about influences beyond the control of the organisation.

6 Assume a new marketing campaign costs £20,000 and manages to bring in an extra 3000 adults. Would it be regarded as successful? **(5 marks)**

 This requires a calculation of the extra revenue that will come in minus the campaign costs. Will there be other costs?

7 Explain why market research is important to the zoo? **(4 marks)**

Straightforward asking you to comment on how it informs decision-making and can be used to make forecasts.

8 How might it best carry out its research? **(6 marks)**

Mention primary and secondary examples and how this may be best gathered. There is plenty of evidence within the case study.

9 Analyse the results of past market research. **(8 marks)**

This requires you to extract information from the data, but don't forget to comment where the data is insufficient. What more would you want?

10 Why has the zoo been able to raise its prices regularly over the past 12 years? **(8 marks)**

Think about the concepts that lie behind such a question. Changes in demand and price elasticity of demand come to mind.

11 Produce and justify a marketing plan to increase customers who might be attracted to events outside normal zoo hours. **(10 marks)**

There are plenty of examples to choose from in the case study. Choose from Santa, safari evenings, Halloween, children's parties, weddings, and corporate functions. You could then comment on the make up of the marketing mix to your example.

Why keep accounts?

starSTUDY

The collapse of energy giant Enron is the largest bankruptcy in US corporate history. In just over 15 years, Enron grew into one of the US's largest companies. However the company's success was based on artificially inflated profits, dubious accounting practices, and – some say – fraud.

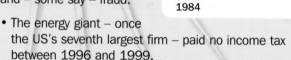

The rise and fall of Enron

Enron share price

- The energy giant – once the US's seventh largest firm – paid no income tax between 1996 and 1999.

- Enron executives bribed tax officials in order to fabricate accounts.

- Share price rose steadily as the profits appeared to grow.

Specification Content
Accounts help a business keep records, monitor and control performance; financial accounts are used by stakeholders to assess performance

1 Why might the executive directors of Enron have tried to cover up the company's real performance?

2 When do you think the problems of Enron's financial records started to be uncovered?

3 Make a list of the stakeholders who are hurt from accounting errors or bad practice and performance described in the examples.

- Shareholders and directors sacked Jean-Marie Messier, boss at France's media giant Vivendi Universal. In two years shareholders have watched the value of their investments drop from $120 a share to about $20 a share. At the same time, debt has risen sharply.

- Two former top executives at bankrupt telecommunications firm WorldCom have been arrested and charged with fraud. 'Corporate executives who cheat investors, steal savings and squander pensions will meet the judgement they fear and the punishment they deserve.' (US Attorney General John Ashcroft)

- A Scottish breast cancer charity has its bank accounts frozen after a judge hears that only a small amount of the millions it raised went on good causes.

- A Devon health trust calls in outside accountants after finding mistakes in its accounts for the last financial year. It found it had an extra £1m debt.

Keeping accurate records

Accurate records are essential to help a business check for errors and monitor how well it is doing by providing the evidence for the accounts. The information can assist managers in making decisions. It can also be used to help support businesses wanting to raise money since it will improve investors' confidence. Lastly, transparent records add to the trust between buyer and seller.

Accurate records are legally needed for the Companies Acts and Partnership Agreements and provide information for the assessment of taxes.

Different stakeholders are interested in different financial documents. For example:

- The tax authorities want to calculate how much tax is due from a business

- Investors want information on how profitable the company is

- Suppliers want to be sure they will receive the money owed to them

- Banks will need to assess the risk of getting back their loan

- Business managers need the data to help them control, monitor and plan

- Unions representing workers will want to know how much the business can really afford in wage increases

- Workers will want to know if their pensions are safe.

What's recorded?

Paperwork in a business is really all about keeping accurate records of its:

- expenditure – or everything it buys

- income – or everything it sells.

Although it is referred to as 'bookkeeping' most businesses now keep their records on the computer. Specialist software makes sure the data entered from a source document automatically updates other financial documents, including the interim final accounts. This allows the business to check the accuracy of its records easily. It is also easy to search the data to bring up exactly the information required, for example overdue payments. What is more, the data can be put into graphs to provide an easier way of looking at how well the business is performing. In this way the software functions as a management information system (MIS) to help monitor and control performance, and predict and plan for the future. This area of accounting is called management accounting. It includes budgets and cash flows. It is mostly used internally by the business.

Accurate financial records must be published annually for all companies. The process is shown below.

The final accounts, often known as financial accounts, include the profit and loss account and the balance sheet. Shareholders will be able to use these final accounts to make judgements on a company's performance.

There is no excuse for managers and directors being unaware of what is going on in their company. If they can't or don't keep close control of their business or they try to cover up problems then they deserve to get into trouble. They will be letting down the stakeholders in their business.

Process of financial accounting

Collecting from source documents	Recording in books and ledgers	Compiling trial balance	Constructing final accounts
• Receipts • Invoices • Cheques • Statements	• Day books • Sales ledgers • Purchase ledgers • General ledger	Summary of all the income and expenditure	• Profit and loss statement • Balance sheet

Critical thinking

1. Who are the main internal and external users of financial information?

2. Why should accounts be both reliable and honest?

3. Accounts must represent a true and fair view of a limited company's performance. Accounts are verified by auditors before being signed by the directors and filed with the Registrar of Companies. How, given this system, do things sometimes go wrong?

4. The UK accounting system is based on principles such as honesty, consistency and accuracy, but should it be based more on law?

KEY TERMS

Management accounts describe financial information that is used to monitor, control and plan.

Financial accounts provide users of these accounts with an accurate guide to the financial performance of the business.

Next steps

1. Search through the BBC news website for news about accounts: http://newssearch.bbc.co.uk

Why budget?

starSTUDY

The Eden Project is a charity whose objectives are:

- To educate without being like a school
- To hold conversations that might just go somewhere
- To research and share this with anybody
- To provide a sanctuary.

This is why they built the centre and this is where the money has gone.

£86 million may sound like a lot of money but, far from being rich, the Eden Project has actually been a lean machine in order to stretch the resources to cover its basic needs.

Success! The target for the first year was 0.75 million visitors. There were 2 million. This produced more revenue, but at peak times they had to turn people away. They needed more facilities to cope with demand.

Source: Eden Project.

Specification Content

The nature and purpose of budgets as an aid to decision-making and control; comparison of budget and actual achievement

	£Million
Buying a large and unusual site and car park with roads and paths to get there.	10
Reshaping the ground to make it safe, useful and dry	8
A couple of decent greenhouses	25
40 acres of plants, some tall	3
50,000m^2 of soil to grow them in	1.5
A nursery to practise in and grow some unusual plants	1
Buildings and contents for visitors and our team	10
Services to keep it all running	7
Paying the team to run it over 5 years	2.5
Exhibits to entertain visitors	2
Advice on doing bits we couldn't do ourselves (including designing and engineering the world's biggest greenhouse)	9
Bits we needed to add to the plan to keep us going in the future	7
Total	86

1. In what ways did the Eden Project's budget plans fit in with the objectives of the project.
2. Why did the charity set aside £7 million as a contingency?
3. What problems would the charity have encountered if it didn't have a financial plan?
4. Why might the charity need to review its plans given the unexpected popularity of the centre?
5. Which budget area has a clear time period?

Planning ahead

The initial objectives of the Eden Project required it to build a centre costing up to £86 million. It was financed by a number of sponsors including the Millennium Commission. The charity employs a number of managers who are budget holders and whose job it is to make sure that the charity works within its budget. The objectives of the Eden Project will need continual review. For example, the extra visitors has resulted in more revenue, but inadequate facilities. Future plans can be adjusted to take account of this.

Decision-making

A **budget** is a financial plan that looks at costs or revenues. Budgets are usually linked to the objectives of a business and show how the strategy will be followed in order to achieve those objectives. Business objectives set out what the managers hope to achieve. They can be both short term and long term. A short-term objective might be the introduction of a new product line or the refitting of a shop. Long-term objectives are concerned with where the business aims to be in a few years' time. For example, Innogy's (the electricity company) strategy to diversify might involve it requiring budgets to take over other businesses.

CONTROL

Someone needs to take responsibility for each budget area. That person will need to monitor both spending and revenues to check whether they are more or less than was expected. The difference between the budget and the actual amount is called the **variance**. A favourable variance occurs where the actual figures are better than budgeted for. This will happen if costs are lower or revenue is higher than expected. An adverse variance means either revenue is lower or costs higher than budgeted for.

All types of organisation need to have budgets, whether they are governments, charities or businesses.

How can budgets go wrong?

Budgets must be as realistic as possible, but there are difficulties.

- Budgeting for something for the first time is going to be more hit and miss than if you have done it before, since you will have learned lessons from the variance in past budgets and built it into current ones.

- Keeping close control is another problem. It is important to note and react to variances as they happen so you can attempt to correct them. Sometimes the variance can be beyond your control. For example, good weather can ensure that building projects are completed within time and within their budget, but a prolonged spell of bad weather can have the opposite effect.

Organisations place different emphasis on their objectives. An order might be accepted or rejected on the basis of the business's objectives. An objective of high profit might lead to the rejection of an order where the level of profit was too low. However, if the objective was to reach a certain sales level it may accept a less profitable order.

Critical thinking

- The channel tunnel train company revealed that its passenger numbers had fallen for a fifth consecutive quarter, declining by 3.3%.

- England's Arts Council has been criticised after 13 of its 15 major projects went over budget, costing £94 million.

- Most building projects under the controversial Private Finance Initiative are being delivered on time and under budget, according to the public spending watchdog.

1 Is the variance positive or negative in each of the examples?

2 How might the first two organisations mentioned react to their budget variance?

3 How should budgets be determined? Think about your school budget.

KEY TERMS

Budget is a financial plan linked to an organisation's objectives.

Variance is the difference between the expected and the actual figures.

Next steps

Find out something about your school or college budget. What is the total budget? How much goes on staffing and how much on maintenance and repairs? What is the Business Studies budget for the year and how is this monitored?

Keep the cash flowing

Specification Content

Importance of cash flow; calculating cash flow and interpretation of cash flow forecast

star**STUDY**

Just Bangers is a new business that makes sausages for sale to restaurants and delicatessens. After spending £8000 on new equipment and a second-hand vehicle, its owner, Jay, has £7000 in the bank. Jay starts making, selling and delivering sausages in March. Since Jay relies on credit sales, his customers have 28 days to pay. This means the sausages sold in March will be paid for in April. Similarly, Jay receives 28 days credit from his suppliers, so the meat he receives in March he pays for in April. Jay makes a cash flow forecast.

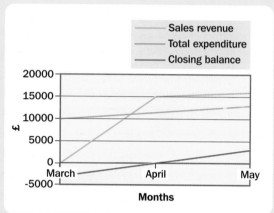

Cash flow forecast

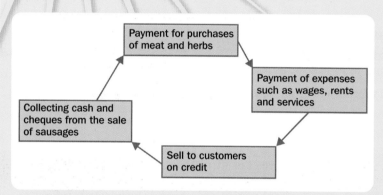

Cash Flow Forecast	March	April	May
Income			
Sales revenue		15,000	16,000
Total income	**0**	**15,000**	**16,000**
Expenditure			
Rent	1,500	1,500	1,500
Services such as power, water			1,000
Purchases of meat and herbs	0	2,200	2,500
Wages/salaries	5,500	5,500	5,500
Motor expenses	1,500	1,500	1,500
Insurance	300	300	300
Other (including marketing)	1,200	1,000	700
Total expenditure	**10,000**	**12,000**	**13,000**
Opening bank balance	7,000	-3,000	0
Balance of cash in and cash out each month	–10.000	3.000	3.000
Closing balance	–3,000	0	3,000

1 Why was no sales revenue forecast in March?

2 What money flows out of Jay's business in March?

3 How short of cash will Jay be in March should his forecast be correct?

4 Suggest how he might meet that shortfall.

5 Why is it important for Jay to be certain that cash flows in before he has to pay the bills?

KEY TERMS

Cash flow measures the actual money received by a business in a time period set against the expenditure of the business.

Cash flow forecast tries to be realistic and predict the cash flowing into and out of the business.

Creditors are organisations that the business owes cash to.

Cash flow

Cash flow measures the money flowing in and out of the business. Money must come in from sales revenue or the business is in real trouble. The business may also receive income from interest earned and from one-off sources such as loans, grants or selling assets.

The cash budget is the expenditure on the day-to-day running of the business. It is also known as revenue spending. Money flows out of the business to pay wages and bills. These bills come from suppliers who usually expect to be paid 28 days after the delivery of the goods. The supplier becomes a creditor.

Sometimes money flows out of the business to pay for fixed assets like property, vehicles or new equipment. This is called capital expenditure because it is spent on long-term operations. The assets purchased will be used for several years to make the product.

Controlling cash flow is essential for business survival. Cash flow problems can lead to business failure. If more money goes out than comes in during a time period, a business may be unable to pay suppliers who may be reluctant to continue to sell to the business.

A business will make a cash flow forecast to predict cash needs and prepare for shortages, for example by getting an overdraft.

A budget is the plan for the future that the business wants to achieve. The cash flow forecast is a prediction of what might happen. They interact because the business tries out its plans by feeding 'what ifs' into the cash flow forecast.

These might include:

- If we accept that order we can pay the suppliers?

- If we accept that order will we need to employ more and what will this cost us?

These are estimates, so it is important to make them as realistic as possible.

If a decision is taken to go ahead, the business needs to record actual income and expenditure on the cash flow spreadsheet. It then needs to look at the variance.

The process

Budget feeds into cash flow forecast.

↓

Needs recognised and fed back into budget.

↓

Decisions made whether to go ahead or not and how to meet any shortfall.

↓

Actual cash flow recorded and compared with forecast to produce variance.

Why worry?

Cash flow problems are responsible for causing over 70% of businesses to fail within their first year. Symptoms of a poor cash flow include:

- wages not paid

- increased overdraft

- later and later payments to creditors

- stocks build up because sales are less than forecasted.

Jay would need to be confident that his forecast is realistic. Jay also needs to make sure there is enough cash to pay the bills. If Jay failed to obtain a loan Just Bangers would be lacking in cash even though it was profitable.

On the other hand, a sound cash flow doesn't always guarantee success. A business could have a positive cash flow but still be unprofitable. For example, the business may have sold off a lot of old stock cheaply. This would raise money from the sales but produce little, if any, profit.

Critical thinking

1 Just Bangers has been asked to consider a contract from a supermarket that would provide an additional £15,000 revenue a month. Some costs remain the same but others would increase. From the evidence in the Star Study identify both these groups of costs and then make a cash flow forecast for June. What cash would Jay need to find before accepting the order? What might be the attitude of the bank if asked for a loan?

2 What are the limitations of cash flow forecasts?

Controlling the flow

Specification Content
Cash budgets and variance

starSTUDY

Just Bangers cash flow and variance after three months trading ('variance' figures in brackets are negative)

Cash flow	March forecast	March actual	March variance	April forecast	April actual	April variance	May forecast	May actual	May variance
Income									
Sales	0	0	0	15,000	13,000	(2,000)	16,000	17,000	1,000
Total	**0**	**0**	0	**15,000**	**13,000**	(2,000)	**16,000**	**17,000**	**1,000**
Expenditure									
Rent	1,500	1,500	0	1,500	1,500	0	1,500	1,500	0
Services such as power, water	0	0	0	0	0	0	1,000	1,100	(100)
Purchases	0	0	0	2,200	2,000	200	2,500	2,700	(200)
Wages/salaries	5,500	5,500	0	5,500	5,500	0	5,500	5,500	0
Motor expenses	1,500	1,200	300	1,500	1,600	(100)	1,500	1,600	(100)
Insurance	300	300	0	300	300	0	300	300	0
Other (including marketing)	1,200	1,300	(100)	1,000	1,000	0	700	600	100
Total	**10,000**	**9,800**	200	**12,000**	**11,900**	100	**13,000**	**13,300**	(300)
Opening bank balance	7,000	7,000	0	(3,000)	(2,800)	(200)	0	(200)	200
Balance of cash in and cashout each month	(10,000)	(9,800)	(200)	3,000	1,100	1,900	3,000	(1,100)	4,100
Closing balance	(3,000)	(2,800)	(200)	0	(1,700)	1,700	3,000	(1,300)	4,300

1 What actually happened to the total sales for the three months when compared to the forecast?

2 What happened to the total costs for the first three months compared with the forecast?

3 Which items were accurately forecast?

4 Which part of the cash flow forecast was the poorest prediction?

5 Although the sales from March would only show up in the April figures, Jay would know in advance what the figure would be as he had sent out invoices. Jay had badly underestimated the sales level. What can be done?

Sometimes things go wrong

BAD PAYERS

Customers who sell things to a business on credit become **debtors**. When customers fail to pay at the agreed time, it can have a major impact on the cash flow. You may need to raise more finance to compensate for the delay in payment.

A business must keep control of its debtors and follow up immediately if payments are late.

DO YOU REALLY NEED ALL THOSE ASSETS?

Buying too many assets can mean increased borrowing and more interest payments. The loans may have to be secured against business assets or even your personal possessions. You may not be able to meet payments.

Buying in bulk can seem beneficial at the time, but holding excessive amounts of stock ties up money in unproductive assets, particularly if the stock is not sold on quickly. Effective stock control is a key to controlling cash flow.

go to→ Find out about stock control on page 198.

PREDICTING DEMAND

Sales may rise or fall unpredictably. A change in demand may be impossible to forecast, but sound market research and effective marketing may help a business to predict the change and reduce the effects.

KEY TERMS

Debtors are organisations that owe the business cash. They are usually customers.

Overdraft is an arrangement with the bank to overdraw on the account up to an agreed sum.

Total forecast	Actual total	Total variance
31,000	30,000	(1,000)
31,000	**30,000**	**(1,000)**
4,500	4,500	0
1,000	1,100	(100)
4,700	4,700	0
16,500	16,500	0
4,500	4,400	100
900	900	0
2,900	2,900	0
35,000	**35,000**	**0**

Next steps

1 Find out about current cost of borrowing and the overdraft rates from a bank.

2 Ask your teacher about the credit periods given for book orders.

Changing the flow

To manage cash flow, a business needs to delay and reduce outflows of cash and speed up inflows of cash to the business.

Increase inflows:

Action	Good points	Bad points
Give customers a shorter credit period	You will receive your payments earlier	Your customers may get a better deal elsewhere
Use a factoring company to chase up unpaid bills	You will spend less time chasing unpaid bills	You will have to pay the factoring business a cut of the money they bring in
General good credit management	Once a system is set up, it leads to good habits	People may need training to run the system so there is a cost

Delay outflows:

Action	Good points	Bad points
Ask suppliers for a longer credit period	Delays payments for supplies already received	Supplier may be worried about your business performance and may not want to risk selling to you
Buy stock only when needed	Less storage and less waste	Need to be sure that suppliers can deliver on time
Lease equipment instead of buying it	Spreads the payments over a period of time	It's not yours to keep
Cut costs through increased efficiency	This reduces outflows	This may reduce motivation and quality

If it all goes pear shaped ...

Many small and even medium-sized businesses go under because they underestimate the importance of cash flow. A business that can't pay its bills is insolvent. Many try to borrow to overcome a problem but sometimes banks will refuse to lend or allow a business an **overdraft** because they are worried about repayments being made. It has been known for businesses with full order books to become insolvent because they have tried to grow too fast.

starSTUDY

Yes ... but ...

'Orders make us profits so why can't we accept this order from France? It's for £280,000.'

'You have estimated the job will cost £80,000 for components, £20,000 power and £100,000 for production plus £50,000 towards cover rent.'

'Yes, exactly my point. We can make £30,000 on this deal.'

'Fine, but hold on, we won't get the money until one month after delivery. That's four months' time. Yet we have to pay out wages, fuel bills and buy in the components. Have you seen our bank balance?'

1 What problem is there in accepting the order?

2 How might the business attempt to overcome this problem?

3 What might happen to the business if it takes the order but can't pay its bills?

What are the costs?

starSTUDY

Amy runs trips to see big bands in the NEC from the south-west. She can purchase tickets for, on average, £20. She spends about £200 promoting the trips through her internet site, by e-mailing past customers, advertising in the local papers and putting up posters. Other costs include the hire of a fifty-seater coach for £200.

Liz Brook is a Product Manager for International Services (roaming), which looks after calling and texting to and from the UK. At the time, Virgin Mobile was charging 55p per minute for all calls to the UK. Within the EU, the roaming partners charge different amounts for rerouting the call. Virgin Mobile averages this out and part of the 55p charge reflects this.

The marketing department at Virgin Mobile is called Brand. It is responsible for promoting the brand of all Virgin Mobile services including international calls.

Source: Virgin Mobile.

1. Identify the costs to each business.
2. Which of these change when there are more customers or calls?
3. Which of these stay the same irrespective of the number of customers or calls being made?
4. Why is it useful for a business to know how its costs change when sales increase?

Business costs

Businesses of all sizes have costs which fall into similar patterns. Some vary according to how much is produced. Others stay the same whether the business is producing nothing or is at full capacity.

The balance between the different sorts of costs will affect the decisions that are made about which products to produce, how many of them and whether to go on producing, so it is important to know what is happening.

Why collect the information?

Managers must have a clear picture of how much products cost to make. Without this information a business has little chance of success, as it is important information for pricing.

go to → Go to page 114 for a reminder on pricing.

Costs are also important when a business wants to monitor progress. Once a budget has been set and targets allocated, knowing how costs are changing is important. The decisions on future plans will depend on the financial information that is coming in.

Although it seems an easy exercise to work out what things cost, it is a little more difficult because allocating overhead costs to a particular item is tricky. Spreading the costs of running the office, for example, is not easy.

What sort of costs?

IN THE KNOW

It is useful for businesses to break down costs into categories in order to understand performance and aid plans.

ONE METHOD OF LOOKING AT COSTS ...

- **Fixed costs** are those that remain the same no matter what output is, within the short run. They include items like rent and management salaries.

- **Variable costs** change with output and include costs such as buying components or materials.

Adding the fixed costs to the total variable costs gives the total costs. The variable costs are not always constant. For example, buying in bulk will often reduce the price paid for components and this will be reflected in a reduction in the variable cost as output increases.

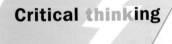

Sometimes costs cannot be easily separated into fixed and variable and are called semi-variable costs. For example, a vehicle delivering stock has to pay a fixed level of insurance and road tax, but the more it is used the greater the fuel bill and maintenance cost.

ANOTHER WAY OF LOOKING AT COSTS ...

- **Direct costs** involve all the costs that can be directly related to the product or service or a cost centre. An example of this would be the food, chefs and waiting staff for a restaurant cost centre within a hotel.

- **Indirect costs** are those that cannot be directly allocated to a specific product or service. This might be the hotel's promotional expenditure or the cost of cleaning, which cannot normally be allocated to just one product or service. Indirect costs are often known as **overheads**. When we add the direct and indirect costs together we get the total costs for the product or service.

    And finally ...

    Marginal cost is the extra cost of producing one more unit. It is the direct cost of producing that item.

- Total cost of producing 500 items is £1000
- Total cost of producing 501 items is £1005
- Marginal cost is £5

It is a useful tool when costing products. Managers must have a clear picture of what each item costs in order to set prices sensibly.

Critical thinking

1. Make a list of all the costs you can think of associated with your school. Identify the
   a. direct or indirect costs
   b. fixed or variable costs.
   Explain your decisions.
2. Draw up a table showing the various types of cost. Complete the table with the costs in each category for the following businesses:
   a. a hairdresser
   b. a website developer working from home
   c. a car factory
   d. a childminder.

KEY TERMS

The **short run** is the period of time when the scale of the operation cannot be changed easily. Any increase in output comes from using spare capacity.

Variable costs, such as raw materials, change with output.

Fixed costs, such as rent, remain the same irrespective of output.

Direct costs are those that can be allocated to a particular product or cost centre.

Indirect costs or overheads are usually connected with a number of products or cost centres.

Marginal cost represents the extra cost of providing an additional product.

Making a contribution

Specification Content

Contribution, its calculation and uses

starSTUDY

The Rondo Theatre is a small provisional theatre in the south-west. In fact it has just 200 seats. It is hiring a comedian for a one-night show. The costs include:

- Publicity   £100
- Paying the comedian   £500
- Overheads such as rent and rates   £100
- Theatre employees booked in advance for the night £100
- Tickets are sold through an agency that charges £2 per ticket sold
- The seats are priced at   £10.

The Rondo Theatre is a simple business with just one product – a ticket for the show – so it is quite easy to work out the costs associated with each sale and the contribution that each item sold makes to costs. In other businesses with more products it is more complex but contribution costing is a strategy which makes it more straightforward.

1. Which of the costs would have to be paid even if no tickets were sold?
2. Which of the costs are directly dependent on each ticket sold?
3. What is the extra cost of selling one more ticket?
4. If 100 seats were sold what would be the total costs and what would be the total revenue?
5. What would be the profit if all seats were sold?
6. How much does each ticket sold contribute to the costs?
7. How many tickets must be sold before the business starts to make a profit?

IN THE KNOW

Contribution and profit

The contribution a product makes is the revenue gained less its variable cost.

For the Rondo Theatre the contribution is the sales price of £10 less the variable cost of £2 giving a value of £8. It means every ticket sold contributes £8 towards covering the costs of the show.

Total contribution is sales revenue less variable costs. So for Rondo it is:

Contribution = Sales – Variable costs
= £2000 – £400
= £1600

To work out the profit, just deduct the fixed costs from the total contribution.

Profit = Contribution – Fixed costs
= £1600 – £800
= £800

The term 'contribution' is used because that is exactly what each item sold is doing. Because variable costs have been deducted already, the extra cost of making the item has been covered. Every £ of 'contribution' goes directly to covering the fixed or overhead costs. Once enough has been sold to cover overhead costs, the business starts to make a profit.

Critical thinking

	Glimmer £	Sparkle £	Starry nights £
Variable costs			
Materials	10	9	14
Labour	8	20	24
Selling price	40	22	60

1. A candle business produces three product ranges. It sells them to retailers in boxes of 25. The following figures are for one box. Overhead costs are £80,000.

   a. How much does each box of candles contribute?
   b. What is the total contribution if 2000 of each line are sold?
   c. How much profit or loss is being made?

2. Why might the level of spare capacity influence pricing decisions for an airline?

Contribution costing

Even a small business has a range of overheads which are hard to share out among the different products or services that are sold. If a beauty salon does manicures, massages and a wide range of other treatments, how do you allocate the rent, coffee, marketing etc. to each service sold? Contribution costing avoids the need to do this because it looks at the contribution that each product sold makes to these overhead costs.

Total contribution is £36,000.

The fixed costs of running the salon are £20,000.

Profit is therefore £16,000.

The great advantage of contribution costing is that it does not attempt to share out overhead costs, which is always difficult, so errors are not built into the decision-making process.

	Manicures	Massages	Make up	Slimming treatments
Sales revenue	10,000	15,000	4,000	20,000
Variable costs	2,000	5,000	2,000	4,000
Contribution	8,000	10,000	2,000	16,000

Is it contributing?

Contribution is a useful idea because it shows whether items that are being produced are beneficial to the business. If there is no contribution because the variable cost of each item is not being covered, questions should be asked. It may be because it is a new product that is getting established and needs some time to make its mark. If no reasons can be found, a business should stop production.

Contribution can tell a business whether it is worth selling something at below full cost. Many businesses will cut prices when demand is low.

In January, newspapers are full of vouchers for low price meals at smart restaurants because everyone has overeaten at Christmas and has stopped eating out. If diners are covering the variable costs of their meal and making a small contribution to overheads, it is better than an empty restaurant.

This strategy avoids upsetting existing customers who are paying full price and the restaurant doesn't lose its exclusive status because this is clearly a special offer for a limited period. These are both problems which affect other businesses when they try to sell spare capacity at lower prices. Many businesses use contribution costing in markets that can be differentiated. 'Off peak' is a concept often used to do this. It can apply to trains, gym membership, flights and other products.

Making decisions

Contribution helps a business to take an overall view of what is going on. Being able to see the contribution of each product in the context of the whole business makes planning and decision-making more accurate.

Better information leads to better decisions but there are some questions that should be asked first.

• Will cutting prices mean that total contribution will never cover the overheads?

• Will cutting prices now make it hard to go back to the old price level?

• Can fixed and variable costs be clearly distinguished?

• Have changes that have taken place in costs been considered?

Remember that contribution can only be looked at in the short run. When fixed costs change, costings will change.

Most important of all – remember that contribution is not all profit. It only becomes profit when all the fixed costs have been paid. Break-even on the following page will make this clear.

KEY TERMS

Contribution is sales revenue minus variable cost. Contribution minus fixed costs is profit.

Break even?

Specification Content

Break-even analysis to support decision making

starSTUDY

'What ifs' at the Rondo Theatre

Price	£10.00
Average variable costs	£2.00
Contribution	£8.00

When the Rondo Theatre is planning an event, the management ask all sorts of questions. Try to answer them. You could use a spreadsheet package to help you.

What if output was?	0	50	100	150	200
Fixed costs	£800	£800	£800	£800	£800
Variable costs	£0	£100	£200	£300	£400
Total costs	£800	£900	£1,000	£1,100	£1,200
Total revenue	£0	£500	£1,000	£1,500	£2,000
Profit/loss	–£800	–£400	£0	£400	£800

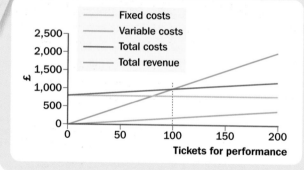

Rondo Theatre's break-even chart

1 How many seats have to be sold to cover all the costs?
2 How much profit will be made if all 200 seats are sold?
3 What would happen if the agent decided to charge £3 to sell a ticket?
4 What would happen if the comedian's fee went up to £600?
5 What would happen if the ticket price was £12?
6 What is the relationship between contribution and the break-even point?

Breaking even at the Rondo Theatre

At the Rondo Theatre the contribution is the sales price of £10 less the variable cost of £2 giving a value of £8. It means every ticket sold contributes £8 towards covering the fixed costs. The fixed costs are those not dependent on customers buying seats. They include paying the performer and theatre employees as well as the rent and the publicity making a grand total of £800. If only 10 tickets were sold then some £80 of the fixed costs would be covered by the contribution and the loss would be £720. To calculate the break-even point, the fixed costs need to be divided by the contribution. For the Rondo, this would be £800 divided by £8 meaning 100 tickets would need to be sold to exactly cover costs. Each ticket sold above that adds £8 towards profit. If the Rondo sold out it would make a profit of £800 as the contribution from the first 100 tickets exactly covers the costs and so the contribution from the last 100 tickets is all profit.

KEY TERMS

Break even is the level of sales at which there is no profit or loss.

Margin of safety is the level of output beyond the break-even point.

Next steps

1 Try to get hold of the figures for a recent school event such as a disco, concert or play. Did it break even? What was the contribution of each ticket sale?

2 How much profit did it make? What advice would you give about pricing to the organisers of the next event?

When will we break even?

Working out when a business will break even is a simple matter once the numbers have been established. You need the following information.

- Fixed costs
- Variable costs

Together, these two tell you

- Total costs

And, finally,

- Sales revenue.

When a business sells its products, it creates revenues that allow it to cover its costs and eventually start to make a profit. The level of sales required so that the total contribution exactly covers the fixed costs is called the break-even point.

To calculate the break-even point a business will often

assume that:

- The selling price remains the same whatever amount is sold
  - Fixed costs also remain the same regardless of output
  - Variable costs vary in direct proportion to output.

The margin of safety is the amount by which sales exceed the break-even point. It informs a business of the amount by which demand can drop before it makes a loss. For example, assume the break-even level of sales for a particular airline flight is 130 tickets and the average sales for Thursday flights has been 150 seats, then the margin of safety would be 20. For Saturday flights past data indicates the average sales rise to 200 giving a higher margin of safety of 70. This information is likely to be extremely useful when deciding ticket prices.

Using break even

The advantage of using break even is that it provides information to managers on the profit or loss that can be achieved. It is easy to see the effect of a change in costs or price especially when using a spreadsheet. The main advantages are that it is simple, quick and cheap.

It does have some downsides (below) and needs to be used wisely with allowances made for the assumptions.

The downsides

It assumes that fixed and variable costs are clearly distinguishable.	Employees, for example, are considered a fixed cost but the Rondo might need more for some events.
It assumes that costs increase constantly.	Economies of scale make bulk buying cheaper.
It assumes that everything will be sold.	It doesn't allow for fashion and changing tastes.
It cannot tell what actual sales will be.	Will you reach break even? It's hard to tell.
It assumes that the price of every item will be the same.	Many businesses give discounts for bulk buys.
It assumes that sales revenue will increase when the price goes up.	An increase in price may lead to a fall in demand. It all depends on elasticity.

Critical thinking

A low cost airline needs to fill about two-thirds of its seats to cover its costs which include:

- Telesales staff
- Advertising
- Crew
- Ground handling
- Insurance and airport landing fees
- Air traffic control fees
- Fuel
- Aircraft ownership costs
- Maintenance

1 Once a plane is scheduled to fly what cost headings will be included in calculating the marginal costs for low cost airlines?

2 Why is the marginal cost much lower for low cost airlines compared with normal airlines?

3 Does the marginal cost help explain ticket prices for these airlines? What other costs are important?

Investment decisions

starSTUDY

Better IT

Virgin Mobile spent some £20 million on information technology in one year. It included specific software packages, hardware, training and maintenance, and backup rescue. Why spend so much and was it worth it? The investment helped the call centre to look after the increasing number of customers more efficiently and provided them with a better quality experience. The aim was to persuade customers to stay loyal and hopefully spend more.

The company is quite new and the PCs still perform well. The Desktop Support team is able to repair any that become faulty. When they can no longer be repaired, they are replaced in small batches.

Mobile marketing

Virgin Mobile's marketing campaign set a target of 6000 new business customers. It bought database information with the addresses of customers who were most likely to convert. Past experience shows that the response rate for mail drops is usually up to 3% whilst outbound calling will produce a conversion rate of 1 to 1.5%. The company can then propose a realistic budget and be fairly confident that the investment in marketing will be successful.

New planes for easyJet

easyJet is investing £4 billion in 120 new Airbus planes between 2003 and 2008. easyJet negotiated with both Boeing and Airbus in order to get the biggest discount and best deal. On top of saving money upfront the Airbus will save a further 10% on running costs.

1 What factors might Virgin Mobile and easyJet consider before making any future investment?

2 What is the difference between the two examples of Virgin expenditure?

3 How many mail drops would Virgin Mobile need to make to convert 6000 new customers?

4 What would be the minimum number of phone calls Virgin Mobile would need to make to convert the same number of customers?

5 What factors might Virgin Mobile consider in deciding whether to use letters or phone calls or indeed whether any of these is worth doing?

6 What type of investment may be necessary in the next few years even if the company did not want to expand?

Specification Content

Reducing risk in circumstances of uncertainty; investment appraisal; pay back period and accounting rate of return

Investment appraisal

When a business invests, it aims to increase net cash inflow above the cash outflow. It usually draws up a break-even chart and puts together a cash flow forecast.

Break-even analysis informs the business of the level of sales necessary to achieve the desired profits. Once the cash flow forecasts are in place businesses can use investment appraisal methods to help it decide whether to go ahead with an investment. There are two commonly used methods of appraising investment proposals.

The payback method calculates the time it takes for the net cash flows to pay back the investment.

Year 0 refers to the time of the investment. By the end of year 2 the cumulative net cash flow is just minus £1000 and the figure becomes positive sometime during year 3.

Year	Net cash flow £	Cumulative net cash flow £
0	(20,000)	(20,000)
1	10,000	–10,000
2	8,000	–1,000
3	6,000	5,000
4	5,000	10,000

In year 3 the net cash flow is expected to be £6000 or the equivalent of £500 a month. So it would take two months to pay back the £1000 required. The total payback period is therefore 2 years and 2 months.

The longer the payback period the greater the risk that something may go wrong. Some businesses will not consider a project unless it pays back quickly. This might be quite short in a high technology business like Virgin Mobile, where the opportunity cost of that funding is the next project that it could use the finance for. Payback is a useful initial filter to see whether an investment is worthwhile, but as it ignores profitability it is best to use it alongside another method. It may also discourage investment. For example, it is unlikely that the Channel Tunnel would have been built because the payback period was so long.

The accounting rate of return measures the profit earned on an investment expressed as a percentage of the initial investment. It does not use cash flows.

Accounting rate of return =

$$\frac{\text{average annual profit from the investment} \times 100}{\text{Initial investment}}$$

The total profit from that investment is added together and divided by 5 to give the average annual profit.

In the example below a hotel is considering introducing one of two new booking software systems. Both suppliers estimate that they will have a useful life of 5 years. The systems will mean lower staff costs and less double bookings. System X should increase profits by £25,000 or an average of £5000 a year and system Y by £60,000 or an average of £12,000 a year.

Software option X

Year	Net cash flow £	Cumulative net flow £
0	(50,000)	(50,000)
1	18,000	(32,000)
2	17,000	(15,000)
3	15,000	0
4	14,000	14,000
5	11,000	25,000

Software option Y

Year	Net cash flow £	Cumulative net flow £
0	(100,000)	(100,000)
1	22,000	(78,000)
2	30,000	(48,000)
3	36,000	(12,000)
4	36,000	24,000
5	36,000	60,000

The accounting rate of return for system X

$$= \frac{\text{£5000} \times 100}{\text{£50,000}} = 10\%$$

The accounting rate of return for system Y

$$= \frac{\text{£12,000} \times 100}{\text{£100,000}} = 12\%$$

On the face of it system Y is the one to go for because its return is 2% per year higher. However, system X would pay back in three years compared with four years and four months for system Y, and system Y earns most of its profit in later years when the predictions are less accurate. By then newer and better software is likely to be available. Also, the cost of system Y is double that of system X.

There are always some questions to ask:

- How reliable are the figures provided by the two suppliers?

- What do current users of the systems feel about them?

- How will staff get on with the two systems? System Y is much easier to use than X and the staff-training package is better.

Investment appraisal will reduce the risk but it is not an exact science.

Is it worth it?

How does a business go about making a sensible decision on investment? Any capital investment is a risk. Sometimes not investing is a bigger risk, as you will lose the competitive edge. Why did Ryanair and easyJet buy new planes? What was the main risk for the Eden Project? Why did Virgin Mobile invest so much in information technology? The idea is a simple one. By investing in capital equipment or a major marketing project a business expects to see an increase in profits. It might result from the increase in revenue being greater than the increase in costs. Alternatively the benefit might come through a decrease in costs since the investment makes the business more efficient.

Like any other business, easyJet will need to consider:

The cost of the actual investment	In this case easyJet agreed a heavily discounted deal of £4 billion.
The life expectancy of the investment	Each plane may have about 15–20 years' passenger service time before it will be sold and converted to freight transport.
The running costs	easyJet expect to make a 10% saving on this because of factors like fuel efficiency, maintenance and ease of getting passengers on and off the plane.
Increased efficiency	The expected revenues and cost savings from running more planes with quicker turnarounds.

Critical thinking

1 Are there any other factors the hotel should consider before making a decision?

2 Using only the accounting return method, which option is best and why?

3 Now considering both the **quantitative** measures which option is best for the hotel?

4 Why is it useful to consider **qualitative** information as well?

KEY TERMS

Net cash flow looks at the returns expected from the investment less the annual running costs.

Cumulative cash flow adds up the annual net cash flow.

Quantitative factors deal with number data.

Qualitative factors are relevant to the decision, but cannot be easily expressed in number form.

Profit or loss?

starSTUDY

Start up

Roger and Kathy are the owners of Indulge. They started out in a small way buying and selling high quality soaps for cash sales in local markets in and around Wiltshire. Their initial budget was £2000, which they spent on buying stock and marketing. They decided to take no wage or salary to keep costs down. To begin with they lived off Roger's income from his teaching and lecturing.

For the first 6 months of trading:

- Sales revenue or turnover was £1900

- Purchased stocks of soap to the value of £1250

- Remaining stocks of £250

- Expenses of £200 for hiring pitches at 5 events and paying for petrol.

1 If profit is the revenue minus the costs what profit did Roger and Kathy make
   a if all stock was counted as a cost along with the expense?
   b if costs included expenses added to the cost of the actual stocks sold?
2 Which method is a more accurate way of calculating profit?

starSTUDY

Getting going

Putting the second phase into operation meant a loan from the bank. Kathy ran the business. A shop was rented and they managed to buy soap-making equipment for £450. They made a range of soaps in quantities that reflected the demand in the first six months.

The second 6 months trading:

- Sales revenue (turnover) rose to £25,000.

- Purchase of £5000 of stock to add to the £250 left over from the previous 6 months' trading. All new stock was ingredients needed to make the soap and package it.

- £750 worth of stock was left over to carry onto the next trading period.

- Expenses went up considerably to £18,500. They had to rent a shop for £5000, pay rates of £4500, and Kathy was paid a salary of £5000 over the 6 months. Other expenses included depreciation, promotion, phone, power, insurance and interest on the loan, adding another £4000 to the expenses.

1 What profit did they make in the second 6 months of trading?
2 Do you think this level of profit is good?
3 What can they do with the profit that was made?

The profit and loss account

At the end of an accounting period, which is usually a financial year, companies send details of their financial accounts to their shareholders. They are used to monitor the performance of a business.

The first stage calculates gross profit.

Gross profit = Sales revenue (turnover) – Cost of sales

The sales revenue is the money that comes in from selling products or services. It is sometimes referred to as turnover.

The cost of sales refers only to the cost of the stocks that a business has used during that trading period. It is calculated by adding the stock purchases during an accounting period to the stock at the beginning of the period and then subtracting the stock held at the end of the accounting period. An example is given below.

Opening stock (at beginning of the accounting period) £10,000

Stock purchased (during accounting period) £60,000

Closing stock (at end of accounting period) (£15,000)

Cost of sales   £55,000

Only the costs of items that have been sold should be included because the other stock is for sale during the next accounting period and should be part of that accounting period's costs.

If sales revenue for the accounting period was £100,000 then the **gross profit** would be:

Sales revenue	£100,000
Cost of sales	£55,000
Gross profit	£45,000

The gross profit tells a business about the costs of its supplies compared with the revenue from sales.

The second stage calculates the net profit. The business has more costs to consider. It may be converting that stock into different products by processing and assembly, or it may be storing the stock or providing places where people can buy it. All these actions incur costs to the business in terms of overheads or expenses and these costs are accounted for in the second stage of the accounts.

Operating profit = Gross profit – Expenses (overheads)

Net profit = Operating profit + Interest received – Interest paid

Expenses or overheads are costs to the business other than stock. It includes items such as wages and salaries, advertising, insurance, depreciation and rent. The cost of fixed assets, such as machinery, shows up in the balance sheet and not as a lump sum in the profit and loss account, since it is best to spread the costs over the lifetime of the fixed asset. It will show up in the profit and loss account as depreciation.

Profit and Loss Account for the Year Ending 31 December	£	£
Sales revenue or turnover		100,000
Opening stock	10,000	
Purchases	50,000	
Total	60,000	
Closing stock	(5,000)	
Cost of goods sold		55,000
Gross profit		45,000
Expenses		
Wages and salaries	25,000	
Advertising	2,000	
Insurance	800	
Depreciation	1,200	
Rent	12,000	
Total expenses		41,000
Operating profit		4,000
Interest earned	100	
Interest payable	(1,100)	1,000
Net profit		3,000

Opening stock = closing stock from last trading period

Closing stock is taken away from the rest of the stock figures

Gross profit = turnover minus cost of sales

Operating profit = gross profit minus expenses

Total expenses are added and placed in right-hand column

Interest payable is in brackets because it will be deducted from the operating profit

The net profit takes into account the net effect of interest paid and received

In the accounts, the sub-calculations are completed in the first column and the final column deals only with the main headings.

What happens to the net profit is the subject of the third stage. This part of the accounts is called the appropriation account.

The retained profit provides an important link between the profit and loss account and the balance sheet, because it becomes a source of funding just like shares. The business will increase its net worth and net assets by the value of the retained profit.

First, companies must pay corporation tax on their profits. It is similar to employees paying income tax on earnings. The Inland Revenue collects it.

Net profit	£3,000
Corporation tax	£500
Profit after tax	£2,500
Dividends	£1,500
Retained profit	£1,000

The remaining profit is retained profit as it is retained or kept in the business to be used to buy fixed assets or to increase the working capital.

Some of the remaining sum is distributed to the owners. For a sole trader and partnership this is in the form of drawings from the business. For a company it is distributed to shareholders in the form of a dividend.

The **profit and loss account** is a record of revenue minus costs to provide profit levels for the trading period. It informs stakeholders of how well the company is performing. It is of most interest to managers and external users such as:

Stakeholder group	What they want to know
Auditors	Records
Government agencies such as the Inland Revenue	That it is receiving the correct tax payments
Banks who provide loans and overdrafts	Know that they will get their money back
Shareholders	What return they are getting on their investment
Potential investors	Compare business performance before deciding which one to invest in
Trade Unions	How much the business can afford to pay its workforce
Suppliers	Want to know if the company is likely to grow and continue to be a good customer
Managers	How well the targets are being met to help them plan ahead

Critical thinking

1 What happens to gross profit if a business manages to find a cheaper supplier?

2 Some expenses are like fixed costs. What happens to the average fixed costs if sales increase? How might this affect profit?

3 Why is profit important to businesses?

Next steps

It is quite difficult to get hold of profit and loss figures of small businesses. However, public limited companies must publish their accounts and you can access these from their websites. Also visit *www.bized.ac.uk*. You need to concentrate at looking at the main headings since these can be complicated documents.

KEY TERMS

Accounting period is the period for which final accounts are prepared. It is usually six months or one year.

Profit and loss account calculates a business's profit or loss for an accounting period. Once the accounting period is over all new revenues and costs will count towards the next profit and loss account.

What can the profit and loss accounts tell us?

starSTUDY

Below are the profit and loss accounts for the first two trading periods for Indulge. Profits have risen, but now it is a full-time occupation for Kathy. Kathy and Roger need to make important decisions. First, whether or not to continue with their business venture. Secondly, assuming that they do wish to continue, what measures they need to take to improve their performance further. Time for some number crunching.

Specification Content

The purpose and limitations of profit and loss

	Indulge profit and loss account for the 6-month period ending 30 December 2003		Indulge profit and loss account for the 6-month period ending 30 June 2003	
	£	£	£	£
Sales revenue (turnover)		25,000		1,900
Opening stock	250		0	
Purchases	5,000		1,250	
Total	5,250		1,250	
Closing stock	750		250	
Cost of goods sold		4,500		1,000
Gross profit		20,500		900
Expenses				
Salaries	5,000		0	
Rates	4,500		0	
Rent	5,000		0	
Other expenses	4,000		200	
Total		18,500		200
Net profit		2,000		700

1 What is the increase in the gross profit between the two trading periods?

2 What is the increase in the net profit between the two trading periods?

3 What has been the increase in expenses between the two trading periods?

How's it going?

Roger and Kathy would not be too concerned about the increase in expenses, as they have budgeted for this. After all, they were expanding by moving into a shop with Kathy working full-time. They have calculated the essential ratios and looked carefully at their costs and revenue data.

They found that average sales are £9, compared with a similar shop in another town of £12. Profit ratios were:

	Second 6 months of trading	First 6 months of trading
Gross profit margin	82%	47.4%
Net profit margin	8%	36.8%

The gross profit margin grew because Indulge started making soap rather than buying it. The net profit margin fell because Indulge had much greater expenses, what with opening and running the shop, manufacturing the soap and operating full-time.

Kathy and Roger felt they needed to further increase sales while keeping expenses under control. Better promotion and adding online sales were serious options. This should improve the net profit margins. They gathered as much reliable information as possible and fed this into a projected profit and loss account.

Interpreting the profit and loss account

Profit is needed for the long-term survival of a business. Part of the profit a business makes is used as a source of finance to help the business expand, but profit also provides a reward for the investors who have risked their money. Managers and owners want to know how the business has performed, so do other stakeholders like banks and suppliers. Some simple calculations allow business performance to be assessed.

Specification Comment

You do not need to learn these two ratios for the AS exam but they are not difficult and do help you to understand what the profit and loss account is showing

Two key ratios are:

1 The gross profit margin measures gross profit as a percentage of sales. This margin will improve if a business can buy cheaper supplies or it can raise prices.

$$\text{Gross profit margin} = \frac{\text{Gross profit}}{\text{Sales revenue}} \times 100$$

For Indulge in the second trading period it was:

$$\text{Gross profit margin} = \frac{20500}{25000} \times 100 = 82\%$$

2 The net profit margin measures a business's net profit as a percentage of sales turnover. It shows how much the business earns for every £1 of sales, after paying for the cost of sales and the expenses. A business can improve this margin if it can reduce its expenses or make them rise at a lower percentage than increases in sales revenue.

$$\text{Net profit margin} = \frac{\text{Net profit}}{\text{Sales revenue}} \times 100$$

For Indulge in the second trading period it was:

$$\text{Net profit margin} = \frac{2000}{25000} \times 100 = 8\%$$

For every £1 of sales Indulge earned 8p profit.

Not all businesses need the same level of profit. Some businesses need to operate on greater profit margins than others mainly because they invest heavily in capital assets. Pharmaceutical industries and software companies have high research and development costs. High profit margins help to provide finance. It is important to compare similar businesses when using ratios to judge performance. Businesses are also interested in looking at trends and it is useful to judge performance over a number of years.

Indulge projected profit and loss account for the 6-month period ending 30 June 2004		
	£	£
Sales		45,000
Opening stock	750	
Purchases	8,750	
Total	9,500	
Closing stock	2,000	
Cost of goods sold		7,500
Gross profit		37,500
Expenses		
Salaries	10,000	
Rates	4,500	
Rent	5,000	
Other expenses	8,000	
Total expenses		27,500
Net profit		10,000

Sales revenue should increase as they expand product range, seek new outlets and sell online

Buying materials in bulk slightly reduces the unit cost of supplies

Kathy feels able to afford to pay herself a better salary

Rates and rent don't change

Other expenses increase with delivery costs for non-shop sales and some depreciation for the website design

The percentage rise in net profit is much greater than the percentage increase in cost of sales and expenses

1 Calculate the projected gross profit margin.

2 Calculate the projected net profit margin.

3 How would Kathy and Roger feel if these margins proved to be fairly accurate?

Next steps

Research the gross profit margin and net profit margins of two or three similar PLCs such as supermarkets. Use data over at least two years to help you comment on their performance. Why do the ratios help you to make comparisons?

Critical thinking

What further actions could Kathy and Roger take to improve sales and what impact would this have on costs?

How does it balance?

Specification Content

The role of balance sheets; sources and uses of funds

starSTUDY

My balance sheet

Assume you are broke and have no possessions. You borrowed £150 from your Mum and then you spent £40 on CDs and £50 on clothes and kept the rest. Your personal balance sheet at the end of the day might look like this:

Assets		Liabilities	
CDs	£40	Loan	£150
Clothes	£50		
Cash	£30		
Bank balance	£30		
Total		£150	

1 What would happen to the total assets and liabilities if you borrowed an extra £50?

2 If you deposited this money in a bank what would your bank balance become?

3 How much cash would you realistically be able to get your hands on in the short run?

What is a balance sheet?

Balance sheets show where finance has come from (source of funds) and how it has been used. It is like a freeze frame of the business at a moment in time. A public company publishes its balance sheets at the end of its accounting period. Whenever the balance sheet is calculated the two sides will balance because it is set up to show the funds that have come in and what has happened to them.

What does the balance sheet show?

The principle of a balance sheet is the listing of all the assets and liabilities.

Fixed assets are those that the business does not intend to sell during that accounting period, such as machinery or vehicles and buildings. These are called tangible assets because they are physical. Some assets are intangible, meaning they have a value but cannot be seen. For example, a business may have an established trademark or hold patents and copyright. Having a well-known brand name and giving it a value provides a more realistic picture of the company, but it is difficult to give intangible assets a value.

Fixed assets only include items a business owns. For example, if the buildings are rented they cannot be included as an asset. Instead the rent becomes a cost that shows up as expenses on the profit and loss account.

Current assets are likely to be turned into cash within the accounting period. This obviously includes cash itself, but also stocks and debtors. Current assets will vary frequently as stock is sold and customers pay. Current liabilities include all creditors who are owed money within a year. Current liabilities are taken away from the current assets to produce net current assets or working capital. This provides an accurate picture of the business.

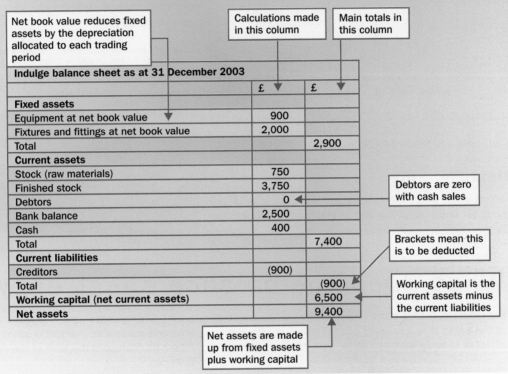

Net book value reduces fixed assets by the depreciation allocated to each trading period

Calculations made in this column

Main totals in this column

Indulge balance sheet as at 31 December 2003	£	£
Fixed assets		
Equipment at net book value	900	
Fixtures and fittings at net book value	2,000	
Total		2,900
Current assets		
Stock (raw materials)	750	
Finished stock	3,750	
Debtors	0	
Bank balance	2,500	
Cash	400	
Total		7,400
Current liabilities		
Creditors	(900)	
Total		(900)
Working capital (net current assets)		6,500
Net assets		9,400

Debtors are zero with cash sales

Brackets mean this is to be deducted

Working capital is the current assets minus the current liabilities

Net assets are made up from fixed assets plus working capital

starSTUDY

At the end of the second 6 months of trading, Indulge prepared their balance sheet. It would show how the funds were used and how the business was financed. This is some of the information they collected.

Assets that they intend to keep: Fixtures and fittings in the shop were valued at £2000 and the soap-making equipment and craft display stand were estimated to be worth £900.

Assets that they hope to turn into cash soon: Finished and unfinished stock was valued at £4500. No one owed them money as it was cash sales. The bank balance and cash totalled £2900 but they owed £900 to suppliers.

To finance all this Indulge has taken out a loan for £4000, invested £3700 from the owners' savings and ploughed back all the £1700 from past profits (drawing out the remaining £1000 for themselves).

1 What is the value of all the assets Indulge intend to keep?

2 What is the value of all the assets they hope to turn into cash soon?

3 What is the total value of the net assets?

4 What is the value of all the sources of finance they used?

Indulge balance sheet as at 31 December 2003	
	£
Fixed assets	2,900
Working capital	6,500
	9,400
Long-term liabilities	4,000
Net assets	5,400
Financed by	
Capital	3,700
Reserves	2,700
Drawings	(1,000)
Net worth	5,400

The standard way of presenting a balance sheet is in a vertical form with the use of finance at the top and the source of finance below.

Indulge is thinking of becoming a private limited company. This way Indulge could attract more investment and the shareholders would have limited liability. Limited companies set out the accounts slightly differently. They balance the net assets with the internal sources of finance. Net assets are lower by the amount of the long-term loans or external finance.

1 What happens to the net worth of Indulge when net assets are balanced with internal sources of finance?

2 Why is it useful for public companies to present their balance sheet in this style?

KEY TERMS

Debtors are people or organisations that owe a business money. They have received sales but not yet paid for them.

Creditors are organisations that are owed money by a business. They have often supplied goods or services on credit.

Capital is the money invested into a business from shareholders or lenders.

Critical thinking

What effect would a net loss in a trading period have on a balance sheet drawn up at the end of that trading period?

Next steps

Research balance sheets from two public companies that are in the same line of business. See what value they give to intangible assets.

What does the balance sheet show?

For example, buying stock increases current assets, but at the same time increases current liabilities. The net effect is to keep working capital the same.

SOURCES OF CAPITAL

There are two broad categories of raising capital. One source is external capital by securing long-term loans from banks. The other is comes from internal capital. This can be in the form of shares and reserves (retained profit). Share capital is the capital that was put into the business when shareholders originally bought shares. Reserves represent the sum of the retained profit of the business.

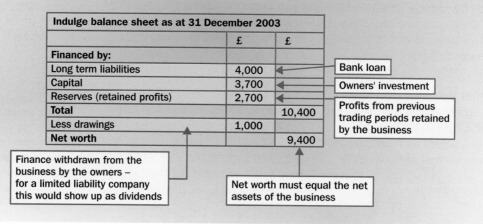

Indulge balance sheet as at 31 December 2003		
	£	£
Financed by:		
Long term liabilities	4,000	
Capital	3,700	
Reserves (retained profits)	2,700	
Total		10,400
Less drawings	1,000	
Net worth		9,400

Bank loan

Owners' investment

Profits from previous trading periods retained by the business

Finance withdrawn from the business by the owners – for a limited liability company this would show up as dividends

Net worth must equal the net assets of the business

What does it all mean?

starSTUDY

Can't pay the bills

K Mart, the discount American store, was forced to seek protection from its creditors and declare **insolvency**. Supplier problems led to empty shelves and the company faced bankruptcy after declining sales and rising debts. The new reorganisation means K Mart is back in business although on a much smaller scale. Shareholders lose everything, but banks will be issued new shares.

Source: http://news.bbc.co.uk/1/hi/business/2968785.stm

1 What evidence suggests that K Mart has not been performing well?
2 Who might be typical creditors for K Mart?
3 Which stakeholders have lost out because of the bankruptcy?

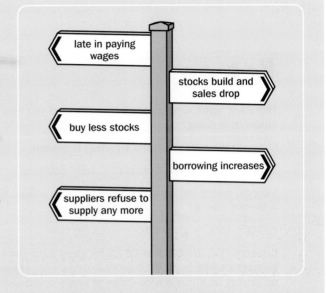

How much profit?

E idos's shareholders are disappointed in the computer games company's late launch of the Playstation version of Tomb Raider. It means that most of the sales of the game will fall into the next financial year. Profit expectations have been significantly reduced. With the company's capital not making as much profit, share prices have fallen.

Source: The Guardian, 28 June 2003.

1 What effect did the late launch have on profits in 2003?
2 What effect did it have on profits in 2004?
3 Why are shareholders upset?
4 Some businesses which have lots of capital invested make small profits. Others with little capital invested make big profits. Where would you prefer to invest and why? How can you tell from the accounts which company is the best bet?

Balance sheet low-down

The balance sheet gives stakeholders all sorts of information about how a business is doing.

- It tells us whether the business is solvent. Can it pay all outstanding debts or liabilities when they are due? A very simple way of using balance sheets to check solvency is to take current liabilities away from current assets to find the amount of working capital. This must be positive. If there is no working capital, there is nothing available to pay the debts.

- It can be used alongside information from the profit and loss account to find out the amount of profit made compared with the investment. This is important information. Often the media suggests that the big profits made by big businesses are somehow wrong but small profits would mean that the investment in the business isn't being used effectively (see ROCE ratio below). A more important question asks how the profit is being used.

- It tells us how much profit has been kept back over the years to use to invest in the assets of the business.

Specification Comment

You will not be asked about the following ratios in the exam but they help you to understand the balance sheet.

KEY TERMS

Working capital is the day-to-day finance used for material and general running costs. On the balance sheet this can be calculated as the current assets minus the current liabilities.

Liquidation means ceasing to trade, usually because debts can't be paid.

Ratios

There are some simple calculations that tell you how a business is doing.

Current ratio tells you if the business is solvent.

Current ratio = Current assets : Current liabilities

Indulge, during the second 6-month trading period, had a current ratio of

£7700 : £900 = 8.22 : 1

It means that Indulge had £8.22 for every £1 it owes. This seems very high, but Indulge needs plenty of stock on display as it has a wide range of soaps and doesn't want to run out of one type. Indulge also makes the soap in batches. It might be better for businesses such as Indulge to take away stock from their calculations.

The acid test ratio does this.

$$\text{Acid test ratio} = \frac{\text{Current assets} - \text{Stock}}{\text{Current liabilities}}$$

For Indulge the acid test ratio $= £7400 - \dfrac{£4500}{£900} = 3.22 : 1$

The business is solvent because it has £3.22 readily available funds for every £1 it owes. The ratio needs to be above 1 : 1 for businesses with a slow turnover of stock. If the acid test ratio falls below this, the business is at great risk of becoming insolvent and may have to go into **receivership**.

A business and investors will want to know how effectively its capital is being used to generate profit. To find this out a business will need to look at the capital employed by the business and relate this to the net profit. It requires taking information from both the balance sheet and the profit and loss account. The ratio used is called the return on capital employed or ROCE. The net profit should be based over a year.

$$\text{ROCE} = \frac{\text{Net profit}}{\text{Capital employed}} \times 100$$

A business has a net profit of £36 million with capital employed of £480 million.

$$\text{ROCE} = \frac{£36m}{£480m} \times 100 \qquad = 7.5\%$$

Investors will look for a business to increase its ROCE. It is more realistic to compare similar businesses, since a business with lots of capital should be making lots of profit.

The next year the business earned a net profit of £40 million using £600 million of capital. The net profit has increased, but the ROCE has fallen.

$$\text{ROCE} = \frac{£40m}{£600m} \times 100 \qquad = 6.5\%$$

The business's capital is not so efficient in generating profit. However, you need to research the underlying reasons. For example, the business may have invested in a new range of shops which haven't been open for the full trading period and have yet to establish themselves, or it may be just about to launch a new product that it has spent considerable resources on for much of the trading period, but the sales will take place within the next trading period.

Getting working capital right

Different businesses need different amounts of working capital. If there is too much, the opportunity costs are high because the money could be used for other things. If there is too little, the business is at risk of not being able to pay its bills. The length of the working capital cycle affects how much is needed. The following questions will help to decide the level.

Does the business:

• buy supplies on credit?

• give credit to customers?

• give more credit than it receives?

• receive more credit than it gives?

The combination of information about the working capital cycle and the evidence from the balance sheet tells the business and its shareholders whether things are working. When a bank is asked for a loan, it would want to see the balance sheet alongside a cash flow statement and profit and loss account.

If a company goes into **liquidation** then its assets are sold off and the money received from sales goes towards paying off the creditors. There is a pecking order of who gets paid first so it is likely that some creditors will lose out. In the Star Study this explains why suppliers were unwilling to supply K Mart, as they are low down the priority list of getting paid.

It's not all doom and gloom and many businesses want to expand. They will be looking for extra finance. They could attract new investors by releasing more shares. They could borrow more or even sell assets they no longer believe are performing well for them. Potential investors, banks and buyers of these assets will be interested in checking the financial accounts before making their own decision. Will the expansion put the business at risk of insolvency? What is the return on capital like compared with similar businesses? What has happened to the return on capital over the past few years? Analysing the balance sheet helps to inform the business and its stakeholders about its performance and supports the decision-making process. Balance sheets on their own are insufficient and should be used along side other financial documents, other ratios and also qualitative information.

go to → pages 16–19 for a reminder on sources of finance.

Critical thinking

Le Meridian Hotel chain whose flagship hotels include the Waldorf and Grosvenor is struggling to avoid insolvency. Fourteen banks are owed £700 million and the company owes £20 million in rent to the Royal Bank of Scotland. The main lenders are desperately trying to reach an agreement, but this might involve them writing off part of their debt.

1 How do you think Le Meridian got into such difficulties?

2 What information would the accounts have given stakeholders about the problems?

3 Who are the main creditors?

4 Why might the lenders be prepared to accept writing off part of their debt?

Next steps

Have a look at the accounts of a business you know. What does the balance sheet tell you about the level of working capital, its profits compared with last year and compared with the capital in the company?

testing–testing

Accounting and finance – assessment

The Carpet Barn

Cai and Ellen had recently set up The Carpet Barn, selling and fitting carpets. They worked out their start up costs and used a cash flow forecast to predict the first 6 months' needs. They needed to fit out the shop and buy a second-hand van and organise suppliers. They found two that would provide 28 days' credit and deliver within 5 working days.

One early decision they made was to buy in a computer system with specialist software. It would save time invoicing and the orders would automatically go through to the suppliers. The complete system would set them back £6000, but would mean not having to employ a part-time cost clerk, saving them £4000 a year.

Cai and Ellen invested £9000 and obtained a bank loan for £3000.

They estimated that the average price for purchasing and fitting a carpet would be £500. The cost of materials comprising the carpet itself, the underlay, and gripper board would be half this price. They would need around £11000 a month to cover business expenses including marketing. They had a budget of £1000 a month for marketing. Cai and Ellen would also pay themselves each a salary of £2000 a month. With all this information they constructed a break-even chart. Since Cai was the fitter and he was on a salary he was counted as a fixed cost.

Cai and Ellen reckoned The Carpet Barn would make around 50 sales each month, bringing in a profit of £18,000 a year. On top of their salary they could draw out a reasonable sum from the profits and still invest some back into the business. If orders went above

Price	£500.00
Average variable costs	£250.00

If sales per month were	0	20	40	60	80
Fixed costs	£11,000	£11,000	£11,000	£11,000	£11,000
Variable costs	£0	£5,000	£10,000	£15,000	£20,000
Total costs	£11,000	£16,000	£21,000	£26,000	£31,000
Total revenue	£0	£10,000	£20,000	£30,000	£40,000
Profit/loss	–£11,000	–£6,000	–£1,000	£4,000	£9,000

The Carpet Barn's break-even chart

	Nov forecast	Nov actual	Dec forecast	Dec actual	Jan forecast	Jan actual	Feb forecast	Feb actual	Mar forecast	Mar actual	Apr forecast	Apr actual	6 months forecast	Actual total
Turnover	24,000	22,000	22,000	20,000	23,000	20,000	25,000	24,000	26,000	25,000	25,000	23,000	145,000	134,000
Total receipts	24,000	22,000	22,000	20,000	23,000	20,000	24,000	24,000	24,000	25,000	24,000	23,000	145,000	134,000
Purchases	12,000	12,000	11,000	11,000	11,500	11,500	12,500	12,000	13,000	12,500	12,500	11,500	72,500	70,500
Expenses	11,000	11,000	11,000	11,000	11,000	11,000	11,000	13,000	11,000	12,000	11,000	11,500	66,000	69,500
Overdraft payment						115		110		85		90	0	400
Total payments	23,000	23,000	22,000	22,000	22,500	22,615	23,500	25,110	24,000	24,585	23,500	23,090	138,500	140,400
Net cash flow	1,000	(1,000)	0	****	500	(2,615)	500	(1,110)	0	415	500	(90)		
Opening balance	3,000	3,000	4,000	2,000	4,000	0	4,500	(2,615)	5,000	(3,725)	5,000	(3,310)		
Closing balance	4,000	2,000	4,000	0	4,500	(2,615)	5,000	(3,725)	5,000	****	5,500	(3,400)		

**** Figures to be calculated. See questions 11 and 12.

80 a month they would need to take on more staff and their expenses would rise.

The first 6 months of trading were disappointing, turning in £500 profit instead of the targeted £9000. They both decided to draw nothing from the business, but looked forward to the second 6 months now that the business had established itself. Cai was in charge of the finances and he made a revised cash flow forecast and predicted sales of the value of £145,000. The revised profit target of £6500 was set for the second 6-month period. (See predicted profit and loss account.)

Two external problems hit The Carpet Barn badly. First, the ongoing DIY programmes on television meant that house owners were buying more laminate flooring as people tried creating the minimalist look featured in magazines and on DIY television shows. As a consequence sales of carpets nationally were falling. The second problem occurred in December when a major employer in the town announced redundancies.

Cai knew within two months that his forecasts were again wrong. After heated discussions with Ellen they decided the business needed more promotion and the marketing budget was increased by £2000 in February. This was followed by an additional £1000 in March and a further £500 in April. They hoped this would help the business get more orders and Cai, ever the negotiator, arranged an overdraft. The bank insisted this would be set against his and Ellen's personal property.

By April they had all the accounts in front of them. They had to make a very important decision.

The Carpet Barn's profit & loss account	Six months ending 30 April		Predicted for six months ended 30 April	
	£	£	£	£
Turnover		134,000		145,000
Opening stock	5,000		5,000	
Purchases	70,500		72,500	
Total	75,500		77,500	
Closing stock	8,500		5000	
Cost of goods sold		67,000		72,500
Gross profit		67,000		72,500
Expenses	69,500		66,000	
Total		69,500		66,000
Operating profit		(2,500)		6,500
Net interest		(400)		0
Net profit		(2,900)		6,500

The Carpet Barn's Balance Sheet	30 April		Previous balance sheet 30 October	
	£	£	£	£
Fixed assets				
Premises	0		0	
Equipment	2,500		3,000	
Vehicles	3,000		3,500	
Total		5,500		6,500
Current Assets				
Stock	8,500		5,000	
Debtors	3,000		3,000	
Bank and cash	0		3,000	
Total		11,500		11,000
Current liabilities				
Creditors	(1,000)		(2,000)	
Overdraft	(3,400)		0	
Total		(4,400)		(2,000)
Working capital		7,100		9,000
Net assets		12,600		15,500
Financed by:				
Capital	9,000		9,000	
Retained profit	(2,400)		500	
Less drawings	0		0	
Total		6,600		9,500
Long term liabilities		6,000		6,000
Net worth		12,600		15,500

assessment questions

(Many of the questions have been designed to make you look more closely at the data.)

1 What is the purpose of budgets? How was the marketing budget monitored and why did it need changing? **(8 marks)**

 The first part requires a straightforward explanation and the second part requires some simple analysis of the marketing budget. You may consider the following approach. What was the amount, what was its purpose, how was it monitored, how was it changed, why was it changed and was the change successful?

2 What happened to the overall budgets on expenditure and revenue over the second 6 months of trading? What might have caused the difference between the budget forecast and the actual performance? **(8 marks)**

 The first part requires you to analyse data from the actual and predicted totals within the cash flow chart. The second part asks you to find evidence in the text or use your knowledge of the subject to support your argument.

3 Using the payback method how long would it take for the investment in the computer system to have paid for itself? **(4 marks)**

 Payback is one way of investment appraisal. A simple calculation is required.

4 Name a variable cost for this business. **(1 mark)**

 Straightforward.

5 State two fixed costs faced by The Carpet Barn. **(2 marks)**

 State two fixed costs and comment on why they are fixed.

6 What is the contribution made by each sale? **(4 marks)**

 Define contribution and show your working.

7 Calculate the break-even point. **(4 marks)**

 Calculate break-even and remember to show your working.

8 What was the forecasted margin of safety? **(2 marks)**

 Use your answer to question 7 along with the predicted monthly sales figure.

9 What would be the average overhead if sales were 40, 50 and 60 a month? **(3 marks)**

 Simple calculation assuming expenses = monthly overhead.

10 Use the data in the case study to explain the difference between profit and
   cash flow. **(6 marks)**

> help! You will need to find the net profit for the second 6 months' trading
> (which is a loss) and calculate the net cash outflow from the cash flow
> forecast. Look at the level of stock increase between the two balance
> sheets to help explain the difference.

11 Calculate the net cash flow for the month of December. **(2 marks)**

> help! A simple calculation of the money coming in that month minus the
> money going out.

12 Calculate the closing balance in March. **(2 marks)**

> help! The opening balance for that month added onto the net cash flow.

13 In which months did The Carpet Barn need to draw on its overdraft facility? **(2 marks)**

> help! You should look at where the closing balance is negative.

14 Comment on the profitability of the business. **(4 marks)**

> help! Compare the profits between the two trading periods. What is the trend?
> Is it good or bad news? What might explain this? Can anything be done?

15 Comment on the liquidity of the business using information from
   the balance sheets. **(4 marks)**

> help! You will need to look at the changes in working capital.

16 What would have happened to the working capital if The Carpet Barn had
   reduced the level of stocks? **(4 marks)**

> help! If less money is tied up in stocks where will it go in the balance sheet?

17 Equipment and the vehicles were depreciated over the 6 months.
   Where would the £1000 depreciation show up within the profit and loss account? **(2 marks)**

> help! Depreciation allocates the costs of a fixed asset over its lifetime, so that
> the profit and loss account shows the fixed proportion that is 'used up'
> each year.

18 The decision Cai and Ellen needed to make was whether or not to cease trading.
   What would you recommend they do? **(12 marks)**

> help! This answer invites evaluation based upon evidence collected from both
> the text and data. Good use of data is essential. Examine the positive
> and negative sides of ceasing trading and comment on how this affects
> stakeholders. Weigh up which is best overall, giving good reasons for
> your proposal.

Human resource planning

Specification Content

An overview of human resource planning

starSTUDY

People at Virgin Mobile

There are nine members of the human resources department at Virgin Mobile. Their role is to recruit, retain, reward and appraise. Others are responsible for training and development.

- Started in 1999 in Wiltshire, a location previously unused as a call centre market

- Needed to train people to meet our own needs

- Over 1200 employees on site mostly looking after customer care meet our own need

- Average age of employees is 30

- High turnover of younger staff means active recruitment

- Maximum of 800 on site on shifts with flexible working to cover 24 hours a day for 365 days a year

- An extra 40 employees a month are needed to meet the growth in demand for customer care

- We must provide enough staff to meet the changes in demand during the day and seasons

1. In what ways do the employees at Virgin Mobile add value?
2. What evidence is there that Virgin Mobile plans its human resource needs?
3. Why does the company take care to plan its human resource needs?
4. Which areas of human resources might the company be most concerned about and why?

starSTUDY

Building T5

Laing O'Rourke won the contract to build Terminal 5 at London's Heathrow airport. The contract says it must be completed on time. To guarantee the staff, some 3,000 building workers will be paid a 'ground breaking' salary of £55,000, following a deal struck between the contractors Laing O'Rourke and union leaders.

1. Why was it important for the contractors to reach a deal with the unions?
2. Why did the company decide to pay high salaries to staff working on the site?

Planning people

Employees add value to your business. That is why they are employed. To add the maximum value employees must be efficient at what they do and effective at meeting the business objectives. Employees must have the right skills and be fully aware of the business aims and objectives. There must also be a demand for their services. There is no point in employing too many because this would be a waste of money and tie up working capital. Employing too few is likely to result in a business failing to meet its objectives. Laing O'Rourke has a key objective to complete Terminal 5 on time. It helps to explain why it was prepared to pay such high wages.

Human resource planning

Human resource planning means employing the right people at the right time. The human resources manager must communicate effectively with the departments within the business and understand their needs. The type of employees recruited must fit in with the culture of the business.

Most businesses find that change is constant and planning must predict what is going to happen.

CAUSES OF CHANGE

- Changes in business objectives and direction.

- Training needs resulting from new products or new technology.

- Changes in demand from new trends or seasonal changes.

- People leave through retirement, internal promotion and by just moving on.

- Trends in work patterns, such as **flexible working**, to allow for personal needs, for example caring for children or the elderly. More older people want to continue working to supplement their pension.

- New employment laws, for example health and safety, and the working hours' directive limiting the hours that can be worked by any one employee.

Getting it right

Employees at Virgin Mobile add value by providing customer service. One factor that contributes to its success is paying careful attention to **recruitment** and training. The human resources department

- regularly meets with the other departments to look at the present mix of employees and at what future requirements will be;

- needs to know when a vacancy arises through someone leaving or gaining promotion.

As well as call centre staff the company needs managers, computer technicians, statisticians for forecasting and planning, marketing experts, administration and maintenance staff. The call centre needs staff 24 hours a day, every day of the year.

Getting the right staff in the right numbers hasn't been easy. Its Wiltshire call centre is not the best location to recruit 40 employees a month. The call centre is at its capacity and the number of customers is increasing. Potential employees are unwilling to commute long distances in this area especially with shift work. The company has looked at **homeworking**, but is reluctant to go down this line as it goes against the ethos of teamwork. It has decided not to expand in Wiltshire nor to relocate the call centre to Asia, but open up a second call centre in the north-east of England.

Critical thinking

1 Why is human resource planning difficult?

2 What things did Virgin Mobile take into account when deciding how best it could find staff to meet the expanding demand?

3 Look at the aims and objectives of Carphone Warehouse and describe the most important elements of human resource planning for this company. To what extent would homeworking be a solution for this business?

Next steps

1 What type of people are required to keep your school or college functioning? How many employees left over the last two years? How much is spent on recruitment? How much of the school's budget is spent on paying its employees?

2 Find out the range of jobs available in a medium-sized business near you.

KEY TERMS

Recruitment involves identifying the need for a job and then attracting appropriate applicants for the position.

Homeworking means working from home.

Flexible working involves employing people who are part-time, full-time, temporary and permanent and on split shifts. It allows businesses to employ people in ways that keeps costs down.

The recruitment process

Specification Content

Recruitment and selection

starSTUDY

The recruitment challenge

Reproduced by permission of Virgin Mobile Telecoms Ltd.
© Virgin Mobile Telecoms Ltd 1999 – 2003.

1 Why might the Internet be a good place to reach potential employees?

2 Where else might a company like Virgin Mobile let potential employees know about vacancies?

3 What is the company looking for in its employees and how might it fit in with its image of 'being young at heart'?

Sainsbury's objective is to meet its customer needs effectively and thereby provide shareholders with good sustainable financial returns. It aims to ensure all colleagues have opportunities to develop their abilities and are well rewarded for their contribution to the success of the business.

Source: J Sainsbury's plc.

Could you manage your own Department?

Department Manager Fresh Foods

To join us you need a serious passion for retailing. We're not just talking a dull 9–5, this is a fast moving, demanding target driven industry.

We are looking for a self-motivated, enthusiastic team player to run our fresh foods department.

- To ensure that customer needs and values are met by developing and motivating the individuals in your team, so that they are fully equipped to contribute to the company's business goals.

- To ensure that current performance management processes are actively used to train, coach and develop the knowledge and skills of colleagues in the department.

- To manage the replenishment, merchandising and quality of goods in the department.

- To meet all statutory regulations regarding price control, health and safety and food safety.

All information © PeopleBank The Employment Network 2002.

1 Which part of the Sainsbury's advert tells you about the type of person the company is looking for?

2 Which part informs applicants of the types of tasks and responsibilities they will have to undertake?

3 How well do you think the advert will lead to employing someone who will contribute to meeting Sainsbury's objective?

4 How does the Department Manager for Fresh Foods add value to the company?

Critical thinking

1 What are the advantages and drawbacks of providing potential recruits with detailed information about the type of person the business is looking for?

2 In what ways could a business discriminate in its recruitment process?

3 What are the advantages and disadvantages of using phone interviews in the selection process?

Next steps

Look up two big companies on the Internet and find out about the types of vacancies on offer and how a potential recruit may go about applying for a post. In what ways are the two companies similar in their approach and in what ways are they different?

KEY TERMS

Aptitude tests measure how good an individual is at a particular skill.

Psychometric testing helps reveal the personality of candidates.

The initial recruitment stages

IN THE KNOW

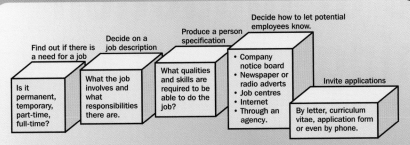

Find out if there is a need for a job
- Is it permanent, temporary, part-time, full-time?

Decide on a job description
- What the job involves and what responsibilities there are.

Produce a person specification
- What qualities and skills are required to be able to do the job?

Decide how to let potential employees know.
- Company notice board
- Newspaper or radio adverts
- Job centres
- Internet
- Through an agency.

Invite applications
- By letter, curriculum vitae, application form or even by phone.

The interview process is essential in testing out first hand whether the candidates have the qualifications, necessary experience and qualities that will support the business in achieving its objectives. References from current or past employers are often called to help verify the candidate's suitability.

A business will need to decide whether it wishes to promote internally or advertise outside the business to fill any identified vacancy. It is not a straightforward decision. The internal candidate will be familiar with the business and is already working towards fulfilling the business objectives, but the external candidate can bring in fresh ideas and use experiences gained in previous employment.

Another alternative is to use employment agencies. They will do the groundwork but charge a fee often related to a percentage of the employee's salary. Agencies are often used when a business needs to fill a position quickly and if the work is short term, usually associated with a timed project.

THE SELECTION PROCESS

The selection process begins once the applications are in. The first stage is usually shortlisting, to decide which applicants to call for interview. Interviews can take a variety of forms, but the most common form is still face to face.

For some jobs, where communication skills are important, candidates may be asked to give presentations. Others might take aptitude tests to check on their skills levels. More senior posts may involve candidates undergoing psychometric testing to find out more about the attitude and personality of the candidates. This is useful for finding out whether the candidate is likely to fit in. For example, a business may want a recruit to be a team player or perhaps someone who questions actions rather than just accepting them.

Some companies who recruit regularly are opting for phone interviews as a way of reducing the costs.

It is important not to discriminate during the recruitment process. First, it is against the employment laws and, secondly, discrimination reduces the number available for the position and therefore the quality of the field.

Methods of recruitment

Although 45% of the local working population has applied for a job at Virgin Mobile in Wiltshire, recruitment is still a difficult problem. Virgin Mobile uses a range of methods to advertise and then select for the posts on offer. It lists job vacancies on the Internet. This is cheap and can reach a large audience. The website gives a brief job description and explains qualifications and experience required. This acts as a filter and some potential applicants may decide not to apply if they do not match the job.

Not all businesses provide a person specification, because some human resources managers feel it is easy for applicants to tailor their applications to this and give a false impression.

Virgin Mobile also uses its intranet to let people within the business know about vacancies. This helps provide equal opportunities for anyone within the company who wishes to seek promotion.

Applicants complete a simple online form and attach a CV. This has the advantage of saving time and the shortlisting can take place electronically. Its simplicity also encourages more people to apply. The human resources department may wish to follow this up with a phone interview before calling people in for final interviews.

157

OCR BUSINESS STUDIES AS: THE COMPLETE COMPANION

The value of induction and training

Specification Content

Induction and training

starSTUDY

To train or not to train?

'Our induction programme lasts five weeks and has been improved in the light of feedback from Customer Service Agents. It starts with a two-week programme of hard and soft skills training. The hard skills focus on using the equipment. The soft skills enable our recruits to get used to doing things the Virgin way. All this takes place in the training centre. The recruit is then attached to a team for a week to undertake simple tasks such as registering customers and working on the phones with an experienced CSA as a mentor. Then there's two more weeks in the training department.'

1 Why does Virgin Mobile bother with the soft skills training?
2 Why does the company allow trainees to operate with real customers half way through the induction period?
3 What different types of costs can you identify in the induction programme?

A survey by *Which?* researchers posing as customers revealed that one in eight gyms questioned had instructors who had not completed first aid training. This is despite the fact that many people who attend gyms have underlying health problems.

1 Why might some gyms be reluctant to provide adequate training in first aid?
2 What reasons would you provide to gyms to convince them that their staff should be fully trained?

Induction

Induction is the first stage of preparing new recruits to reach the standard of performance expected of them. It is necessary because businesses need to ensure that new employees feel comfortable enough to want to stay and that they are well informed about the ethos and objectives of the business.

Elements of induction programmes	Benefits
Familiarisation with the work environment including how to use equipment, work in a secure way and follow health and safety procedures	Provides new recruits with basic skills and knowledge of how to work
Introduction to team members	Provides sense of belonging to the business and being part of a team
Introduction to amenities such as social facilities	Makes new recruits feel wanted
Awareness of the culture and objectives of the business	Ensures new recruits work in the way the business wants them
Administration arrangements such as what to do when ill, and who to contact if there is a problem	Helps ensure new recruits are aware of systems so that the business is run more efficiently
Attachment to a mentor	Helps recruits to settle in and any problems to be solved quickly

Preparing people

TRAINING helps employees carry out tasks necessary to perform effectively in their jobs. It is an ongoing process that applies to existing employees as well as new ones. It is necessary because of the continuous change in technology and the desire to improve processes. When a business changes its ethos and objectives it will need to set up training programmes. Training also develops individual skills and can be a motivating and rewarding experience.

ON THE JOB TRAINING is where employees learn how to carry out their tasks in the workplace. It may be demonstrated or a supervisor may coach the employee through it. Trainees will not be as efficient at their job as experienced employees and are often likely to make more errors. The trainee will be given simpler tasks and be under the eye of a mentor. On the job training is more likely to be job specific.

OFF THE JOB TRAINING refers to training that is not in the immediate workplace. It can take place on sites such as at special training centres or in conference rooms. Another alternative is to send employees away to specialist courses organised by experts in their fields. This can range from one-day courses at specialist training centres through to day release at colleges. Some courses result in qualifications that meet national standards. These courses are more likely to be skills-based training for general employees. Managers, however, might focus on more strategic issues and the latest business theories.

MULTI-SKILLED TRAINING involves making some employees able to undertake a number of tasks and means it is easier to cover for absent colleagues. Wider responsibilities also improve motivation.

Good training

Any training is an investment in human capital. Although induction and training are expensive it can be more expensive in the long run to cut back on training budgets. Big companies constantly monitor and evaluate their training programmes. At Virgin Mobile, the human resources department asks those who went through induction and training how to improve it and changes programmes as a result. This brings a sense of ownership and is likely to produce better results.

Poor or ineffective training can also result in a loss of income as customers go elsewhere. In a manufacturing business badly trained employees will produce poor quality work and there are costs involved in correcting mistakes, both in the extra time taken and in the waste of materials.

If training seems to bring such benefits why are many business poor at it?

- Training costs time and money. Training an employee on the job requires an expert supervisor who is therefore not working. The trainee usually carries out simpler tasks slowly.

- A business may train employees who then use their new skills and experience to get a job elsewhere, so other businesses benefit. Some businesses will therefore be choosy about the people they train and the level of training.

- Training budgets are often trimmed in a recession. Large businesses anticipate a decline in skills requirement and small businesses may need to cut costs just to stay alive.

Critical thinking

Businesses don't always want to spend money on training for fear of losing staff once they are trained. This doesn't help the economy and may make the UK less competitive than it should be. What should be the role of the government in terms of improving the skills level of the UK workforce?

Next steps

Find out about the training and induction programme in a local business. How is it monitored and evaluated? Do you work part time? What training and induction have you been given? Was it sufficient? How does it compare with full-time employees?

KEY TERMS

Soft skills training focuses on getting the employee to work towards the objectives of the business in the style the business wants.

Hard skills training is associated with the skills of using equipment such as computers and machines.

Mentor – someone in the business whom a new employee can turn to for advice. The mentor will keep comments in confidence.

Rights and duties

starSTUDY

Airbase closes

No service personnel will be made redundant in the closure of RAF Lyneham. The base is set to close by 2012 as part of a strategic review of military airbases. A defence spokesperson said: 'The early announcement will allow our recruitment planners to take account of the reduced manpower requirements. We will reduce staff numbers through natural wastage and redeploy others.'

Source: BBC.

Specification Content
Severance, principles of employment law and the rights and duties of employees and employers

1 What do you understand by the terms 'natural wastage' and 'redeployment'?

2 Why has the defence department given such a long notice?

3 How easy is it for businesses to give such long-term notice of redundancies?

Elev8 closes

Workers made redundant at an Ammanford call centre are pinning their hopes on the council finding a new tenant for the building. Some have already found jobs as far away as Swansea. Those who lost their jobs when Elev8 shut were still waiting to hear from the receivers if they would receive any redundancy pay.

1 Why might Elev8's call centre have failed?

2 What happened to all the workers at Elev8?

3 Why might the ex-workers not get redundancy pay?

A better deal

Hundreds of biscuit factory workers in Leicestershire are to have improved redundancy packages offered to them after negotiations between managers and representatives of the Union of Shop, Distributive and Allied Workers (USDAW). The union is urging its members to accept the offer that is above the statutory minimum. The factory is to close next year.

Usdaw
Union of Shop, Distributive and Allied Workers

1 Why might the union recommend that the workers accept the redundancy terms?

IN THE KNOW

Being dismissed

Dismissal is different from redundancy in that the employee is not entitled to any extra payment because the employee has been in breach of his or her contract of employment. The contract of employment is an agreement between the employer and employee. Both employee's and employer's responsibilities are clearly set out within this. By signing this, an employee agrees to accept the terms. The employee can be dismissed if he or she has broken the contract.

The contract can be broken by:

- going on strike

- gross misconduct (stealing, destruction of property, fighting or putting employees and customers at risk)

- continual lateness or high absence levels

- being unable to do the job.

Out of a job

REDUNDANT?

A person is redundant when the job they were doing no longer exists. It might be caused by:

- changing technology, such as new robots taking the place of welders

- a move to a different location

- a fall in demand for the product or service

- business failure.

Whatever the circumstances, employment laws provide protection for the employee. A major principle is that employees must be treated fairly and there are rules that the business must follow. These may be supplemented by negotiations between the employer and the employee's representatives, which is usually a trade union. The employers must always try to give as much notice as possible.

WHO GOES?

Stage 1 Natural wastage is when people who leave are not replaced.

Stage 2 Voluntary redundancy is when the organisation asks for volunteers to leave.

Stage 3 Compulsory redundancy occurs when the other two stages have been exhausted and there are still too many people employed.

Employees who volunteer or are compulsorily made redundant will receive a redundancy payment. Unions try to negotiate higher rates than the statutory minimum set out by law. The redundancy payment is related to the employee's wages and the length of time in service.

NOT FAIR?

An employee who feels unfairly treated might take his or her case to an Employment Tribunal, an independent body which considers the case and comes up with a ruling that is either in favour of the employer or the employee.

Employers have responsibilities and must make sure they have followed proper procedures as set out in law.

An employer cannot dismiss an employee for not being able to do the job properly unless the reasonable steps have been taken to help the employee improve by providing support and training.

If an employee is continually late the employer must provide sufficient warnings, both verbal and written.

The tribunal will look to see if the employers have contravened employment laws. Employment laws are complex and there are many of them. They govern areas such as breaks, paid leave, notice of resignation, pension rights, health and safety, discrimination, equal opportunities, dismissal, redundancies, union rights and employer rights.

Critical thinking

1 What is the disadvantage of voluntary redundancy to the business?

2 Why are older employers usually more costly to make redundant?

3 What are the advantages and disadvantages of operating a 'last one in first one out' redundancy policy?

4 Why is it important that rights and duties of employers and employees are backed up by law?

Next steps

1 Look at your local newspaper's website for stories about cases at the local Employment Tribunal.

2 Find out more about up to date employment issues by visiting http://www.employmenttribunals.gov.uk/england/enghomeind.html and http://www.bbc.co.uk/ and search the news for unfair dismissal and redundancies.

3 Visit union websites for issues and campaigns:

http://www.usdaw.org.uk/

http://www.unison.org.uk/

http://www.troubleatwork.org.uk/

http://www.tgwu.org.uk/

http://www.bbc.co.uk/radio1/onelife/work/rights/law_intro.shtml

4 Just in case you want to research employment laws try http://www.dti.gov.uk/

KEY TERMS

Trade union is an organisation that represents the interests of its members who are workers.

Why worry about labour turnover?

Specification Content

Causes and consequences of changes in labour turnover

starSTUDY

Why do they go?

'We recruit the best people in the country. It's an expensive process and we want to keep them.'

'Working at a call centre isn't everyone's idea of a great job but we want to make sure that when people join us – they stay.'

'There are lots of people round here who would like to work but child care is always a problem.'

'There's a lot of demand for people in our business. We train them – then off they go to a business which pays more.'

'The turnover rate has been so high that we're having trouble getting orders out on time.'

'Everyone who leaves is given an exit interview.'

1 Why do businesses worry about a high staff turnover?

2 Why can a high turnover be expensive?

3 Why might the introduction of a crèche reduce labour turnover?

4 What questions might the company ask people who are leaving?

5 Why is this information important to the human resources department?

6 What do you think a business can do to reduce turnover?

Critical thinking

1 Why is it important to compare labour turnover information over a period of time?

2 Why is it important for large businesses to break down labour turnover data into different departments, different skills levels, gender and different job roles?

3 Why might labour turnover data need to take into account the trends in the number of part-time employees compared with full-time employees? What might explain a high labour turnover in a specific department?

Next steps

1 Calculate the labour turnover in your school over the past academic year in terms of teaching and non-teaching staff.

2 How many of the staff moved on to new jobs and how many retired?

3 Why might either a low or high labour turnover over a few years be seen as a problem in a school?

Labour turnover

The attrition rate, or labour turnover, measures the percentage of people leaving an organisation over a time period. It is calculated by expressing the number of staff leaving the business in a year as a percentage of the average number of staff in the business.

Average number of employees   1000

Number leaving in the last year   250

Labour turnover   1000/250 × 100 = 25%

People leave for perfectly sensible reasons. For example, they might get promotion or they might retire. Students

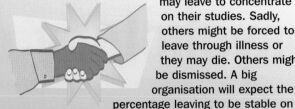

may leave to concentrate on their studies. Sadly, others might be forced to leave through illness or they may die. Others might be dismissed. A big organisation will expect the percentage leaving to be stable on average. However, they will keep a close watch on comparisons with other similar industries and also look at the trends. Is labour turnover increasing or decreasing? If so, they will want to know why.

There are many causes of a high labour turnover.

Poor recruitment and selection means you may employ the wrong type of people who are not suitable and will not enjoy the job. Such people are not likely to stay long.

Poor induction and training means the recruits don't understand the business objectives and systems. New recruits are less likely to positively identify with the business.

Lower wage rates or poorer working conditions compared with local employers, especially if unemployment is low in the region.

Training can be too good and the employees gain transferable skills that are in demand elsewhere. For example, the RAF spends huge sums training pilots to a high standard. The RAF contracts these pilots for a set number of years to prevent them quickly moving into commercial airlines.

A lack of promotion opportunities within a business will force employees to look elsewhere.

Poor or ineffective leadership reduces the commitment of employees.

Low labour turnover can be viewed as being unhealthy because the business may lack new ideas and enthusiasm. Businesses can also recruit people who already come with the skills required and this would save on training staff within. A low labour turnover may result in a business looking to recruit externally rather than promote from within.

Why keep people?

Businesses generally want to attract the right employees and keep them. Recruitment and training are expensive processes, so costs rise every time they have to be repeated. More human resource staff are needed and time must be devoted to on the job and off the job training.

A high turnover also makes running the business more difficult. Experienced people guide a business –if they leave frequently, it can be hard to guarantee production, so orders may be late. This will annoy customers who may look elsewhere for future purchases.

The culture of the business can also be affected because people's commitment is reduced if they see others leaving frequently. It is difficult for management to sustain a positive environment when employees stay for only a few months.

Some jobs tend to have a higher turnover than others. More than one-fifth of call centres have a

staff turnover of over 40%. Many recruits leave within the first three months. The industry employs over 400,000 in the UK, but call centres are finding it increasingly difficult to recruit employees with the correct skills. Many companies are setting up new centres in India and South Africa.

A company may need to review its recruitment and selection process so that it presents a more realistic picture of what the job involves. The process might be part of a staff retention programme, which might investigate the pressures of the job, and how they could be reduced.

The human resources department can use more of its time and resources to improving the quality of the experience of the staff. Improving the conditions under which employees work includes providing more sociable shift patterns as well as providing an attractive working environment.

The science and psychology of motivation

star**STUDY**

Jethro's is a fast food fish restaurant operating in a busy Cornish seaside resort. Customers demand to be served quickly and they want to eat in a clean environment. Jethro knows what's best and he wants to maximise his profits. Jethro gives each employee straightforward tasks to do. At busy times two employees have the job of taking orders, another two clear the tables, one makes sure the litter bins are empty and that the floors are clean. Two cook the fish and two cook the chips. Lastly, one employee is responsible for the drinks. He has separate fryers for the fish and chips and has a specialist machine that dispenses hot and cold drinks. Most of his employees are part-time and staff turnover can be high. However, because the tasks are straightforward it is not costly to train them and by concentrating on one task

they quickly become proficient. He only employs two full-time staff and these are trained to complete a number of tasks when the restaurant is less busy. Although wages are at a given rate per hour, Jethro gives a bonus related to the turnover generated in each shift.

Future Publishing produces a range of specialist magazines including those devoted to computer games, mountain biking and music. Each magazine has a specialist team of writers whose task is to produce a thoroughly accurate, well-written magazine within the time allowed. The production editor organises the team and ensures everything runs smoothly. There's also a deputy editor who takes responsibility for what goes into the magazine. Lastly, there are two writers. The writers are encouraged to be creative and are delegated tasks. The editor encourages teamwork both through regular meetings and getting the team to support each other. The most important meetings are those at the beginning and end of the publishing cycle. The first meeting decides what is to go into the magazine and the post-publication meeting allows the team to review what went well and what could be improved. Employees are paid a salary.

Specification Content

Taylor's scientific management and Mayo's human relations approach

1 How do these businesses differ in their attitude to their employees?

2 Which business offers its staff greater responsibility and allows more initiative? Why do you think this is so?

3 Which business instructs its staff to undertake simple repetitive tasks? Why might this seem an appropriate method?

4 Can they both claim to encourage teamwork?

5 What effect do the different approaches have on the staff?

Critical thinking

1 To what extent do you agree with this statement: 'A motivated worker will be more productive'?

2 How much are you motivated by your current studies?

Next steps

Consider two businesses in your area and investigate how they organise their employees.

KEY TERMS

Motivation is the willingness to work because you enjoy it.

The **scientific approach** uses technical research to help establish how to achieve the highest output per worker.

The **human relations approach** uses psychological and social ideas to help improve motivation.

Taylor: scientific management

IN THE KNOW

Around 100 years ago an American engineer, F.W. Taylor, carried out scientific investigations on how to make workers more efficient. He undertook a series of observations looking closely at time and motion. He believed his results showed that with repeated tasks and the proper equipment each worker would become more efficient and productive. He advocated the division of labour and de-skilling of the workforce. Managers needed to keep tight control and provide the workers with clear-cut instructions. The workers' job was to do what they were told. Henry Ford used these principles

to mass produce cars by providing workers with discrete, uncomplicated, repeated tasks using purpose-built equipment. Many other businesses followed.

Taylor believed that the incentive to work hard was to link pay to the amount produced. This piece-rate paid workers more per unit after a threshold was reached. Those who did more work would receive more pay. This scientific approach seemed to treat workers more like machines than people, and factories adopting his approach saw a big increase in union membership because this approach alienated the workers.

go to → Go to page 169.

Mayo: human relations management

IN THE KNOW

Elton Mayo, a follower of Taylor, conducted research in which the conditions of a group of women workers at a factory at Hawthorne near Chicago was varied every few months. The results were discussed with the group. Each change, such as work layout, rest break times, refreshments and varied bonuses, led to an increase in

productivity. Productivity even improved when the group went back to the original conditions, suggesting that the causes of change could not wholly be explained by scientific management, but was based on human relations management.

MAYO'S FINDINGS

- Group felt more of a team and wanted to contribute to the experiment.
- Workers were pleased that the managers showed an interest in them.
- Women gained satisfaction from making decisions themselves.
- Workers' expectations of each other might be influenced by informal relationships rather than the formal ones.
- Communications between people on the same level and between them and managers had an influence on morale and production.

His findings had a huge impact on business thinking. Businesses organised themselves in a different way. Personnel or human resources departments were

established and the organisational structures were designed to take account of formal groups with an appointed leader and clear objectives.

Which method?

go to
Find out more about Herzberg on page 167.

Different businesses organise their employees in different ways. There is no right or wrong method. Jethro's approach is more scientific as he instructs his employees to undertake tasks in order to increase efficiency. The staff can perform their tasks well, but may find the jobs narrow and boring. He tries to reward them through bonus payments. He could allow them to decide how to operate the business. This would provide them with increased responsibility.

Members of the writing teams working for Future Publishing have individual and group responsibility for their magazine although the ultimate accountability for the quality of the magazine and

the meeting of the deadlines falls to the publishing editor. He or she must have confidence in the quality of the team to deliver the goods. The publishing editor would still need to provide clear instructions but the team has an opportunity to propose amendments which will be considered. Giving the writers responsibility helps to motivate them and fosters a good team spirit. Frequent communications, both formally at meetings and informally across the office or by e-mail, help to boost morale. Future Publishing firmly believes in human relations management as put forward by Herzberg.

Needs and satisfaction

Specification Content

Maslow and Herzberg's theories of motivation

starSTUDY

Terry didn't do too well at school but he was good at practical things and could work with numbers. He related well to others and had a streak of determination. He became an apprentice engineer at 16 learning how to convert specialist vehicles. He was promoted to supervisor and was well respected and trusted by his fellow workers. He was promoted to sales manager because of his experience, knowledge and negotiation skills. Things were going well and he felt proud of his achievements, especially given his limited academic qualifications. However, when the firm started to suffer Terry was made redundant.

Terry and a colleague used their redundancy money to set up in business. A nice house, BMWs and great holidays followed. Terry sold to his partner and set up on his own. Success followed until competition became so fierce that Terry had to close down. He felt he'd let down his workers.

What do you think was the most important need to Terry when he

1 started his career

2 became a supervisor

3 became a sales manager

4 was worried about being made redundant

5 worked with his colleague to set up a new business

6 sold the business to his partner

7 saw his business fold?

Maslow: hierarchy of needs

IN THE KNOW

Elton Mayo had introduced psychology to the field of business management and Abraham Maslow, an American psychologist, subsequently developed the hierarchy of needs.

He wanted to know why people worked. He came up with a hierarchy of five groups of needs. It is a 'hierarchy' because once they have totally achieved a lower order need they may wish to achieve the next order up in order to maintain their motivation. Not everyone will achieve all the needs, even though they may strive to do so. For example, a threat of redundancy may change an individual's focus back to a lower level.

Maslow's hierarchy of needs

Highest order need — 5
4
3
2
Lowest order need — 1

Maslow's levels of need	For employees to reach the level a business should
Self-actualisation means you have achieved your target and reached your potential	Encourage employees to meet new and demanding challenges
Esteem needs include status, recognition and self-respect	Recognise achievement and provide promotion prospects and responsibility
Social needs such as the desire for friendship and a sense of belonging	Have good social facilities, promote effective communication
Safety needs – security and a stable and safe environment	Offer of job security, a clear job role, and safety at work
Physical or basic needs include food and shelter	Reward employees with adequate pay

Business managers use Maslow's ideas to improve motivation. For example, Terry's potential for leadership was recognised by his employer and he was promoted. Such people can be singled out for extra training especially if they are likely to stay loyal to the business.

Today, many businesses use employees on a part-time basis. These will be on the lower level of needs. If Maslow is correct such businesses will find it hard to get their workers to take on responsibility since they have not reached the safety needs.

Critical thinking

1 How does Terry's story relate to the hierarchy of needs proposed by Maslow?

2 How might a business go about ensuring hygiene factors are in place and providing for motivators?

3 To what extent does Terry's story fit in with the two-factor theory?

Herzberg: hygiene or motivation?

IN THE KNOW

Frederick Herzberg was an American psychologist whose research in the 1950s led to his two-factor theory. They are factors which lead to

- job dissatisfaction – known as hygiene factors
- job satisfaction – known as motivation factors.

Both of these are equally important for businesses. Managers can reduce dissatisfaction by addressing hygiene factors, but they must provide opportunities for motivators to increase the level of satisfaction. Not providing motivators does not lead to dissatisfaction.

He made an interesting distinction between motivation and movement. The latter persuades people to go to work but has nothing to do with how they work once they get there. Pay will persuade you to work and therefore is a hygiene factor. Giving a bonus would just make the worker do enough to achieve that bonus but not their best. To achieve this there must be motivators.

Hygiene or maintenance factors	Motivators
Culture and ethos of the business	Achievement
Level of supervision	Recognition of your efforts
Pay (wages and salaries)	Work itself
Relations with others	Responsibility
Working conditions	Advancement

WHAT HAPPENS IF HYGIENE FACTORS DECLINE?

A dissatisfied worker may show:

- Greater reluctance to respond to change
- Increase in lateness
- More absence
- Work becomes poorer
- Increase in industrial disputes.

WHAT HAPPENS IF MOTIVATORS ARE PUT IN PLACE?

Businesses must react to success by finding new challenges and new methods. They should foster innovation and motivate employees so:

- There will be a greater desire to meet the firm's objectives
- Employees adopt a more positive approach to change
- Employees show greater initiative
- Employees care more about the quality of their work.

Although Herzberg's research used a limited sample of accountants and engineers, business leaders have successfully adopted it. Its advantage over Maslow's hierarchy of needs is that it offers a practical approach to improving motivation.

Businesses can improve hygiene factors by reducing the level of supervision, providing rest areas, developing better relationships between bosses and employees and giving employees more status.

Herzberg proposed job enrichment as a method of improving motivation, because it gives employees responsibility. To enrich a job means a range of tasks and challenges, some of which are beyond the employee's current experience. They should be complete, meaningful units of work with direct, immediate feedback. This view opposes that of Taylor who said tasks should be simple and repetitive.

Many businesses have taken on Herzberg's ideas and moved away from the traditional assembly line. Canon, for example has shifted from mass production using conveyor belts to cell production, to give employees more responsibility.

Job rotation is where an employee has a regular change of activity in order to make the job more interesting. It does not increase responsibility, but does increase flexibility and makes employees multi-skilled; therefore when someone is absent the others can cover. In an office, this might involve spending some time each day answering the phone, filing, word processing and photocopying.

Job enlargement is a general term used to describe anything that expands the range of the job. It therefore includes job enrichment and job rotation.

Critical thinking

1 Does Maslow's theory work for all people? If not why not?

2 What do Maslow's and Herzberg's theories have in common?

3 Why do you think Herzberg was against piece rates as a means for motivating workers?

Next steps

1 Find someone who really likes his or her job and explore the reasons why.

2 Now find someone who is dissatisfied with his or her work and ask for the reasons.

3 How well do their explanations fit in with Herzberg's ideas?

Rewards and motivation

Specification Content

Monetary and non-monetary motivation; management by objectives; delegation; empowerment; payment methods

starSTUDY

Keeping the best

Microsoft has some of the best people working for them at their UK headquarters in Reading. The company spends a lot of money finding and training them and really wants to keep them. They do not pay the highest salaries but the rewards are wide ranging.

The Microsoft campus is spectacular, with a lake where charity rowing teams train, a forest and picnic tables.

There are wireless links throughout the campus so that people can open their laptops anywhere, mobile phones linked to the e-mail system, and broadband at home for everyone.

The Wellbeing Clinic offers everything from a mechanical massage chair to well-man clinics.

The 'bump' club helps pregnant mothers before their 18 weeks' fully paid leave. There are on-site nurses and a doctor, and even a facility to donate bone marrow. And more:

- a crèche
- four cafés
- a subsidised restaurant
- Xbox games terminals for entertainment
- £260,000 social budget for sports, outings to shows or trips abroad
- free private healthcare for 'life partners' and families
- a four-month sabbatical (unpaid) after four years
- a chance to buy days off.

Microsoft gave 9.6% of UK pre-tax profits to charity and matches fundraising by up to £7500 per person, per year.

1 Explain Microsoft's reward system in terms of motivation theory.

Just money?

Ask most people about why they work they will place money at or near the top of their list. In fact, motivation theory suggests that money is not all we want. The range of possibilities is wide, although many industries and styles of work have traditions of particular types of reward.

Critical thinking

1 It is not easy to isolate the effects of initiatives aimed at improving motivation, even using indicators such as lower labour turnover and reduced absenteeism. This is because other influences come into play. What might these other influences be?

2 A sceptical business will be worried that improving motivation will cost money and time and not prove worthwhile. What arguments could you use to persuade such a business that it could save money and increase turnover?

KEY TERMS

Appraisal is a method used to assess the effectiveness of an employee's performance by comparing goals set with outcomes.

Ways to reward people

FINANCIAL REWARDS

SALARIES are usually paid to managers and professional staff. They do not usually receive overtime pay. Their annual pay is divided into monthly instalments.

TIME-BASED WAGES are calculated according to the number of hours worked. Overtime, night shifts and bank holidays are often paid above the basic hourly rate.

WAGES are the most common method of payment for production and unskilled workers.

COMMISSION is often paid to sales staff to encourage them to sell more. They may be paid a low basic rate, but receive a commission for each sale they make. Examples include people selling cars or furniture.

PIECEWORK is calculated according to the amount produced. It can boost productivity by encouraging people to work harder, but work may only be completed to an 'acceptable quality' and there may be more waste.

PERFORMANCE-RELATED PAY

provides an opportunity for employees to receive extra payments (usually less than 6% of their basic pay) for being good at their job. It encourages employees to work towards the company objectives. Great if you get it, but demotivating if you don't. Employees must reach agreed targets with their appraisers and review these at the end of the appraisal period. Many businesses complete this annually. To make it more acceptable, staff often receive training to improve performance in their weaker areas.

There are some strong arguments against rewarding individuals in this way, certainly if you believe Herzberg's ideas. Performance-related pay might damage team spirit as some staff might feel the system is unfair, with favouritism shown towards some individuals. Also the level of the award may not be significant enough to motivate people.

A more recent development is to encourage greater teamwork by organising groups of workers into cells. The members of each cell will receive bonuses if monthly targets are met.

go to → Go to page 190.

Profit sharing gives employees a share of the annual profit as a bonus. This encourages employees to have a greater sense of being part of the business.

Shares are often given to employees as a reward. It is thought that they will work harder if they think the share value will rise. They may, however, sell them for fear that the price will fall.

Fringe benefits, such as company pension schemes, discounts and out of work social facilities, help to develop a sense of staff loyalty and reduce staff turnover.

NON-FINANCIAL MOTIVATORS

Herzberg's ideas were taken up by businesses. Job enrichment, job enlargement, job rotation and teamwork are all types of non-financial motivators. The ideas have been developed and taken further to include more delegation and the empowerment of workers.

Delegation means passing the authority down the levels of the hierarchy so that the delegated employee undertakes tasks. The boss must be able to trust the delegate to carry out the tasks and the delegate will want to be sure that the boss is not just handing down boring and time consuming tasks, otherwise resentment will build up. The boss is still accountable.

Empowerment is a step further than delegation and recognises that employees are often in the best position to make the decisions since they are the experts in their field. It allows freedom for employees to decide what to do and how to do it. For example, a manager of a travel agency might be allowed by head office to decide the best mix of holidays to sell since that manager will best know his or her customers.

Getting it right

A business will look for evidence that it is getting value from the measures it has taken to improve motivation. This may come in the form of positive appraisals, a reduction in absenteeism, lower labour turnover, an increase in productivity, a drop in complaints from customers, and an increase in customers.

What style of leadership?

starSTUDY

Specification Content

The impact of leadership styles on performance; autocratic, democratic and laissez faire leadership; McGregor's Theory X and Theory Y.

1 How do you think the boss and the staff feel about their role in each picture?

2 Why is the style of leadership important in a business?

3 Think of a situation when the first type of boss is effective.

4 Think of a situation or type of business in which the second type of boss is effective.

5 What problems might the third type of boss have?

Leading people

Leaders – who may be the ultimate boss in a business or the leader of a team – can influence the way people work. The style of leadership is often a mix of an individual's personality, the culture of the business and the circumstances at the time. Some people are great in a crisis but not so good at the everyday things. Others might panic when problems arise.

Leadership styles

IN THE KNOW

AUTOCRATIC LEADERS take an authoritarian approach. They tell people what to do and expect them to get on with it. They are not prepared to discuss their decisions and don't want any feedback. They 'know' what's best for the business and won't listen to anyone else.

Employees can find this undermining because their expertise isn't valued. It is unlikely to be effective in a creative environment where people like to share ideas and discuss the way forward. They will be demotivated because they want to share in the decision making and don't feel trusted. In a crisis or with people who need a lot of support, an autocratic style can be effective. People know what they have to do and get on with it.

DEMOCRATIC LEADERS expect staff to be involved in the decision-making process. Their contribution is valued and they are aware of it. This helps people to become more confident in their work and develop their abilities to the full. It provides a motivating environment in which responsibility is delegated and people are trusted.

PATERNALISTIC LEADERS will listen to people's points of view but then take no notice of them. This is unlikely to be successful because staff soon realise what is going on. There is no point in asking someone's opinion if you don't really want to listen.

LAISSEZ FAIRE LEADERS don't really lead at all. They wait for a crisis and then step in. They may be too busy to worry about what other people are doing or just too lazy. Some people thrive in such conditions because they love to manage themselves. Others are left feeling confused.

Theory X and Theory Y

Douglas McGregor in the 1950's analysed the way managers carried out their roles. He found two types, which he identified as Theory X and Theory Y.

Theory X managers assume	Theory Y managers assume
Workers need money to motivate them	Workers seek job satisfaction
They must be supervised to make sure they perform	Workers will respond to rewards and to recognition
Workers respect tough, decisive bosses	Low performance is the result of uninteresting work or poor management
Workers lack the ability to make decisions	Workers can work on their own
Workers avoid responsibility	Workers seek responsibility
Workers lack initiative and ambition	Workers can show initiative if trusted
So: a Theory X manager will be unwilling to delegate responsibility. As a result, people get bored and think more about pay than other rewards of the job. These managers tend to be autocratic.	So: a Theory Y manager will discuss issues and encourage people to contribute their ideas in a democratic environment. These managers tend to be democratic.

WHAT'S BEST?

It depends on the circumstances. A Theory Y manager is likely to get more out of the staff because they are happier and better motivated. A Theory X manager might be more effective in a crisis.

Is there a right answer?

Most successful businesses have good management teams. It is, however, hard to judge what is best because situations can be very different. It is also not always easy to train people to change their style. At best, managers should be able to adapt their style to match the situation. A crisis might need a quick, autocratic decision. A fall in sales might need a brainstorming session with staff to come up with some ideas in the light of the evidence. Using a range of expertise is likely to be more productive than one person's views.

The type of leadership which is appropriate on a particular occasion depends on a variety of factors. These include:

- The personality of the leader
- The skills of the leader
- The skills of the workforce
- The amount of risk involved
- The type of task
- The speed needed to get the task done
- How quickly things are changing.

Many employees expect to be treated in a more democratic way. The domineering boss may end up being neither liked nor respected, with a workforce which does not rise to the occasion when there is a crisis. In some businesses, the distinction between workers and management is disappearing. Everyone is a team member who has the same conditions of employment, eats together in the same canteen and dresses in the same way. The manager still manages but from a different position in the organisation.

Critical thinking

If the appropriate leadership style varies according to the circumstances, how do you think a leader should manage the following situations:

1. An order has come in which is going to be difficult to produce in the time available.

2. The quality of output seems to be falling.

3. Customers have been complaining that the staff in the shop are not helpful enough.

4. The press has got hold of a negative story about the business which isn't true.

5. A member of staff has been sacked for dishonesty but some employees don't support the decision.

6. There's a flu epidemic and 25% of the staff are ill.

KEY TERMS

Leadership is the process of influencing others to work effectively to help meet the organisation's goals.

What structure?

Specification Content

Principles of structure, span of control, hierarchy

starSTUDY

What shape and why?

1   Draw diagrams to show the business organisation

   a when it was first set up

   b when the two managers were appointed

   c in the future.

   Use the information on these pages to help if you get stuck.

2   Why does a business need to bring in experts like this as it grows?

3   Why is it important for Jim to delegate responsibility?

4   Why do you think it is important to have clear lines of responsibility in a business?

5   What problems do you think might arise if you get too many levels in the hierarchy?

6   What conflict is Jim facing as his business gets bigger? How might this affect his motivation?

The business had grown since it was set up. Production was still under Jim's control as this was how the company began. In the early days, he'd done everything – even the books. There were eight people working in production and he knew them all well. He'd taken on a bookkeeper and that had worked for a while but things were very different now.

He'd appointed managers for marketing and finance and several people now worked in each department.

It was getting a bit too big for him to manage the whole business as well as looking after production but it was a hard decision for him to take. He wanted to run the business but it was the shop floor he really loved. Sitting in an office all day was not really his cup of tea but there was probably little option if he wanted to keep an eye on everything that was going on.

Organisations and structures

All organisations, from the Brownies to BP, have a structure. Getting the organisation right, so that it achieves the tasks intended, is not always easy. Different structures have different benefits and work most effectively with different sorts of people and different outcomes. Jim's business is developing a hierarchical structure – which many do as they grow. He can bring in experts but he must learn to delegate responsibility.

A simple hierarchy

Next steps

Draw up an organisation chart for your school, college or an organisation that you know. Explain how it works. Does it reflect what actually happens?

Formal organisations

An organisation chart shows the roles and responsibilities of people in a business. In a small business it will be very simple. In a multinational, it will provide an outline of the structure.

UNDERSTANDING ORGANISATIONS

- All organisations have a HIERARCHY. Tall organisations have many layers. Flat organisations have few.

- Tall hierarchies have long CHAINS OF COMMAND because there are many people between the chief executive and the operators on the factory floor. Flat organisations have short chains.

- SPAN OF CONTROL shows the number of subordinaters under the control of a boss. A narrow span gives more control. A wider span means more delegation and can increase motivation. It is likely to be greater in a flat organisation. It has been suggested that span should not be more than five if a business is to run efficiently.

- CENTRALISATION leads to decision making being kept to the top layers of an organisation. This gives tight control and focused strategy, especially when finance, marketing and other key functions are organised from head office. On the other hand, it can lead other parts of the organisation to feel that they cannot make decisions about factors that affect them first hand.

- ROLE defines what an employee should do. It is set out in the job description. A poorly defined role can lead to inefficiency.

- AUTHORITY comes from an individual's position in the hierarchy. The Finance Director has authority over the Finance Manager and the Accounts Manager.

- A subordinate is ACCOUNTABLE to a superior. A superior is RESPONSIBLE for people directly beneath them in the hierarchy. This can be a positive experience or it can appear to be a threat if mishandled.

Is it manageable?

A formal structure works best when roles are the key factor in an organisation. Marketing, for example, is clearly in the hands of the marketing department rather than being spread through product groupings. It also provides clear lines of communication and procedures for dealing with problems.

Much is dependent on the quality of leadership from the top and at different levels. The match of leadership to the organisation is critical to the success of the structure. The ability to delegate is also important. A boss who can't let people get on without interfering will demotivate employees because they are not allowed to take responsibility.

People do not always behave as a structure implies. They may create other groupings within an organisation which may affect how people's roles work. If this happens it can cause difficulties because their objectives may conflict with those of the whole organisation.

There is not, of course, one structure which perfectly suits all organisations – or even all parts of one organisation. The finance department might need a formal structure with a clear chain of command but the design department might work in a very different way. This may be because of the culture which exists in different areas. A whole business may have a culture of its own but within departments of a big organisation there may be local cultures. This can be reflected in the organisational structure, and the way people dress and address each other.

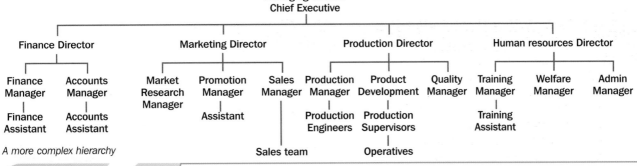

A more complex hierarchy

Critical thinking

1 Use the terms included in 'Understanding organisations' to explain the workings of the business with a complex hierachy.

2 Explain how motivation is affected positively or negatively by the structure of an organisation.

Structure and purpose

Specification Content

Types of structure: centralised and decentralised

starSTUDY

Future Publishing: getting the right shape

Future Publishing produces 52 magazines on computing, computer games, hobbies and sports from their offices in Bath. Each magazine has a team that is responsible for putting it together and getting it to the newsagents. Within the business, there are other teams that specialise in marketing, production, distribution, finance and the other functions needed to get magazines to customers.

The magazine team is responsible for the content and design of each edition. Members of this team are also responsible for liaising with

the other teams to keep everything running smoothly and ensure that each edition reaches the news-stands on time.

1 What drives Future Publishing?

2 Why is it more efficient to have specialist teams involved in marketing, finance, production etc. rather than having specialists in every magazine team?

3 Are there likely to be more or less layers of hierarchy in this sort of structure? Why?

4 Is the organisation likely to be more or less flexible? Why?

5 Why are people likely to be more motivated when working in this type of structure rather than a hierarchical one?

6 Why might senior managers feel threatened in such an organisation?

Making a match

Future Publishing has developed a structure that meets its needs. The creative people who organise and write the content for the magazines need a flexible environment in which to work. Getting the products printed and distributed to the shops requires a different sort of approach.

The formal hierarchical structure doesn't fit the bill for many organisations because of the nature of the work and the people involved. As a result, a range of alternative structures has developed. They are often more decentralised and flexible.

Right business – right structure

One size does not fit all. Devising a structure and making it work is a challenge for many organisations. Some spend millions on reorganising only to find that there are unexpected effects.

A formal hierarchy is unlikely to be effective in a business which must respond quickly to change or where people are expected to work creatively. It can be frustrating when decisions have to be made much higher up the ladder as it often takes time and the people involved may not have been party to earlier discussions.

It can also be frustrating for people who want to take responsibility quickly and are full of good

ideas. They may have to wait until others have moved up the ranks before them.

Some businesses do need this formal structure because of their size or the need for safety. Rules and regulations mean that things are done correctly. A multinational, for example, must have very clear lines of command if corporate objectives are to be achieved.

Many organisations are a mix of several cultures. They may develop because of the type of people in different areas of the business. This is probably a good solution providing they can all communicate with each other and understand that corporate objectives have to be achieved.

Shapes for a purpose

MATRIX

A matrix structure combines functional departments with task-focused groups. Such businesses generally have a flattish hierarchy and a wide span of control. Someone working in marketing will be answerable both to the head of marketing and the magazine team leader. This may be of concern to people who are used to clear chains of command but it has been found to save time because it shortens lines of communication – which run between groups rather than up to the top and down again. People often succeed in such organisations because they work effectively rather than climbing the hierarchical ladder.

The group focus is often the product. The scale of a group can vary. Many hotels work as a group but refer to head office for setting objectives, financial management and marketing etc. Businesses that run a cell structure will generally be a matrix organisation.

BUT ...

The matrix structure can lead to problems if project groups have to fight for the attention of the functional departments. In a business where project groups depend on the IT department for programming time, deadlines can put pressure on relationships between groups when one feels it is getting more attention than another.

Senior management can find the structure unnerving because power lies quite low down in the structure. They have to balance the challenge of less power with the ability of groups to achieve their outcomes quickly and flexibly.

	Finance	Production	Marketing	Distribution
Playstation 2	✓	✓	✓	✓
PC Answers	✓	✓	✓	✓
What guitar?	✓	✓	✓	✓
Official Xbox Magazine	✓	✓	✓	✓

WEB STRUCTURE

At the centre of a web culture is a powerful leader. It is often the person who set up the business. Decisions are made at the centre and people often try to second-guess the outcome. A business built on this structure is often quite flat because there is no role for middle managers.

BUT ...

The culture will depend greatly on the boss.
If the leadership style gives people freedom once decisions have been made, staff will find it motivating. If they feel scrutinised all the time, they will be less so.

PERSON CULTURE

Some small organisations revolve round a group of stars. They are often people who are renowned in the field and work within an organisation that is designed to support them as effectively as possible. Many are creative organisations like advertising agencies or architects.

Such organisations are generally very flexible and can initiate or respond to new circumstances very quickly.

BUT ...

A bunch of stars can be hard to control. They tend to spend money beyond budget because they consider the outcome to be more important.

Critical thinking

Two major pharmaceutical companies were planning to merge but failed because the culture and organisation of the businesses were very different. Why do you think it was such a big stumbling block? Can you suggest any ways of motivating staff to adapt to a new environment?

Next steps

1 Do any of these structures match an organisation that you know?

2 Does the organisation match the objectives and nature of the business?

Effective management

Specification Content

Management by objectives; delegation

1 What is the objective of this business?

2 What is the focus of attention for these managers?

3 What are they missing?

4 Why does this put the business at risk?

5 How might the objectives have been set?

6 What benefits are there in having clear objectives?

Management by objective

The idea of management by objective was formalised by Peter Drucker in 1973. He was convinced that a clear line of objectives for all levels of a business should stem from the mission statement. The development of the objectives should involve everyone at every stage. It means that each employee can see why they are doing what they are doing – and how it all fits together.

If it is to work, objectives must be very precise, realistic, in a fixed time period and agreed by all concerned.

MANAGING

Whether a business uses management by objectives or a more informal method, managers need to be able to organise themselves and other people. Once the objectives have been put in place, managers must plan, organise, lead and control. In anything other than a very small organisation, they can't do all this by themselves so must learn to delegate. The owner of a small but growing business often finds this very hard to do. Having organised everything and made all the decisions, handing over responsibility can be a challenge.

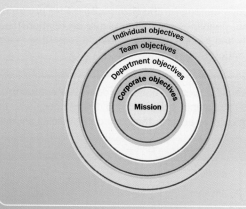

From mission to individual

Benefits	Problems
Motivation is greater because people are involved in setting objectives.	Time consuming meetings have to be held to set objectives.
Priorities are clear so people should be able to decide what tasks are most important.	External factors can make targets impossible to achieve.
Benchmarking results from setting objectives. Everyone knows what the targets are and aims to achieve them. If things are not going according to plan, changes can be made.	Inflexible targets do not allow for a changing market. Managers may be obsessed with targets and unaware of changes in technology or other products which might affect them.
Targets are realistic because they are agreed together and people in the organisation understand why they have been set.	Traditional organisations may find it hard to work this way. People have to be trained for a different approach.

Delegation

In businesses large and small, delegation has to take place if everything is to get done. The owner or manager does not lose responsibility for the business but must be prepared to hand over authority so that the individuals concerned can carry out their tasks effectively. Once the marketing manager has worked with the team to develop a plan, the team members must be allowed to make their own decisions about the best way to carry out the tasks. They should be able to spend money, as long as it is within the budget and can be clearly seen to be helping to meet the targets.

RULES OF DELEGATION

- Is the task clear to both sides?
- Is the timing clear?
- Are other people involved clear about the task?
- Can the members of staff carry out the task? Do they need training?
- Have the persons concerned got enough authority - either themselves or through the business structure?
- Do they and others know the limitations of their authority?
- Are reporting requirements clear?
- Do they know where to go for help?
- Is everyone involved kept informed?
- Does everyone know that the manager is still accountable?

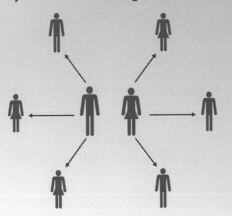

WHAT MAKES DELEGATION DIFFICULT?

Sometimes delegation just won't work.

- A business may be too small to allow delegation.
- An autocratic leader may not allow it to happen.
- Customers may want to see the boss, not the person responsible.
- Work might be confidential.
- Staff may not have the necessary skills.

Sometimes delegating can take more time and be more expensive than carrying out a task single-handed. This may work in the short run but if it continues, it can mean that resources are not being used effectively. Spending some time training people will mean that they can do the work in future so the manager can concentrate on other things. The pressure of targets and deadlines can mean that this doesn't happen.

Critical thinking

1. Why can it be difficult for someone running a small business to delegate as the business grows?

2. Why is it important for people running a business to delegate tasks to others?

3. Why does effective delegation motivate people?

4. How can the structure and leadership of a business affect people's ability to delegate?

Next steps

1. How is authority delegated in your school, college or a business that you know?

2. Are the managers good at letting others take responsibility for carrying out their tasks – or do they interfere?

KEY TERMS

Delegation is the handing over of authority to someone else to carry out specific tasks.

testing–testing

People in organisations – assessment

Case study A: More nurses needed

The Royal College of Nursing represents many nurses and has warned that the NHS is in a 'race against time' to replace the 50,000 nurses who will retire over the next five years. The government needs to keep up their efforts to recruit more nurses, and to work even harder to retain those we already have.

On average, 10% of nurses on wards came from agencies or the staff bank which leads to a lack of continuity.

The radical restructuring of pay aimed at making sure that the most skilled nurses receive the highest pay was welcomed by the RCN. However, many nurses leaving or considering leaving the profession do so because

of poor morale, stress and a frustration that they could not meet all their patients' needs. Most of those leaving are the most senior staff, therefore creating gaps that are difficult to fill.

Source: BBC News Online

assessment questions – Case study A

1 What do you understand by the terms 'recruitment' and 'retention'? **(4 marks)**

 Straightforward definitions testing knowledge.

2 What is workforce planning and why is it important in a large organisation like the NHS? **(6 marks)**

 You will need to select evidence from the case study or from another study to apply your knowledge about why workforce planning is important.

3 What might explain the high labour turnover in the past and what has been proposed to reduce it? To what extent do you believe these proposals will be sufficient? **(12 marks)**

 This question requires knowledge, application, analysis and evaluation. To get high marks you will need to make sensible conclusions as to the extent that the proposals work. Don't forget that you can state what further information you would require to provide a more reliable answer. Try to bring in key theories or ideas about motivation.

Case study B: Prudential to relocate call centre

Thanks to modern telecommunications, India can process the same work as UK call centres – with a saving of about 40%. Many of the Indian call centre workers are graduates. They answer the phone to customers in Britain calling about car insurance or cable TV. They need extra training so that they are aware of British customs. They are paid much less than British call centre workers – but more than most Indian graduates. It is considered high status here to work in an air-conditioned office.

Source: BBC News Online

Prudential has agreed not to force through 850 redundancies at its Reading call centre. The job cuts would have been part of its plan to transfer call centre work to India. Leaders of the Amicus union declared victory after the UK's second largest insurer agreed that nobody would have to leave the company against their will.

assessment questions – Case study B

1 What do you understand by the term 'redundancy'? **(2 marks)**

 Straightforward definition testing knowledge.

2 Explain why businesses like the Prudential have decided to transfer call centre work abroad? **(4 marks)**

 You need to select from the evidence to provide at least two reasons and short explanations for the proposed move.

3 Analyse the concerns Prudential might have about such moves? **(6 marks)**

 Although costs are much lower there are problems for Prudential both in the UK and in India. Don't forget to analyse both areas.

4 What arguments might the Amicus union have used in its negotiations with Prudential? How might the Human Resources Department plans be affected by the decision to make no compulsory redundancies? **(8 marks)**

 You should apply your knowledge about redundancy and recruitment to see the issue from the perspective of the union and then the company.

Case study C: Amazon.co.uk

Amazon is recruiting for departments across the company. These include product areas like books, electronics and photos through to support systems like customer care, information technology, finance and marketing. The company encourages online applications. Here is some of the information it provides for potential recruits.

Should I send samples of my work (writing, code, designs) with my application?

If you're selected for an interview, we may request samples of your work, so please do not send them with your initial application. However, if you have public copies of your work available that can be seen online, please include the link on your CV.

How long does it take you to decide whether I'll get an interview?

Our process is simple. We search the submitted CVs and then contact the people we'd like to learn more about (usually within 2–3 weeks after new CVs come in).

What is your interview process?

The process is variable. For some positions we begin with a phone interview. If there's interest on both sides, we invite you to an on-site interview, typically with the hiring manager and managers from other areas of the business. A candidate can expect to have two rounds of interviews and, depending on the role, some form of assessment or presentation to perform.

What are the benefits of working for Amazon?

- Shares in the company. All Amazon.co.uk employees are allocated a number of Amazon.com restricted stock units when they join. Additional performance-based annual stock is granted and depends on eligibility and start date.
- 22 days paid holiday (pro-rata) per year.

After successfully completing your probationary period of three months:

- Pension plan
- Life assurance
- Disability insurance
- Private medical insurance through BUPA.

We operate in small working teams. As we grow, we continue to promote cross-functional teamwork, so it's possible that the people you work with will have all sorts of experience from other parts of our company. This team diversity encourages creativity, an open exchange of ideas across groups, and a respect for the challenges and trade-offs present across our business. Our hands-on approach to work is really demonstrated during peak selling times: no matter what your role, you will have the opportunity of spending time at our distribution centre ensuring that products get to our customers in time.

If you join us you'll be able to:

- Learn from smart, focused people who care about their work
- Gain from challenging, interesting projects that have a huge impact on our success
- Work in a casual but accountable environment in which hard work, initiative, and smart decisions are rewarded
- Play an important part in continuing our leadership in e-commerce by bringing new ideas to the table and launching new businesses
- Be rewarded by a great career opportunity and the chance to participate financially in the company's long-term success.

Source: Amazon website.

assessment questions – Case study C

1 Identify the stages in the recruitment process described by Amazon in the article above.

(4 marks)

This is best tackled by looking at the stages chronologically. You may come up with four or five stages.

2 Analyse the advantages of Amazon using the Internet and for some positions having a phone interview.

(4 marks)

Straightforward analysis.

3 Recommend other methods that Amazon might use to let potential applicants know about vacancies.

(6 marks)

This asks you to apply your knowledge in a logical way. There is a degree of analysis required for you to earn full marks.

4 How does Amazon structure the company? **(6 marks)**

 You must select from the evidence and apply your knowledge of relevant organisation structures.

5 Evaluate the methods that Amazon uses to motivate its employees. **(10 marks)**

 Your evaluation must be underpinned by knowledge of motivation theories and business ideas such as enrichment. You could divide your answer into financial and non-financial motivators. Since this is an evaluation you should comment on the relative merits of the methods used and question what Amazon has in place to check that its methods are motivating staff.

Case study D: Co-operative Bank

We believe the Co-operative Bank is a great employer, and this has been reflected both in our staff surveys, and also through the various awards we've won.

The Bank is an ethical bank supporting principles of human rights and not dealing with businesses that have links to oppressive regimes. It is committed to providing equality of opportunity for all potential employees and welcomes applications from all individuals for advertised jobs that match their skills and interests.

We believe our achievements are attributable to our way of working which is based on:

⟳ Customer-focused teams and projects

⟳ A flat organisation structure working across functions

⟳ A lot of hard work from focused and flexible people who can rise to a challenge.

We consult with managers and staff, to find out their opinions about the Bank and their jobs within it. We are committed to carrying out this type of survey on a regular basis to ensure that we remain in touch with the views of our staff in everything we do.

Source: Co-operative Bank.

assessment questions – Case study D

1 Why might the Co-operative Bank be so committed to equal opportunities? **(6 marks)**

 Use evidence from the case study to relate to knowledge of objectives and empowerment. Shouldn't all businesses be committed under employment legislation?

2 Define the terms flat organisation structure and flexible employee. **(4 marks)**

 Straightforward definitions testing your knowledge.

3 Evaluate the benefits and drawbacks of a flat structure to an organisation like the Co-operative Bank. **(12 marks)**

 You must consider both positive and negative aspects of having this type of structure. You should relate it to the business ethos and culture. Has the business anything in place to reduce the impact of the negative effects? If not what would you recommend?

Being efficient

starSTUDY

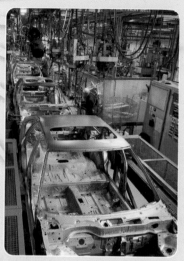

Specification Content
The study of operations management should focus on the way in which organisations manage business processes efficiently in order to satisfy customers

1 Why are cars and wedding dresses made in different ways?
2 Which method produces more units per week?
3 What investment is needed before you set up a car plant and a wedding dress business?
4 How does this affect the return you expect?
5 How would you measure the effectiveness of the people working in the businesses?
6 How would you measure the effectiveness of the machinery and equipment used in the businesses?

Production or productivity?

Production is simply the amount that a business produces in a given period of time. There would be little point in comparing the production of a small wedding dress business with a major car plant.

A much more useful measure of output compares the relationship with the resources used and the output. This is known as productivity. It is one way of judging the efficiency of a business.

Measuring productivity

IN THE KNOW

Productivity is important to a business because it has a direct impact on costs. Greater productivity makes a business more competitive as it can produce things at a lower unit cost.

Productivity can be measured in two ways:

- LABOUR PRODUCTIVITY compares output with the number of people employed. If 10 people are producing 500 items a week, costs will be lower per item than if they were making 300 items per week. If people become more efficient their productivity rises, and costs per item produced fall.

- CAPITAL PRODUCTIVITY compares output with the capital used in the business. Installing a new machine often increases productivity because more modern equipment is designed to be more efficient.

WHY IS PRODUCTIVITY IMPORTANT?

Businesses need to keep a close eye on productivity because competitors are always trying to get a step ahead. It is equally important to make sure that, in trying to achieve greater productivity, quality doesn't suffer. Just turning up the speed of a production line may mean that more is produced from the same resources but if there are faults as a result, customers will buy from somewhere else. If the faults are picked up and put right before leaving the factory, costs per item may rise rather than fall because such actions are expensive.

If a car company, for example, is wanting to close one of its plants, productivity often plays a key part in the decision. If looking for a location for a new plant, it will turn to national data on productivity because it will want to set up in a country where people work effectively. It is therefore important to watch both labour and capital productivity at both plant and company level.

In many industries, competition is cut-throat. The low cost airlines, for example, have been slashing ticket prices and the traditional airlines have been seeking ways to compete. When BA set about installing a staff management system it was perceived as a threat to staff because they assumed that the aim was to expect greater flexibility. The result was a strike, which stopped flights over the busiest weekend of the year. The company lost many millions that weekend. It shows how careful a business must be when it sets about increasing productivity.

Being more productive

IN THE KNOW

There are several ways in which a business may increase productivity. They involve making the production system more efficient by changes to equipment or people.

Whether in the primary, secondary or tertiary sector, businesses can use these strategies to become more productive.

Train people more effectively. Businesses are sometimes reluctant because of the costs and if staff leave it is perceived as being wasted. It may, however, attract high quality staff who are looking for effective development.

Buy modern machinery. New machinery is generally more productive but a business must be careful to make the right investment decisions. Markets can be fickle and the product people want today may be different tomorrow, so equipment needs to be flexible.

Motivate people. Using strategies to encourage people to work more effectively can enhance productivity. If people are contented and feel well looked after, they are more likely to meet targets.

Manage the business efficiently. Managers must watch both the production system and people constantly if productivity is to be improved. They can be more interested in production than productivity because of the way the business is organised. A system of continuous improvement encourages managers to be alert and spot strategies to improve productivity.

Critical thinking

1 Why is productivity critical to a business?

2 Why can it be difficult to raise productivity in service industries? Which strategies might you use? How might these be the same or different from strategies used in manufacturing industries?

3 Spam e-mails are a nuisance and the number received by businesses is soaring. Why are businesses worried?

Next steps

1 Choose two businesses that you know and identify ways in which they have improved productivity.

2 Can you suggest any ways in which they might improve productivity in future?

3 What might prevent them doing so?

KEY TERMS

Productivity is a measure of efficiency. It can be capital productivity, which measures output against capital invested, or labour productivity, which is measured against the number of people employed.

Production is the amount a business produces in a given time period.

How big?

Specification Content
Factors affecting operational scale; tactics for short run over capacity production and impacts of under capacity

starSTUDY

Under the Christmas tree

1. Why would a business want to meet all its orders?
2. What advantages are there for running a factory at full capacity?
3. What problems arise if the factory is running consistently below capacity?
4. Why is it difficult to deal with erratic demand?
5. What should it do to try to predict demand for next year?
6. Why can it be hard to predict demand for products like Christmas toys?

Too much or too little?

Businesses generally want to use all the capacity they have because it uses resources most effectively. A little bit of spare capacity is generally acceptable because it gives some flexibility. If a big order comes in from a customer who might become a regular, any business is going to want to be able to fulfil it quickly.

A little space also means that there is time to service the equipment and avoid breakdowns.

Over capacity means that expansion is possible provided that demand is likely to continue at the higher level. Problems arise when there is constant spare capacity.

Capacity utilisation

Capacity is the total amount that can be produced by a particular business. It will depend on the buildings, equipment and people employed. When all of these are used fully, the business is at full capacity. Providing it knows the total amount that can be produced, a business can work out current capacity utilisation using the following formula.

Whether a business produces tangible items or a service, the same applies. A hairdresser will know how many clients he or she can deal with in the course of a week and a bank will know how many staff it needs on the tills to keep the queues down.

The main reason for wanting to work as close as possible to full capacity is to spread fixed costs as widely as possible. Fixed costs do not change with capacity so if output is only half of the possible level, unit costs will rise.

$$\text{Capacity utilisation} = \frac{\text{Current output}}{\text{Maximum possible output}} \times 100$$

Hitting the spot

Toys Unlimited didn't manage to get it right from one year to the next. But it is in a business in which demand is notoriously hard to predict. Once a business has decided that there is a long-run problem with capacity, changes have to be made or competitiveness will be lost. If there is spare capacity, many firms will turn to the marketing department to try to sell more. It might mean making slight changes to the product to broaden the market – a waterproof version for swimmers

perhaps. If this fails there will be a need for a more severe solution – a cut in capacity.

If demand exceeds capacity, growth is required, but a business must be convinced that the increase in demand will be sustained. Many small businesses have expanded because of large orders from supermarkets. Trouble sets in when orders disappear after heavy investment has been made to increase capacity.

How to change capacity

IN THE KNOW

Capacity can be increased by changing working patterns. If it has been calculated initially on the basis of one shift per day, a second and third shift can raise capacity very quickly providing there are enough people with the right skills. Overtime can also help in the short run. Such a solution may be effective in service industries as well as production industries. A hairdresser with more customers than time may find that staying open in the evenings is a popular move especially with people who are at work all day.

Orang's salon is open from 10 a.m. to 10 p.m.

Capacity can be changed by investment in new factories, offices or shops. This also involves training new employees, so there is considerable expense involved, but if demand is growing steadily, it is a sensible strategy.

Capacity can be reduced by shutting down existing parts of the business – or rationalisation. This may mean that people have to be made redundant – skilled labour is therefore lost and motivation within the business will be affected. It is always difficult to manage a business that is contracting. Again the short- and long-run expectations must be taken into account when decisions are made.

Questions to ask

Before any business makes a decision to change capacity there are some questions to be asked.

To grow ...

• Is the business really at full capacity or could it be made more efficient within the existing capacity?

• Is an increased level of demand likely to be sustained?

• Is time critical? Will other businesses take your place if you can't meet orders?

• Can the business afford to borrow?

• Are there any activities that can be contracted out to avoid expansion?

To shrink ...

• Will demand increase by itself?

• Why has demand fallen?

• Can demand be increased by attracting new customers with differentiated products?

• Can costs be cut to attract new customers?

Critical thinking

Seasonal industries have to work on the basis of low capacity utilisation for much of the year. Draw a rough graph of how it might look for a seaside hotel. What might the hotel do to even up utilisation across the year and to keep costs under control?

Next steps

1 Are any businesses near you expanding or contracting?

2 How are they going about it?

3 Try to work out why it is happening.

KEY TERMS

Capacity utilisation shows the extent to which existing capacity is being used.

Rationalisation usually involves cutting capacity in order to produce more efficiently.

Is bigger better?

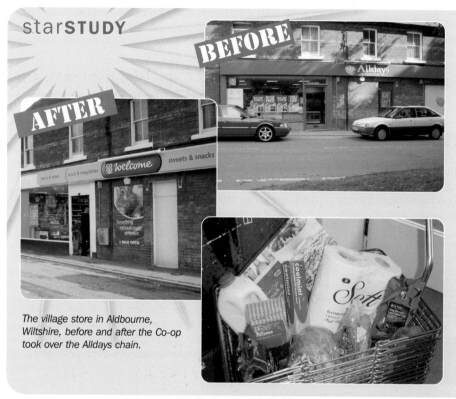

starSTUDY

BEFORE

AFTER

The village store in Aldbourne, Wiltshire, before and after the Co-op took over the Alldays chain.

Specification Content

Economies and diseconomies of scale

1 What effect did the takeover have on the number of outlets where Co-op products are sold?

2 What effect do you think this had on total sales of Co-op products?

3 Why do you think this led to an increase in efficiency for the Co-op?

4 What effect should an increase in efficiency have on the competitiveness of the business?

5 What effect do you think the takeover had on the management of the organisation?

6 How might the takeover affect capacity utilisation? How important do you think this was in the decision to go through with the takeover? Why?

Economies of scale

IN THE KNOW

BUYING IN BULK works for bigger businesses because they order large quantities of raw materials for production or managing the organisation. A car producer will order millions of tyres in the course of a year and may need to install thousands of new computers in its offices. The larger the order, the greater the discount, so the lower the unit cost of the end product.

TECHNOLOGY can be used more effectively by larger businesses on many occasions. A firm that has very large orders will need equipment that allows it to produce cheaply and efficiently on a large scale. A smaller business will not be able to invest in such equipment because it probably hasn't got the financial resources and would have lots of spare capacity if it did so. The unit cost of each item would rise it the equipment wasn't used efficiently as the fixed costs would be spread over fewer items.

MANAGEMENT can specialise in a big business. In a small business, the entrepreneur often has to do everything – and may not be very good at it. Hiring experts for finance, marketing, human resources or production can lead to an increase in efficiency because they make better decisions and fewer mistakes.

MARKETING is an expensive process and it generally takes a considerable spend to be noticed. A big business will therefore benefit because it can spread the cost over more sales. Whether marketing involves television adverts, running a national sales team or any other type of promotion, the cost of selling 1 million items can be little different from 5 million.

FINANCE is often hard to raise for small and new businesses. Big, well-established businesses have a track record, so banks tend to lend them money more cheaply and easily. This all helps to keep unit costs low.

RISK is spread when a firm makes more than one product. Most big businesses, as they have grown, have diversified to sell a range of products. Some even make products which are safe in recession. We all continue to buy birthday cards whatever the state of the economy, so having them as part of a portfolio makes the business more secure.

Some economies of scale affect a whole industry. An industry which is concentrated in one area will develop local suppliers, a skilled labour force, as well as training and local government support. Information sources develop as an industry grows. These provide help for all businesses in the industry.

The benefits of growing bigger

Businesses grow by expanding their activities or taking over other businesses. However it happens, it leads to a bigger scale activity. This may mean more shops, offices or factories – or larger shops, offices or factories. The objective of growth is often to become more efficient. This cuts costs and increases competitiveness. As it grows, the business benefits from economies of scale which lead to increased efficiency. They arise because the business can produce on a larger scale and can be managed more efficiently.

But can it get too big?

Being a big business obviously has many advantages but things can go wrong. People often find it hard to work in big organisations because they feel like a very small cog in a very big wheel. Unless a business works hard to avoid this feeling, people can become very disillusioned and demotivated. Once this happens, it is hard to restore a dynamic environment.

Diseconomies of scale

IN THE KNOW

WHAT CAN GO WRONG?

LACK OF MOTIVATION causes inefficiencies. People like to be treated like individuals and their contribution to be appreciated. The motivation theorists, Mayo and Herzberg, have written about the importance of valuing staff. In large organisations, it can seem hard to find the time to develop this sort of relationship between managers and staff. Once people lack motivation, their productivity falls and unit costs start to rise.

NO-ONE KNOWS WHAT IS HAPPENING in some large businesses. If communication links are not developed productivity will suffer because people will feel alienated. In small businesses it is easier for people to talk to each other and explain what is happening. In bigger businesses things often have to be written down instead. Such messages often go unread and therefore the staff remain uninformed.

CO-ORDINATION of a big business is very time consuming. It takes meetings and planning to make sure that everyone knows what they should be doing. If information doesn't get through, poor decisions may be made on the basis of false assumptions.

SO REMEMBER THE PEOPLE ...

Spending money on enriching jobs and training people to manage an organisation better can seem to be an unnecessary expense. The shareholders of a public company are always looking for a good return on their investment and such training cuts into profits. However, a business is probably wise to look at the big picture and appreciate that profits are likely to be slight if the workforce is discontented.

Managers need to remember that there can be problems when growth is proposed. The economies of scale are often stressed in such proposals but the needs of the organisation are often forgotten. The profits may therefore be lower than expected.

Critical thinking

1 Work out which economies and diseconomies of scale might affect the Co-op in its takeover of Alldays.

2 How can motivation theory be used to overcome diseconomies of scale?

Next steps

Compare a large and small business that you know and work out how economies and diseconomies of scale affect them.

KEY TERMS

Economies of scale cause a fall in costs per unit as an organisation grows larger.

Diseconomies of scale cause unit costs to rise as the business grows larger.

How to produce?

Specification Content

Organising production: job, batch and flow

starSTUDY

Making products

Each one is different

They are all just the same

When one batch is finished the machines are cleaned thoroughly before changing flavour

1 Explain why each product has to be made in a different way.

2 How is technology used in each example?

3 In which examples are labour costs a relatively low proportion of total costs? Why?

4 Which type of production gives employees most satisfaction? Why?

5 What problems do you think can arise with employees in the television plant?

6 What sort of production is easier for a small business to organise? Why?

7 Which types of production allow a business to spread its fixed costs furthest?

8 Can you think of an example of one-off products that are made using high technology? (See pages .)

Different product – different production

There are almost as many ways of making things as there are products but they can be divided into three main categories. The examples above show job, batch and flow production. A business needs to pick the most appropriate method for the product it wants to make because the cost implications are very different. In making the decision, it must consider whether the items are all the same or all different, how many the market wants, how much money is available to invest and the objectives of the owners.

Critical thinking

1 Draw up a chart which shows the advantages and disadvantages of each type of production.

2 How are the following items provided: a haircut, a personal stereo, a new garden wall, a croissant from a local baker, a croissant from a big bakery, a T-shirt from a high street retailer.

3 What steps must a business which uses flow production take to ensure that time is not lost because the line stops? How does this help to keep costs down?

KEY TERMS

Job production is used for one-off products.

Batch production is used when groups of items are made at the same time and move from stage to stage together.

Flow production is used to mass produce items by keeping them on a continuous process which moves them from stage to stage.

Job, batch or flow?

Job production is used to produce any one-off product. The size and shape is of no importance. It can range from a wedding dress to a spaceship to Mars. The one thing they all have in common is that they are specially made for the purpose.

It is an expensive process because it needs specialised staff who concentrate on the project. The outcomes are usually of high quality because the staff are highly motivated as each job is unique. They may use very little equipment, as in the case of the wedding dress, or masses of very specialised technology for a Mars probe. Unit costs are going to be high because each item takes a lot of time and, in some cases, investment.

Small businesses often use job production because they begin with the skills of the person who sets up the business. A window cleaner, for example, is using job production methods.

Batch production is the most effective way of working when products have similarities but are different. Yeo Valley's output is almost all of this kind. It produces yoghurt and other dairy products – but in different flavours.

It is flexible because if the supermarkets want more lemon yoghurt than strawberry, the machines are set up for a longer run. Printing works on a similar principle. The presses run for a long period every time a new Harry Potter book is in production but for a much shorter period when a new Business Studies textbook is nearing publication.

Unit costs will be lower because the equipment can be used over and over again but time will be lost when the switch is made from one batch to the next.

Flow production involves producing long runs of the same item. In this system the product moves directly from one stage to the next. It often uses a conveyor belt that passes through a variety of stages. Many cars are produced on an assembly line so they move continuously from the initial stages of putting the chassis together through to the paint shop.

Such systems are very expensive to set up, so they are used by big businesses. They need careful planning and a great deal of investment. They are a combination of specially designed equipment and computers needing sophisticated programming. Once in place, they are expensive to change. A new car design means restructuring the line – or even starting from scratch. They tend to be used for products that have a consistently high level of demand. Many food products and sweets are made in this way.

It is critically important to keep the line flowing. Stoppages mean loss of production and, because no one can do anything, the losses will be heavy. Another problem that occurs is that staff become bored and motivation drops because they are doing the same thing all the time.

Although the initial costs are very high, the volume that can be produced means that these fixed costs are spread over millions of items, so unit costs can fall quickly.

Personalised flow

Developments in technology have meant that businesses can use flow production but make products to the requirements of the customer. Triumph motorbikes are made in this way. A purchaser orders a bike of a particular specification and the information is fed into the computer system. This ensures that the right parts are in the right place and employees receive instructions at each stage. Many car firms have moved to this flexible approach because cars come with many alternative specifications of colours, doors and extras. The process means that a business can have the benefits of both flow and job production.

Is this a threat to the small firm which specialises in job production? Probably not, because people buy handmade products because of the status attached and the hand finishing associated with it. A machine is unlikely to be able to make a wedding dress with a perfect fit and millions of individual beads.

Raising efficiency

Specification Content

Organising production: cell and lean

starSTUDY

Reforming production to create real value

Canon has shifted from mass production using conveyor belts to a cell production method, in which small groups of employees undertake the entire production process. The shift is in line with our worldwide production system reformation aimed at eliminating labour and space inefficiencies. The beauty of cell production is that it puts the art of creation back where it belongs – in the hands of real people, rather than machines and systems. Spearheading cell production are teams of multi-talented individuals, who we call Experts, themselves overseen by Super Experts, who excel in all facets of the production process. Super Experts also provide sound guidance in such areas as parts procurement, machine tool refinements, product inspection and final installation. Initiatives such as these, which encourage employees to improve their skills, are being broadened to cover all companies in the Canon Group.

Source: www.canon.com

1 Why has Canon moved to cell production?

2 How does it work?

3 Why are people important in cell production?

4 Why do you think it works better than mass production using conveyor belts?

5 What extra responsibilities do Super Experts have? How does this help the cell, the individual and Canon?

People, process and prices

Businesses are always looking for ways of increasing efficiency. Cell production has removed the problems associated with flow production because staff are working in small groups on one particular item that they see through the production process.

Another strategy has been to look carefully at the process and ensure that it is constantly being improved and there is no 'fat' in the system. Lean production means that every stage is watched to speed up the process and cut wastage.

The advantage of lean production is that it keeps costs down and therefore gives a business a price advantage. If a business can speed up the time it takes to get a product to market, it will also have competitive advantage from being innovative.

Cell production

Cell production means teamwork. Instead of working on a production line which leads to boredom and reduced motivation, staff with different skills work together on a complete product or a complete stage of a product. They are in competition with other teams and rewards are often associated with meeting targets.

In many cases where cell production has been introduced:

- productivity has risen
  - output has increased
  - costs have been cut
  - absenteeism has fallen.

Lean production

LEAN PRODUCTION aims to cut costs and ensure the efficient running of a business. It can be applied to every aspect of production from design to distribution.

LEAN DESIGN means getting the product to the shop floor very quickly. This has been helped by the development of computer-aided design which allows drawings to be turned into products quickly and easily. It can cut the time taken to develop a new car by nearly half. When staff feel that their decisions are going to become reality quickly, it focuses the mind on getting it right.

JUST-IN-TIME PRODUCTION means that stock levels are kept to a minimum. They arrive when required – no sooner, no later. A factory doesn't need large stock rooms and saves money because stocks do not have to be paid for until they are needed for final production. When stocks arrive, they go straight to the place where they will be used.

There is pressure not to make mistakes because there are no stocks to rework the product. As orders for components and raw materials are put in when production is about to begin, there is less chance of over-production. When a business makes its products on the basis of an expected market for them, things can go wrong if demand is lower than expected.

LEAN PEOPLE do not have boring repetitive jobs. They probably work in cells. They are all responsible for solving problems and can maintain the equipment they use. If a machine goes wrong, everything doesn't stop until the engineer turns up. This means teamwork, so they have to meet to discuss what is happening and how to achieve the targets.

LEAN QUALITY means everyone is responsible, not just the checker at the end of the production line. The aim is that nothing goes out faulty because rectifying the situation adds to costs. Mass production is cheap, so some argue that a few faults are worth the price. The lean producer would disagree because there is less reworking and waste of materials. Total Quality Management – or TQM – is one approach to achieving quality.

go to → Find out more about TQM on page 195.

KAIZEN, as in the Canon story, involves the staff in ensuring quality and looking out for opportunities to improve the process. This way, waste is eliminated and groups are responsible for ensuring that their team performs well. It requires well-trained, highly qualified employees.

In practice

Lean production should not be regarded as a cheap way of making things because it cuts down on staff and other resources. People have to be empowered through training and job enrichment to work this way. Some employers use it as an excuse to cut the workforce and reduce the time available for things to be done. When treated this way, it doesn't work. Employees get disillusioned and are unable to perform at the level required. Mistakes will be made and costs will rise.

Critical thinking

Lean or mass production?

Draw up a chart showing the costs and benefits of each form of production. What sort of products do you think are best suited to each production strategy?

Next steps

Why do you think quality is important for a business? Use some examples from businesses you know.

KEY TERMS

Lean production is a strategy that involves cutting out waste but ensuring quality.

Cell production uses teams of multi-skilled employees who work together to make a whole product or a particular stage.

Just-in-time production keeps stocks to a minimum to avoid wastage. They arrive when they are needed.

Kaizen is Japanese for continuous improvement. Employees constantly provide ideas to improve the process and therefore improve competitiveness.

Why quality?

starSTUDY

Perfect pizzas

Canadian Pizza (UK) makes pizzas for Tesco, Asda and Morrisons and supplies pizza bases to other manufacturers. There had been 128 customer complaints at one of the manufacturing plants when a new senior management team arrived. They decided something had to be done to improve quality.

The British Standards Institute (BSI) came to the rescue. It provides quality standards and helps businesses to achieve them. Canadian Pizza had to produce a document setting out its business procedures, write a quality manual for internal use and assess its

quality management systems. Once this was all in place, a BSI assessor visited to check that everything was up to scratch. Once it had achieved the award – known as ISO 9000 – the inspectors continued to visit to ensure that the standard was being maintained.

The effort paid off. Complaints fell to 19 at one plant and there were no complaints at all about the 6 million pizzas produced at another plant. Wastage fell from 5% to 2–3% and training is now an integral part of the process.

Source: www.bsi.org.uk

Specification Content

Quality: importance; methods of ensuring quality

1 Why did Canadian Pizza's new management team decide to improve quality?
2 What might have happened to the business if nothing had been done?
3 How does the BSI process help a business to be more efficient?
4 What gains do you think can be made once the standards are in place?
5 How does it help in the long run?
6 Why does having achieved the standard help marketing?

What is quality?

Everyone knows that quality is important but it is surprisingly hard to define. Customers want quality but it will be related to the price they are prepared to pay and the degree of competition in the market.

In a perfect world customers want a product that looks good, does the job, is reliable, lasts as long as it is wanted, comes with good after-sales service and is value for money.

From the business point of view, the quality of design is the starting point. Whether producing a pair of designer sunglasses or the motor for a lawn mower, if the design is good, the end product can be produced efficiently and as cheaply as possible. The production process itself must be quality driven in order to meet the specifications, avoid wastage, not break down and be workable for staff.

This design specification can be driven by a powerful customer. When Nissan buys in components for its cars, they are made to its specifications. When supermarkets give contracts for ready meals, they set the specifications.

The law also influences specifications. There are laws about health and safety. These are monitored by trading standards officers. Industries also have their standards with Kitemarks of approval.

go to →
page 66 to refresh your memory on Health and Safety legislation.

The important thing to remember is that quality is always changing. Just think how the quality of music equipment has changed in the last ten years.

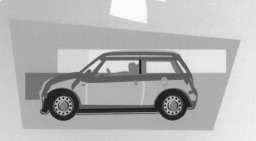

Achieving quality

Businesses want to achieve quality in their field. Canadian Pizza became much more effective once it had established quality standards and embedded them in the business.

Once a product is recognised as being of good quality:

- customers return
- brand builds a good reputation
- marketing costs may be reduced
- retailers want the product on their shelves
- the product is perceived as value for money, so its price can be higher than the competition.

Once a product has developed a good reputation, a business has to work hard to maintain it. Measures must be in place to ensure that things only get better, so there must always be a search for ways to improve.

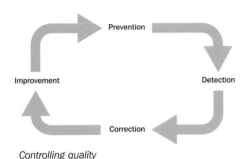

Controlling quality

Quality control

IN THE KNOW

Most businesses have systems for checking that their products are up to quality. If you phone a helpline, you often hear a message saying that calls may be recorded to check on quality. This keeps employees alert because they never know when they might be recorded. It also gives the customer a 'feel good factor' because they feel they are important to the business.

A system might involve

- checking the raw materials as they come in
- checking at each stage of production
- checking the finished products.

Each of these stages often involves sampling because it would be too expensive to check every one. There are different ways of checking.

- Inspectors may be employed specifically for the job. They may not be popular with other employees and often find the job repetitive and boring – which leads to mistakes.

- Everyone may be responsible. This leads to a greater sense of ownership of the product and, as Herzberg suggested, can be more motivating than just sitting on a production line.

- Many mass production systems have built-in alerts which warn staff when something has gone wrong.

BUT SOMETIMES IT ALL GOES WRONG ...

If products that are not up to scratch reach the customer, insuperable damage may be done because reputations are hard to rebuild. If customers start complaining, it is important that the message gets to those who need to know. A business needs a system to feed customer views to people who have the power to change things.

A business which carries out market research might be alerted to problems by people's responses. If customers try things and don't come back, it can be hard to find out why. Building quality questions into research on a regular basis can help to prevent issues building up.

Critical thinking

1 What aspects of quality are important to Levi's jeans, Pizza Hut, BT, Volkswagen?

2 Explain why. What would happen in each case if quality slipped?

KEY TERMS

Quality control involves ensuring that products meet their specification.

Improving quality

starSTUDY

Something wrong?

A small business had been receiving a significant number of complaints that its bars of soap were not up to standard.

A hairdresser noticed that some regular customers were not returning.

A call centre's customers were complaining that the staff were unable to give the support expected.

A supplier to a major car manufacturer had a whole delivery returned because it was not up to standard.

A games machine business became aware that its competitors' products were more sophisticated.

E verything seemed OK but the managing director felt that the business might get left behind if nothing changed.

> **Specification Content**
>
> Approaches to quality: quality assurance, TQM and continuous improvement; interrelationship between motivation, training and quality

1 What effect will these problems have on the businesses?
2 Look at the strategies on these two pages to decide how each business might solve its problem. Explain your choices.
3 What are the implications for the business?

Who's involved?

Inspection is often necessary but unpopular, so systems of self-checking have been developed. Many such systems try to involve everyone so that quality control is not just the responsibility of the few. As motivation theory suggests, giving people responsibility enriches their jobs, and they become more effective employees. If the whole staff is to participate in quality assurance and the search for improvement, they need greater levels of expertise, therefore training is an important part of the process. This, in turn, enhances motivation. By building quality into all stages of production, costs should fall because there should be less wastage and fewer inspectors.

Critical thinking

1 Explain why ISO 9000 helps the marketing strategy.
2 Why is motivation likely to be stronger in a business that takes improving quality seriously?

Next steps

1 Find out whether any businesses in your local area have ISO 9000.
2 Check their websites or annual reports.
3 Do they explain why they have done it and how it has helped?

KEY TERMS

Benchmarking results from comparisons with other businesses or industries.

Quality strategies

TOTAL QUALITY MANAGEMENT (TQM) is

built into the system and involves all employees being responsible. At each stage, employees aim to pass the best quality output to the next part of the process. Products will be checked to ensure they meet safety standards but all other quality checks will be carried out by departments.

It is important that senior management is seen to be part of the process because others will lose faith in the system if they aren't.

Benchmarking involves measuring the business against best practice elsewhere. It has become established as a strategy for businesses both large and small. It is usually carried out on separate aspects of the business. If there is a problem with customer service, it is useful to have a look at firms that do it well. This is done through forming an alliance with them so that they will share the information that needs to be analysed and applied to the business, to enable targets to be set. The process should be carried out in consultation with everyone involved. People often feel threatened by such processes, so careful preparation and training is needed.

KAIZEN, or continuous improvement, is a

philosophy that underpins the way a business works. Everyone is responsible for quality and looking out for ways of improving all aspects of the business. It is a strategy that was originally developed in Japan but the practice has spread round the world.

If it is to work effectively, every employee needs to be empowered so that they feel they can make decisions. This means being well trained. People work in teams or cells.

 go to → *Find out more about cells on page 190.*

Find out more about cells on page 190.

Members develop expertise so they can identify and solve problems and work out how to improve the process. They will meet frequently to discuss their activities. This will only work, of course, if sensible ideas are accepted.

Targets are important because they help to identify problems and show whether the system is working.

Persuading management and other employees to work within the system means the business must develop a democratic structure in which everyone feels free to contribute their ideas. This means trust between different levels of staff because some people may see extra responsibility as a burden rather than an opportunity.

QUALITY CIRCLES are often part of a Kaizen

strategy but can be used independently. Groups of employees meet to discuss issues related to their work. A meeting might focus on a particular problem or look generally for ways to improve output.

... IN PRACTICE

Some larger businesses set up quality assurance departments to organise the process and take responsibility for ensuring that quality targets are met. In a smaller organisation, one person may be responsible.

People in the department will work with others to set targets and oversee strategies that are in place. Benchmarking, for example, takes planning, development and implementation. It therefore needs managing.

The quality assurance department will also manage quality accreditation. This enhances the role of quality because it provides a very public measure of the way the business works. Accreditation like ISO 9000 is often part of a business's marketing as well as its quality strategy.

Continuous improvements to quality can only be achieved by well-trained employees. It is unrealistic to expect staff to contribute in this way if they lack the expertise to deal with problems and come up with new ideas. Training generally increases motivation, which leads to improved quality, so the whole process is interlinked.

DOES IT COST TOO MUCH?

Some people who run businesses argue that strategies to improve quality are too expensive to implement and run:

- Training is expensive
- People need time to meet and discuss the work of a cell
- Change means more cost
- Quality strategies need managing
- Accreditation involves costs.

Shareholders are often looking for a quick return so investing in the long term may be unpopular. In a market with little competition, it can be tempting to ignore quality issues. There are, however, few businesses today that are unchallenged. Applications for registration for ISO 9000 now come from all round the world.

Inevitably, the decisions made about setting up a quality system will depend on the power of customers, shareholders and employees. In some companies these will all be in favour but in others it may lead to conflict.

The ins and outs of stock

Specification Content

Purpose and costs of stock; determination of buffer stock, reorder level and quantities, lead time; construction and interpretation of stock control chart

starSTUDY
At a halt

1 What effect do all these problems have on the business?

2 Why does the business not keep masses of stock?

3 Which of them are the result of internal problems and which are external?

4 Can you think of a solution to each of these problems?

5 Having lots of stock of finished products means that orders can be met but why should it not be the usual situation?

Why keep stock?

If a business hasn't enough stock, production will grind to a halt. If a shop runs out of stock, customers will go elsewhere. Keeping **stock control** is therefore important. It takes careful planning within the business to manage stock levels, ensure they are of the right quality and are in the right place at the right time.

Choosing a supplier

Some clues to help the purchasing department to make the decision are:

• Has the supplier got ISO 9000? If so, it has quality systems in place.

• Has the supplier provided samples to judge quality?

• Will the supplier give discounts for bulk purchases?

• Is the supplier happy to discuss adapting its products to meet your needs?

• Will the supplier provide contacts with existing customers to check for satisfaction?

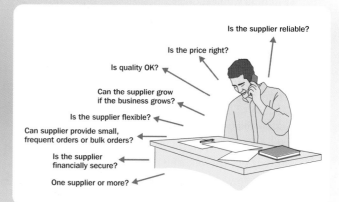

Is the supplier reliable?

Is the price right?

Is quality OK?

Can the supplier grow if the business grows?

Is the supplier flexible?

Can supplier provide small, frequent orders or bulk orders?

Is the supplier financially secure?

One supplier or more?

Managing stock

A business may have three different types of stock to manage:

- raw materials and components from suppliers

- work in progress that is produced within the business

- finished stocks that are awaiting orders coming in and dispatch to customers.

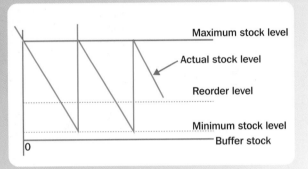

If any stocks build up or run out, it is clear that stock management isn't working. Stocks are expensive to hold so any business wants to keep them to a minimum. It is equally expensive to run out because it can bring the whole business to a halt. A hairdresser without shampoo would soon lose customers! A car plant with no wheels would have trouble rolling new vehicles off the production line! Whatever happens, keeping stocks for too long has an opportunity cost because the money lost could be used for something else.

Stocks are expensive because:

- they need storage space, so the factory or office has to be bigger

- if money is borrowed to acquire them, interest payments need to be made

- if cash flow is a problem, the business might be at risk of being insolvent

- they may deteriorate, become obsolete or be stolen if held for a long time.

On the other hand, not being able to meet orders threatens a loss of reputation. It can be hard to repair the damage when this happens.

Most businesses try to use old stock first and keep newly arrived stock until later. This is essential in the food industry for obvious reasons, but is good practice in any business because if stocks are left for a long time, they might deteriorate or become obsolete. This is known as stock rotation.

There are times when a business wants to build up stock. Easter eggs are made for a long time before Easter but do not hit the shops until the spring.

STOCK CONTROL CHARTS

In order to check that stocks are adequate – and under control – a business will keep charts to show what is happening. These are usually computer based.

When stocks are delivered, they reach the maximum level. As they are used up, the quantity falls. It reaches a point when another order is triggered. Businesses often hold a buffer stock to allow for delays.

The chart should not be a rigid guide. It needs to be used with other information. When a shop expects hot weather it will want to increase stocks of ice cream and charcoal. If the weather forecast proves wrong, the chart will show that stocks have remained high and the reorder level will not be hit for a while.

Critical thinking

1 Draw up a chart showing the costs and benefits of keeping stocks.

2 Give some examples of businesses that are likely to build up stocks of finished goods.

3 Draw up a stock control chart for a product of your choice in a supermarket. Label it showing factors that would influence the speed of use of stocks.

KEY TERMS

Stock control involves systems that ensure that adequate supplies of stocks are in the right place at the right time.

Stock rotation ensures that older stocks are used first.

Opportunity cost is the cost of the next best alternative that is missed because of a decision that has been made.

Buffer stocks are kept to protect a business against delays in the arrival of stocks.

Controlling stock

starSTUDY

Keeping the shelves full

Specification Content

JIT as a means of controlling stock

Customer: 'Why don't you order more at one go – then you won't run out so often?'

Manager: 'We haven't anywhere to put it here. There's no warehouse. Everything comes off the truck and goes straight to the shelves. Anyway, the system usually adjusts the amounts ordered when we know demand will be high.'

Customer: 'So why does it go wrong?'

Manager: 'Humans aren't infallible! Some of the people on the checkout confuse the fruit. I'm always running out of pink grapefruit – checkout staff keep putting them through as white. Sometimes the warehouse is out of stock. Sometimes it's beyond their control. Where does that wine come from – Chile was it? If the boat gets held up, there isn't much we can do about it.'

Customer: 'Well thanks for explaining. I do hope it arrives soon.'

Customer: 'You're out of my favourite red wine again. What's gone wrong?'

Manager: 'I'm sorry. I'll have to find out what's happened.'

Customer: 'The manager of the wine department ought to get his orders in on time.'

Manager: 'Oh, it doesn't work like that. When people buy things, the information is sent straight from the till and stock is reordered as levels fall.'

1 Explain how the stock control system works in the supermarket.

2 How has IT helped the process?

3 Does the store hold any buffer stocks?

4 Why does the supermarket use just-in-time stock control?

5 Why is any system going to go wrong sometimes?

6 How can the business work to minimise such difficulties?

7 Where do you think the customer will buy the red wine?

8 What effect will this have on the supermarket's profits?

Keeping the stock moving

Receiving stock when expected is critical for any business. The supermarket may lose a customer because, in going elsewhere for the red wine, she might discover that another supermarket provides a better service – and never return.

Businesses work hard to make stock control as effective as possible and information technology plays a major role. It has enabled businesses to use just-in-time stock control practices much more effectively.

Speeding up the stock

JUST-IN-TIME (JIT) stock control aims at zero buffer stocks. A manufacturing plant without a warehouse has stock delivered straight to the point on the factory floor where it will be used. As the last items are used up, the next arrive. As many firms now make products to order instead of just hoping they will sell, there is no need to hold stocks of finished products either. An order comes in and stock is immediately ordered on a just-in-time basis.

A JIT system cannot be installed overnight. Any business has to be convinced that its supplier can manage to deliver the right product at the right time on a regular basis. Normally it would take effect gradually. Stocks are cut as close as possible to zero as trust is built up.

Using a JIT system means developing a close, trusting relationship with suppliers because you are dependent on them. Production will halt if stocks don't arrive on time.

JUST-IN-TIME HAS ITS UPSIDES AND DOWNSIDES ...

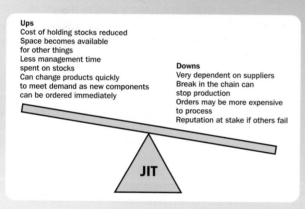

Ups
Cost of holding stocks reduced
Space becomes available
for other things
Less management time
spent on stocks
Can change products quickly
to meet demand as new components
can be ordered immediately

Downs
Very dependent on suppliers
Break in the chain can
stop production
Orders may be more expensive
to process
Reputation at stake if others fail

JIT

KANBAN is a system which helps just-in-time to happen. It involves having cards – or kanbans in Japanese – on individual components or batches of components. As they are used, the cards, which contain a barcoded number, are fed into the computer-based stock control system. More items are ordered and brought to place on the factory floor where they will be used. It empowers employees because they have the responsibility for ensuring that the order goes in – or they will be unable to meet their targets and hold everyone else up.

THE ROLE OF IT is clearly central to the development of JIT systems.
Businesses set up systems to meet their needs. A supermarket's system will not just link to the warehouse but to the suppliers who supply the products. If the shelves empty quickly, the supplier is asked to increase deliveries.

However, the quality of the system often depends on people inputting data accurately. A failure of the system can lead to chaos as stocks fail to arrive.

BUT ...

- Just-in-time has been referred to as just-in-trucks. Guaranteeing deliveries when the route includes the M25 round London or the M6 round Birmingham can be difficult and makes production extremely erratic.

- Someone in the supply chain needs to hold stocks. Imported or seasonal resources are unlikely to arrive at 6-hourly intervals, as a producer might want. Apples grown in the UK are stored throughout the year – until the supermarkets want them.

- Stock control systems have mainly been aimed at big business but are increasingly being used in medium-sized businesses, but the small operator may still need to use a traditional approach. It may be too time-consuming to tailor a standard package to the particular needs of a small business.

- JIT may be inappropriate for a business which suffers erratic demand. It may be necessary for someone to work out expected demand and plan accordingly. It may also be necessary to hold stocks – just in case.

Critical thinking

1 Look back to the problems in the star study on page 196. Can you give any further advice to overcome the problem?

2 Identify some businesses that can use just-in-time effectively and others that can't. Explain why.

3 Explain, using motivation theory, why Kanban can empower people.

Next steps

Ask your local shop how it controls its stock. Are the shelves usually well stocked? How does this compare with your local supermarket?

KEY TERMS

Kanban is a system of stock control involving barcoded cards that are used to reorder when stocks run low.

Hankins Joinery

Hankins Joinery is a small family-owned business. Some 50% of its sales revenue comes from wooden components supplied to Millers plc, a large office furniture manufacturer. About 30% of Hankins sales are components supplied to a total of five other businesses. Most of this is made in batches. The remaining 20% of sales is for bespoke furniture that it makes using job production methods especially for individual customers who make orders through the Internet or visit the show room attached to the factory.

- Hankins sales revenue   £4 million

- Full-time equivalent employees   50

- Organisation by function. Finance manager and general manager, sales manager, purchasing manager, production manager, administration manager who is also the human resources manager

- Millers sales revenue   £80 million

- Full-time equivalent employees   400

Hankins has reduced the price it pays for wood supplies by becoming a member of a buying consortium. The consortium has managed to lower the price it pays per cubic metre of wood by guaranteeing to buy in bulk from the timber mills in Sweden on a regular basis. The consortium makes weekly deliveries to Hankins. Hankins are pleased with the prices, but sometimes the quality of the wood is poor and needs to be sent back.

Hankins has a large area of the factory given over to stocks. The bespoke orders have a shorter lead time if Hankins doesn't need to order stock and await delivery. The same is true for the orders it gets from its furniture manufacturers. Hankins management knows that it often gets orders precisely because of its quicker delivery. That is the prime reason why the buffer stock represents about 50% of maximum stock levels. Certain types of wood can be difficult to store and the stores department operates a stock rotation system.

Millers have decided to invest in the JIT stock control system and have approached the management of Hankins with a proposal for a big increase in its orders so long as Hankins can deliver every day rather than the current fortnightly arrangement. Hankins would become a preferred supplier. Millers would buy four types of wooden component. Hankins would also be required to improve its quality control. It's a big decision, because it would mean Hankins moving towards its own JIT approach and cutting out job production and bespoke orders.

The management decided to meet with representatives from the production team, purchasing department and members from stores. The employees would have to be brought on board if business was to change. If not Hankins would lose a major part of its market.

The initial meeting discussed the proposal and decided that before Hankins could go ahead it would need to think of ways of improving delivery, quality and becoming more productive.

Representatives were sent to other businesses and on training courses to find out more about the ways the business could set up cell production, operate its own quality control system and become a JIT operation. The production team would see a shift in culture. The proposal would be to set up four different production cells, but would need a greater production area. The purchasing department had to explore finding new suppliers who could deliver quality wood on a daily basis. It might cost more in purchases, but there would be savings elsewhere. The gross profit would fall, but the net profit rise.

Decision time was approaching and a final meeting was called.

1 What is meant by the terms 'JIT stock control system' and 'cell production'? **(4 marks)**

 Straightforward understanding required.

2 Explain how Hankins organises its production. What are the advantages and disadvantages for Hankins of operating in this way? **(4 marks)**

 The first part of the question is applying production methods to the case study. The second part invites you to make a simple analysis.

3 Why does Hankins keep a large buffer stock? What problems might Hankins face in keeping such a high level of stocks? **(8 marks)**

 You will need to know what buffer stock is and then provide a reason why Hankins feel it is important to keep large stocks. The last part asks you to come up with a couple of problems about holding large stocks. Try to relate this to working capital.

4 What comparisons can you make between the size of Hankins and its main customer, Millers? How else might you compare their sizes? **(6 marks)**

 The first part asks you to select appropriate data from the case study. If you are making comparisons try to use ratios, e.g. 'A is 50% of or half of B'. The last part hints that if more data were available you could make better comparisons. You should know one or two further ways of comparing size.

5 Discuss the advantages Millers has by being bigger. How does Hankins manage to survive despite it being small? **(16 marks)**

 Always try to recognise the key concept that can be used to support your answer. Start briefly with explaining economies of scale and then explore the different types of economies by applying it to the case study. Most businesses are small so they can survive just like Hankins.

6 Evaluate the proposal to have closer ties with Millers and accept its offer of increased orders, but daily deliveries and improved quality. **(16 marks)**

 There is so much you can write about here, but you don't have to include everything. You could look at a couple of options: (1) Do nothing and lose the contract; (2) Make the changes as required. What are the good points about making the changes and what are the obstacles and problems? Can these be overcome? Are the disadvantages greater than the advantages? It doesn't matter which view you take as long as you can back up your arguments with evidence based on sound analysis.

End of Part 2 assessment

Paper 2: Business decisions

- Time allowed 1 hour
- A total of 45 marks available
- Answer all questions

> Words that are highlighted in green are key ideas that might be useful in your answers. A good idea for the real exam!

Note: comments in red are made by the authors.

Tariq is a qualified hairdresser who has just purchased Style Design, an existing hairdressing salon in his local area. Tariq employs two qualified full-time staff and a junior member of staff. The junior is half way through a two-year training scheme, which includes attending one day per week at a local college (day release).

Style Design is the only local outlet for a well-known and profitable brand of shampoos, conditioners and hair care products. Stock is ordered whenever an item runs low (Stock control). Some items sell out very quickly while others remain on the shelves for long periods of time. There is a lead time of ten days.

The majority of the salon's current customers are over the age of 40 (Market segment). Tariq has been looking at the client database set up by the previous owner. (See Table 1 below.)

Age of clients	Average spend	Average frequency of visits
0–16 years	£10	8 weeks
17–21 years	£40	6 weeks
22–40 years	£35	2 weeks
41–50 years	£30	4 weeks
51–65 years	£25	4 weeks
Over 65	£15	4 weeks

(Speech bubble: Second biggest spend but most frequent customers)

Table 1: Average customer spending per visit

Tariq plans to give the salon a more modern image. His new target market is younger and more affluent. He knows that he will have to spend a considerable amount of money on both refurbishment and new equipment (Investment). He has therefore drawn up a cash flow forecast.

Receipts	July £	August £
Opening cash balance	10,000	(4,675)
Revenue from hairdressing	15,000	16,500
Sales of hair products	300	300
TOTAL INFLOWS	25,300	12,125
Payments		
Fixtures, fittings and equipment	19,000	
Wages	6,000	6,000
Rent and rates	1,200	1,200
Salon consumables	3,000	3,300
Stocks of hair products for retail sales	150	150
Electricity and other expenses	250	250
Insurance	300	
Advertising	75	75
TOTAL OUTFLOWS	29,975	10,975
Balance carried forward	(4,675)	1,150

(Speech bubble: One-off payment)

(Speech bubble: Negative figure carries on to start of August)

Table 2: Cash flow forecast for July and August

Tariq will use the following assumptions to help him draw up the cash flow forecast for September:

- Revenue from hairdressing will continue to rise by 10% per month

- Salon consumables such as perming solutions and tints will also rise by 10% per month

- Advertising expenditure will be 20% higher than in August

- All other cash flows will remain the same as in August.

Answer all questions.

1 a Outline two methods that Tariq could use to segment his market. **(4 marks)**

   b Analyse Tariq's plans to change the target market for the salon. **(8 marks)**

2 Evaluate the advantages and disadvantages to the business of day release as a method of training the junior member of staff. **(12 marks)**

3 Calculate the closing cash balance for September based on the information in Table 2 and Tariq's assumptions. **(7 marks)**

4 Evaluate the factors that Tariq should consider in deciding his stock control policy. **(12 marks)**

Paper 3: Business behaviour

- Time allowed 1 hour 15 minutes

- A total of 60 marks available

- Answer all questions

Oaks Holiday Tours Ltd (OHT) & Thornwood Coaches OHT was set up in 1975 by James and Jayne Oaks. They began with one coach taking day trips to the Lake District from their base in Settle, North Yorkshire. As the population's demand for travel increased (outward shift in demand curve), OHT expanded into 7-day and 10-day holidays throughout the UK. However, by 1985 the vast majority of OHT's holiday destinations were to Europe (Table 1). OHT employs secretarial and administrative staff who make the necessary hotel bookings and plan the tour itineraries. It also employs full-time and part-time telephone reservations staff. However, OHT does not employ any coach drivers, nor does it own any coaches. This is because OHT sub-contracts out the individual holiday tours to coach companies throughout the UK. At any one time there may be as many as 30 coaches and 20 sub-contractors taking OHT customers to and from their destinations in Europe. The majority of OHT's customers purchase their holidays directly from the company. Brochures are sent out each year to anyone on the company's database who has purchased a holiday from OHT in the past five years. It also advertises in the majority of travel supplements in the better quality newspapers between December and June (promotion methods, above the line, direct). Although research suggests that the majority of OHT's customers initially find out about the company by picking up a brochure in a high street travel agent, most still book direct over the telephone. The next 12 months will see OHTs website grow in size; the intention being that customers will be able to book holidays over the Internet. James and Jayne are proud of OHTs reputation in the industry and put strong emphasis on quality. In the last five years OHT has won awards for 'Best UK Coach Operator', 'Best Coach Operator to France' and 'Best Long Stay Coach Operator'. The majority of OHT's holidays are fully booked, although a few run with as many as 20 empty seats (break even) on the coach. However, Jayne, who is the firm's Marketing Director, is most proud of their customer feedback. She sees this as more important than any award (Business objective and monitoring). Customer feedback is encouraged by asking every customer to complete a questionnaire as they travel back to Calais on the final day of their holiday (primary research). As part of plans for diversification, OHT is currently looking at the feasibility of introducing 'fly-drive' coach holidays. Customers would fly to their starting point, travel around their chosen location by coach for eight or nine days and then fly back to the UK. This would further increase the range (product range) of countries to which OHT could provide holidays. It may also help to reduce the age profile (market segmentation) of its customer base (Table 2). Jayne recognises that she will have to spend a considerable amount of money developing new promotional methods if the Fly-Drive concept goes ahead. Thornwood Coaches, a coach operator based in Chatham, Kent, is just one of the many sub-contractors that OHT currently uses. Like all sub-contractors of OHT it has to provide an air-conditioned 49-seater coach not more than five years old. The coach must be painted in OHT's green and white livery (brand). Adrianne Thornwood, the owner of Thornwood Coaches, first took on an annual contract with OHT three years ago. She saw it as a

Source: Module 2, OCR, June 2003.

way of gaining a regular income to supplement her main source of revenue from day coach tours and longer UK holidays for her regular customers from north Kent. However, she is now becoming increasingly concerned about the small profit margin that the OHT contract provides, and has been examining the financial figures (Table 3) with her accountant, Sunil Ambrose.

Relate to product life cycle and Boston Matrix

	1980	1985	1990	1995	2000	2005 forecast	
UK	14	5	3	2	2	1	Big decline
France	13	12	8	6	5	2	
Benelux	17	19	19	17	18	19	stable
Germany	22	23	18	14	12	12	decline
Switzerland–Austria	16	20	23	20	19	21	
Italy	10	11	15	18	18	21	Strong growth
Spain	8	8	10	12	10	10	stable
Eastern Europe	0	2	4	11	16	14	
Total revenue (£m)	0.9	1.2	2.2	3.8	4.8	6.1	

Market share

Table 1. OHT holiday destinations (% of sales revenue)

If market share remains the same, revenues are still growing (see total revenue information)

	1980	1992	1994	1996	1998	2000	2002
0–17	1	1	2	3	3	4	2
18–29	3	5	5	6	8	8	9
30–39	5	6	7	7	10	10	14
40–49	19	22	21	24	24	26	25
50–59	52	46	41	35	29	27	25
60+	20	20	22	23	26	25	25

Table 2. Age profile of OHT's customers (%)

Main tour		Operational excursions (Stresa)	
Drivers' wages	760	Local tour guides	72
Diesel	900	Diesel	100
Road tolls and taxes	210	Extra road tolls and taxes	20
Drivers' lunch allowance	110	(Innsbruck)	
Miscellaneous	100	Local tour guides	60
		Diesel	64
		Extra road tolls and taxes	12

Table 3. Typical costs for Thornwood Coaches (10-day Swiss Glacier Express)

Adrianne said, 'I am paid a fixed price of £2430 (sales turnover or revenue) by OHT for each 10-day tour. Out of this I have to pay all operating costs, including driver's wages, diesel, road tolls, taxes and any other expenses. If the tour goes smoothly, I make a profit of less than £400 per trip (work out net profit margin = $(400/2430) \times 100$). But most weeks the coach returns with some minor damage that eats into the profit. I sometimes wonder whether the contract with OHT is worthwhile. 'Sunil was less pessimistic about the data they were examining. He felt that Adrianne was putting too much emphasis on the profit figure. 'What you must remember is that the regular cash that this contract provides is just as, if not more, important than any profit (cash flow). What is highly unsatisfactory is for one coach to be idle for too many days of the year (efficient use of resources). You need to investigate ways of hiring it out, especially during the winter (seasonal demand). This will help to maximise your capacity utilisation, argued Sunil. 'That's easier said than done. Remember it is painted in OHT's livery. Most of the other firms I do business with will not hire a coach with a competitor's name all over it,' replied Adrianne. At the conclusion of the meeting, Adrianne turned her attention to a very different matter. A married couple who she has employed as a driving team for the past three years, primarily for the OHT contract, wanted to speak to Adrianne about the future. For 30 weeks of the year, Rob and Linda Davies operate OHT's highly popular 'Swiss Glacier Express' 10-day tour, staying for 3 nights in Lugano, Switzerland and

4 nights in St Anton, Austria. One night is spent in Brussels travelling out to Switzerland and back from Austria. The tour includes two optional excursions: to Stresa on Lake Maggiore and Innsbruck. (Both optional excursions are charged for separately, and any profit from these remains with Thornwood Coaches.) Although they enjoy their job, Rob and Linda are considering whether they wish to continue working the OHT contract for the 2004 season. Spending 10 days with a group of passengers is demanding work. As well as sharing the driving, Rob and Linda must also load and unload the passengers' luggage at each hotel, serve hot and cold drinks when not driving, deal with any problems or complaints and liaise with hotel staff. For this they are each paid a flat rate of £38 per day (motivation and reward). In addition they receive a lunch allowance from Adrianne of £5.50 each per day and get their breakfast, evening meal and board provided free of charge by the hotels (fringe benefit). Linda began the meeting by outlining her concerns to Adrianne. 'We are basically on duty all day from 7.00 am until 8.00 pm or later. Even when we arrive at the hotel the customers expect us to sort out their problems and answer their questions. We are not really getting the minimum wage and we even have to pay for our own uniforms. I would be better off working on the checkout at the local supermarket.' Rob added, 'Also, we are away from family and friends for 10 days out of every fortnight. Quite often you end up giving us local jobs to do during the other 4 days so we hardly get any time off. If it wasn't for the tips we get at the end of the holiday I would pack this job in tomorrow.' Linda felt now was the time to put forward an idea she had about increasing their earnings. 'I am usually the one who organises the bookings for the optional excursions. Most of the time the coach is less than half full on these extra trips; breaking even is a real issue. If we were able to keep some of the extra income generated from these trips we would work harder at encouraging the customers to go on them. This would increase our pay and still improve your profits (empowerment, responsibility, risk and reward).'

'At the moment we might as well discourage the passengers from going on these extra trips. At least we would then get a couple of extra days off during the tour,' Rob added. Adrianne quickly replied, 'I doubt I can afford to do that. Remember the local tour guides have to be paid out of that money as well as extra diesel and road tolls. The way finances are at the moment I may even have to take a cut of your tips.' 'Well if that's the case I might as well start looking for a new job tomorrow,' said Linda angrily, as she stormed out of the meeting, closely followed by Rob. After Rob and Linda had left, Adrianne sat and thought about the problems she faced. Could she afford to hand over some of her income to Rob and Linda? If she did not, then how else could she avoid losing such good drivers?

Answer all the questions.

1 a On a typical excursion to Innsbruck (see Table 3) there are 20 passengers. If the price charged for this excursion is £8, using break-even analysis, calculate the margin of safety. **(6 marks)**

b Evaluate ways in which Thornwood Coaches could increase its profit from the OHT contract. **(10 marks)**

2 With reference to appropriate motivational theory, evaluate monetary and non-monetary ways in which Thornwood Coaches could motivate its drivers. **(16 marks)**

3 Discuss suitable promotional methods that Jayne Oaks could use if OHT introduces fly-drive coach holidays. **(16 marks)**

4 Evaluate the extent to which management of capacity is important in the context of the case. **(10 marks)**

Source: Module 3, OCR, June 2003.

Examination advice

How is the examination organised?

Unit 2871, Businesses, Their Objectives and Environment. A written paper of 1 hour's duration with questions based on a pre-issued case study. (45 marks)

Unit 2872, Business Decisions. A written paper of 45 minutes' duration. This is a data response paper with a set of four compulsory questions. The question paper assumes candidates' knowledge of teaching module 2871. (45 marks)

Unit 2873, Business Behaviour. A written paper of 1 hour 15 minutes' duration. Four compulsory questions based on a pre-issued case study. The question paper assumes candidates' knowledge of teaching module 2871. (60 marks)

What the examiner is looking for

The syllabus has four broad aims.

The aims of the syllabus	This means
Critical understanding of organisations, their markets and the process of adding value.	*You can identify the main forms of business and how their legal identity affects their choice of finance, objectives, reporting to shareholders and internal decision-making.*
An awareness of the perspectives of a range of stakeholders in these organisations.	*You can list the different types of stakeholders and say how they influence and are affected by the business.*
An understanding of business issues – economic, environmental, ethical and international.	*You can apply a PEST analysis to a particular business.*
The ability to make decisions by evaluating the information available.	*You can make judgements and recommendations about business behaviour.*

The examiner will measure your ability to meet these aims by testing the same skills in each unit. The AS level course is designed to test all of these skills by requiring you to answer questions **in context**. This means that the exam board will not reward high marks (if any) for the simple recall of knowledge.

Each unit uses a case study. Units 2871 and 2873 use a seen case study and unit 2872 uses an unseen data response question. You will be presented with text and numerical data to interpret. The questions on the examination papers are based on the stimulus materials and your answers must address the issues in the case. You will need to select the most appropriate knowledge from the syllabus and use your knowledge to answer the questions in light of the particular circumstances to the case.

To test how well you are meeting the aims of the syllabus there are four levels of skill that a candidate can display:

Level 1 Demonstrates **knowledge**

Level 2 **Applies** knowledge and understanding to the case

Level 3 Uses knowledge to **analyse** problems and issues in the case

Level 4 **Evaluates** the significance of ideas and makes judgements.

In the AS course, less emphasis is given to the skill of evaluation but it is still necessary to achieve the higher grades. The marks available for the answer and the command words used can inform you which skill is being tested in the question. Generally speaking, a question with about 4 marks is looking for knowledge that is explained in the context of the case. Knowledge that does not relate to the case will only receive 2 marks at the most. You must always say how the concepts relate to the case to gain the full 4 marks. A question with about 6 marks is looking for you to apply your knowledge with relevance to the case. Questions set for 6–10 marks require you to analyse the information. Between 10–15 marks and you are expected to show a well-structured answer which is relevant to the case and which evaluates arguments.

Several students find analysis and evaluation difficult. You can demonstrate analysis by assessing advantages and disadvantages or discussing the cause and possible consequences. Evaluation is more difficult. It means discussing whether the advantages outweigh the disadvantages or to assess which consequence is more likely. You must also state why you believe this. The biggest mistake that you can make is to just summarise points that have already been made.

Imagine that you were called for jury service. You would listen to the prosecution give evidence for one side of the case and the defendant gives evidence for the other side of the case. Each person may give different information or they may have different views on the same information. This is the analysis of the case. You will then have to form an opinion of guilty, not guilty or insufficient evidence to convict. This is giving your evaluation. By making a judgement you are stating which side of the argument you believe. In the examination you can demonstrate evaluation by making a judgement that weighs up the arguments, considers the feasibility of your ideas and may discuss the short term compared to the long term.

Be aware that the examiner assumes that you will display the highest skill and that you do not need to slavishly work through each level. Aim for evaluation from your first paragraph on the larger questions and the examiner will award this accordingly.

Guide to command words

Level 1 (1–2 marks)

- Define   Give the exact meaning of a word or concept
- Identify   Highlight the main idea
- State   Write a series of points

Level 2 (3–4 marks)

- Explain/Describe Give a detailed explanation
- Outline   What are the key aspects

Level 3 (6–10 marks)

- Analyse   Show the cause and effects on the business in the case study

                  Analyse the advantages and disadvantages

Level 4 (10–15 marks)

- Assess   Consider the value of something
- Discuss   Give reasons from both sides of the argument for your ideas
- Justify   Provide arguments to support one view
- Recommend   Provide some solutions which are supported by your arguments
- Evaluate   Give a final judgement that is justified

Before the examination

You should review at least three past papers and identify the pattern of questions that are asked.

To be a good athlete you have to train. Athletes don't just turn up on the day of the big race and have a go. The same training is needed to do well in any examination. Your training is by practising some answers using past examination papers. The mark schemes and examiners' reports are also available a few months after the examination. They are worth studying as they highlight common errors made by candidates and give useful hints on how to focus your ideas in answering particular questions.

During the examination

First of all read the question carefully and highlight the command word. Many students change the question in their mind and do not follow the command word. Brief plans for large questions can often help you stay focused so that you do not go off at a tangent and explain your ideas fully.

Secondly, consider the **context** and register some initial thoughts which will keep your answers **in context**:

- What are the objectives of the firm?

- Is it large or small?

- Is it a producer or retailer?

- Is it a service provider or manufacturer?

- Who are the customers?

- How competitive is the market?

- Is the good essential or a luxury?

Underline parts of the case study that you could use to give examples from, to show how you have **used your knowledge in context**.

Use your time carefully. There is nothing to be gained from writing a lengthy answer for a four-mark question. You could provide sides of work for the answer as you know that part of the syllabus very well but the examiner will not be able to give you any more marks than is set down on the paper.

You can often use trigger phrases to structure your ideas and signal to the examiner that you are using all your skills.

Skill	Trigger Phrase
Evaluation	'Overall...' 'The biggest impact on the business will be...because' 'The impact on the business will depend upon...' 'In the short run...but in the long run...' 'The most significant argument is...because'
Analysis	'However...' 'On the one hand...on the other hand...' 'The result of this will be...' 'The cause in this case is...' 'The relevance of this is that...'
Application	'This will mean that...'

Some textbooks will give you long lists of external influences that affect a business. It is worth developing a few ideas in depth rather than listing lots of ideas too briefly. Consider which ideas are most relevant to the case as only a few will be. Develop the ideas and work them through the levels of skill so that you end up with a fully reasoned and evaluative paragraph at the end of the larger questions.

Remember that there are marks for the quality of your written communication and this can sometimes be the key to achieving a higher grade. You should always work in continuous prose and not provide bullet point lists.

The examiner can only mark what is on the script. If the examiner were able to visit every student and assess them with a conversation then several more candidates would do better than they do. Your written answer is the only way you have of expressing how well you know the syllabus and can make a business decision. Use the opportunity wisely to communicate your ideas in full.

Business terminology is very specific and you should have clear definitions for key words and concepts. Repetitive learning strategies help you to cement these definitions into your mind. The examiner will not give you the benefit of the doubt for sloppy definitions.

Many students find Business Studies easy to understand and have a working knowledge of many issues. This arises as they have experience of part-time jobs, work experience and listening to their parents talk about their issues in the workplace. Many students, however, find it difficult to get a top grade in Business Studies. This is because top grade answers require more than everyday knowledge and experience. They require your thoughts and judgements to be supported by theory and detailed background knowledge.

Don't lull yourself into a false sense of security. If you have not covered the syllabus in detail, you will not be awarded the highest marks.

How is your examination paper marked?

After you have sat your examination, a team of examiners will compare at least ten scripts. These scripts are used to reach a common understanding of what is expected from candidates. Examiners will then mark several hundred scripts over a period of three to four weeks. Chief examiners will ask for samples from examiners to test for quality control and consistency of marking. When marking is finished, the principal examiner will then decide upon the grade boundaries which can vary from year to year depending upon the questions set and any general misunderstandings that were made by candidates.

Assessment answers

The nature of business: magic in Paris

1 What is a stakeholder? Identify examples of stakeholders from the evidence. (3 marks)

A stakeholder is an organisation or individual who has an interest in the business. The Euro Disney shareholders want financial rewards and the 12,000 Euro Disney employees wish to have secure jobs. The 13 million customers want a good experience and the 25,000 jobs in surrounding hotels and support services all depend on the company being successful. The public sector has made significant investment in the local infrastructure and now depends on taxes paid by Euro Disney and the support businesses.

2 State why the banks would be interested in the performance of Euro Disney? (2 marks)

Banks will have provided Euro Disney with large long-term loans or overdrafts and they would want to be sure of receiving the interest payments and making sure that Euro Disney would be able to pay back what it owed. They will have been very concerned in 1992 when Euro Disney made a loss.

3 Discuss the effects of the rescue package on stakeholders (lines 14–42). (14 marks)

The rescue package was necessary because costs were greater than revenues. A key part of the package was to reduce costs. The stakeholder group – employees – would clearly be affected since the number of administration staff had to be cut and many people lost their jobs. Also, those working in the resort and dealing with customers had to accept more flexible working. This would mean fewer full-time jobs and less favourable shifts. The change would be difficult for the employees to swallow, but their unions negotiated lower working hours without a pay cut and actually over 600 new jobs were created.
The banks want Euro Disney to turn in profits and to have more cash coming in than going out. Cutting costs, especially in winter when customer numbers are lower, helps achieve this. The second part of the strategy was to do with expansion and this would worsen the cash flow in the short run, as more money would go out of the business than come in. Euro Disney wanted to invest in new attractions and facilities designed to increase the number of customers. The banks would be reluctant to loan all the additional sums needed. So Euro Disney issued more shares, but shareholders need to be convinced that their investment would be successful in the long run, if not the short run. Evidence that the strategy was successful for these stakeholders comes in from increased customer numbers and customers spending more. This resulted in higher

annual turnover, bigger profits and greater employment opportunities. However working conditions may have worsened.

4 Explain the term 'added value' (line 20). In what ways is Euro Disney attempting to add value in looking after its customers? (4 marks)

Added value is the difference between the total cost of resources and the price that is charged for the product or service. Euro Disney hopes to add value by providing customers with services they want. The money spent on customer research informed the company that it needed to provide more attractions and introduce the Fastpass system to reduce waiting time. This required greater investment in physical resources. But it is also important to employ staff with the right skills and training to ensure high levels of customer care. Although these actions cost money by looking after its customers, Euro Disney can charge more.

5 What were the operating costs for the company in 1994 and in 2002? What might account for the difference between these two sets of figures? (8 marks)

The operating costs in 1994 amounted to €626 million in 1994 and had risen to €900 million by 2002. Increasing unit labour costs and supplier prices may account for some of the increase with the rest reflecting the increased supplies and extra workers employed to meet the increased demand as customers stay longer and spend more. For example, hotel occupancy rates have risen year on year. This means more meals and more hotel staff will be required to maintain the level of service.

6 Why is it important for Euro Disney to pay dividends to shareholders? (4 marks)

Dividends are the share of profits paid to shareholders as a return for investing in a company. Euro Disney needs to reward shareholders for the risk they took when investing in the company. Their investment has helped Euro Disney finance the development of new facilities such as the Walt Disney Studios in 2002.

7 Identify two resources that were required to increase added value. (2 marks)

Resources are all the things that Euro Disney needs to buy to provide the service for its customers. The added value is the difference between the cost of these resources and the price that visitors to the resort pay. The resources include the attractions in the two theme parks, and the people, food and other items that are needed to run the 7 hotels, 61 restaurants, 52 shops and the 12,000 employees who look after the 13 million visitors.

8 For one internal stakeholder and one external stakeholder to Euro Disney suggest why it is important to look after their interest. (6 marks)

Each employee is an important stakeholder for Euro Disney. There are 12,000 of them and their skills are vital to look after the 13 million customers who visit the resort each year. If the employees feel unhappy they will not provide the level of customer service that the Euro Disney Company needs to be successful. This is why it was important for the company to have the agreement of unions before introducing new working arrangements. Disney has strong relationships with suppliers who provide food, drink and merchandise. Many of these are well known such as Nescafé, McDonald's and Coca-Cola. There are also suppliers of water and electricity. It may be that their brand names will be enhanced if Disney do well. The suppliers would like contracts with Euro Disney especially if Euro Disney is their main customer. The suppliers would also want to get paid on time. On the other hand Euro Disney is a stakeholder for them and would be interested in their performance.

9 To what extent do you think Euro Disney has kept its stakeholders happy? (14 marks)

Customer numbers were high when Euro Disney opened, with 11 million customers. This has risen to 13 million a year, but more importantly they are staying longer and spending more. Disney has reacted to their needs by improving customer care (e.g. the Fastpass system) and providing more attractions. Euro Disney undertakes constant research in order to meet customer needs. This is a service industry and it is essential to keep customers happy. Although a huge amount has been invested in attractions this would be wasted if the customer care from the 12,000 employees was not excellent. Part of this stakeholder group have had to accept more flexible working in terms of shifts and part-time contracts in order to make the company more efficient. Fewer workers are now employed at non-peak times. However, it is important for Euro Disney to look after the interests of their employees and they have a shorter working week, good training, and employee communications have improved.

The main shareholders are the parent Walt Disney Company and Prince Alwaleed. They are interested in the long-term success and therefore have supported the investment in extra facilities such as the Walt Disney Studios. These seem to have paid off as the trend for operating profit has been on the increase. Shareholders would want to monitor performance and analyse why the profit fell in 2002. More data would be needed to provide a more accurate picture. For example, it would be useful to know the dividends per share over the last few years. If more shares had been issued, the dividends may have fallen.

Suppliers want a positive relationship with Euro Disney. However, Euro Disney is a big company and may use its power to try to squeeze the prices it pays suppliers. Euro Disney may argue that getting it right for employees will help them to get it right for the customers. More customers should lead to more profit and this will make the shareholders happy.

Classification of business: magic in Paris

1 Disney Resort Paris operates in the tertiary sector. Identify the other two sectors of economic activity and provide an example of each that would support the Disney resort. (4 marks)

An example of a primary activity that supports Euro Disney would be farms that supply food. However, most of these may not directly supply Disney, but rather food processing industries that represent an example of a secondary economic activity.

2 What type of legal structure is Disney Resort Paris? What responsibilities does this legal structure place on the owners? (4 marks)

Disney Resort Paris trades under the name Euro Disney and is the equivalent of a public limited company or plc for a British registered company. Its shareholders own it. The two main shareholders are its parent company, The Walt Disney Company, and Prince Alwaleed. They own over half the shares between them. The shareholders have liability should the business fail, but it is limited to the value of the shares they own. That's not all, because the company can be sued if it does damage.

3 Evaluate the suitability of this type of legal structure for Euro Disney. (14 marks)

Being a public limited company offers advantages and disadvantages. Euro Disney believes the advantages win. For example, Euro Disney has made huge investments to improve the attractions and facilities at the resort and has plans to continue to do so. Only recently the company opened Walt Disney Studios. All this needs finance. While some comes from loans and some from keeping back past profits, the remainder may come from issuing more shares. This is much easier to do if anyone or any business in the world is allowed to buy them.

The drawback comes in the form of risking losing control. Others can purchase the existing shares in the world stock markets. There could be a takeover. The loss of control is unlikely as the Walt Disney Company owns about 40% of all the shares and it would be reluctant to sell. Another issue is that the company may have to compromise on long-term investment in order to provide short-term gains for its shareholders. The company would be worried about a fall in the value of shares. Some experts view this as a necessary discipline and control on the business that is for the good.

4 In what ways has the development of Euro Disney supported small businesses in the area? (4 marks)

Being a large company Euro Disney will need to trade with a whole range of businesses of different sizes and different types of ownership. Some businesses will be suppliers to Euro Disney. For example, local electricians may have maintenance contracts with the hotels. Local bakers may supply the top hotel with quality fresh produce. Euro Disney is not so much worried by the legal structure of its partners, but by their ability to supply or with customers their ability to pay. Other local small businesses benefit indirectly from the existence of Euro Disney, such as local taxi services and so on.

5 There are many measures that can be used to identify the size of this business. Suggest two measures most suited to Euro Disney and one least suited. Give reasons for your choices. (9 marks)

The size of a business can be measured in a range of ways. For Euro Disney it could be by the 12,000 workers it employs, or by the size of the development covering a land area of nearly 20 sq. km. You could look at the value of the capital employed, which measures the amount of money invested in the company. The level of profits provides another indicator. The level of turnover of over €1000 million suggests that this is a big company. Perhaps the share of the market would also help indicate its size.

Turnover of over €1 billion combined with the 12,000 employees both indicate that this is a big business. By looking at changes over time it is possible to assess whether the company is growing. It is best not to rely on one measure alone. For example, the number of employees may fall even though the turnover may increase as the business uses its employees more effectively.

Using profit levels may be misleading. A business may perform badly in terms of profit one year, but then recover over the next few years. For example, Euro Disney only made a €6 million profit in 1994 compared with €110 million two years later, yet turnover only increased by around 20%. It also needs to be related to the investment in the business. One with much investment would expect to see a good return.

6 Using turnover to measure the size of the company calculate how much the company has grown by between 1994 and 2002. (4 marks)

Turnover in 1994 was €632 million and this rose to €1076 – an increase of €444 million or about 70%

7 What do you understand by the term 'profit'? In which year was the largest operating profit made? (3 marks)

Profit is what is left after costs have been deducted. The largest operating profit was €185 million earned in 2001. However, the 1998 profit margin was highest.

8 Analyse different reasons why Euro Disney needs to raise finance and provide examples of how this may be raised? (8 marks)

Euro Disney would need to raise substantial finance to help set up the business in 1992. There would be land to buy, the park facilities to build plus the hotels and infrastructure. Much of the finance would have been raised from shares or equity and bank loans, which represents debt.

Another reason for requiring finance is to help in emergencies. This protects the business when it is not performing well. Euro Disney had a cash flow problem soon after opening as its target revenue was not met and its labour costs were well above the budget. It may have asked for more bank loans or increased its overdraft.

Euro Disney would require extra finance to help expand the business. Euro Disney wanted to develop attractions and open up a new theme park. Finance could be raised through further loans matched by issuing new shares. Euro Disney may wish to introduce a new computer system. One way of financing this would be to lease the computers with the right to buy at the end of the lease. This way the cost is spread out over the period of the lease.

Finance is also needed to maintain the day-to-day running of the business. Euro Disney needs sufficient working capital to pay suppliers, interest on loans, not to mention its 12,000 employees. Most of the working capital is earned from turnover, but in some winter months this may be insufficient. Often an overdraft is arranged to cover this.

9 What is the difference between the public sector and private sector? In what ways has the public sector contributed to the success of Euro Disney and the region? (6 marks)

The public sector includes activities undertaken by local and national government. The main objective of the public sector is to serve the community. The private sector includes all organisations, which are owned by individuals or groups. The main objective of the private sector is to make a profit. The public sector authorities in the Disney area wanted to develop the region to create jobs and increase prosperity to the underdeveloped community. When Euro Disney approached them they reached a joint agreement where Euro Disney would locate in the area so long as the public sector improved the infrastructure including the road and rail links. There was also agreement that the public sector should provide schools and a college to improve the skills of the new community. By delivering the infrastructure the public sector has made Disneyland Resort Paris much more accessible to millions of potential customers. In return the presence of Disneyland Resort Paris has brought in many jobs as well as tax revenues for the authorities. They each seem to have benefited from each other.

Objectives and strategy: Amazon delivers; the Royal Mail

1a Provide two pieces of evidence that suggests Amazon is a market-oriented business. (2 marks)

b Is the Royal Mail market or product oriented? Explain why. (2 marks)

A market-oriented business aims to make a product that matches what the customer wants. Amazon calls itself a customer company and is highly innovative in its efforts to provide 'an unparalleled on line shopping experience'. The Royal Mail might be regarded as more product oriented as its focus was on its product, namely delivering mail. However, it must change this focus especially in the light of losses and increasing competition.

2 Giving an example using Amazon, what is an aim? (2 marks)

An aim is the idea or vision of where the organisation needs to go if it is to be successful. Amazon wants to be the world's most customer-centric company. It is a very challenging aim. Aims are sometimes incorporated into mission statements.

3 What objectives did the Royal Mail set itself? (4 marks)

An objective is a target that can be measured. It is used to drive activities. The Royal Mail had an objective to turn its loss into a profit. Other objectives might be to reduce the number of strikes by its employees and to lower the pollution by a set level of its activities.

4 Suggest an objective that Amazon might set itself. (2 marks)

Amazon might have an objective to grow by a certain amount each year. This should fit in with its aims of being the world's most customer-centric company. Happy customers will buy more and so the business will grow.

5 What is a strategy? How did strategy change in each organisation? (6 marks)

A strategy is like a plan in that it shows how the objectives will be met. Amazon felt the need to change strategy even though its aims and objectives remained the same. This change was required to keep it competitive. It involved the company becoming distributors (holding stock and being responsible for delivery) as well as e-commerce sellers. A high investment was required for this long-term strategy.
For the Royal Mail the objective of turning a loss into a profit required a strategy to improve efficiency and involved cutbacks in staffing and also closure of loss-making sub-post offices. It also wanted to improve employee relations and might have set objectives on absence and strike days.

6 Construct a simple SWOT analysis for each organisation. (8 marks)

Amazon		Royal Mail	
Strength	Super well-known website that is easy to use	Strength	Infrastructure in post boxes and sorting offices
Weakness	Complex IT system could go wrong	Weakness	Inefficient
Opportunity	Extended range of products sold	Opportunity	Develop the post bus in some urban areas.
Threat	Too dependent on the Internet as an outlet	Threat	Much more competition soon

7 Contrast the culture differences between the two organisations. What recommendations would you make for the Royal Mail in order to improve its culture? (14 marks)

Amazon claims it has a positive culture and treats its employees with respect. The cross-functional teamwork means employees have a chance to meet and work with employees from other areas of the business. They are encouraged to be creative and exchange good ideas. The workers are likely to be more motivated. If they own shares they may work more efficiently to help Amazon improve its

profits since they will receive a share of this.
The past strike record of the Royal Mail suggests that the culture has not been a positive one. It is difficult to change things around, especially when the organisation has to cut back the numbers of workers it has. The lower strike rate may reflect some success in the Royal Mail changing attitudes. Perhaps the Royal Mail needs to listen to its workers more and let them come up with some ideas to improve its competitiveness. This may help to bring about a more positive culture.

8 What is meant by 'social responsibility'? To what extent is the Royal Mail meeting the social objectives of its customers and its owners? (14 marks)

Social responsibility is the business's agenda to meet the needs of its stakeholders. Royal Mail customers want letters delivered on time at an affordable price. They will also want to use local post offices for transactions involving pensions, licences and the like. A more efficient mail service may achieve more reliable delivery, but to be cost effective some rural areas may lose out, as deliveries in these areas are expensive. Closure of post offices must mean longer journeys for many. However, the post bus would be seen as something positive for the community. Being a public sector organisation the owners are the government. It wants the levels of pollution to fall and would give the thumbs up to the Royal Mail's strategy of having less journeys and using less polluting fuels. Recycling its old bikes for charity is a socially responsible action, but even better would be to encourage greater use of bikes to deliver mail.
There seems to be a trade-off between some stakeholders especially at a time when the organisation needs to reduce its costs.

External influences: the market

1 What evidence is there that demand to see films has changed? (4 marks)

Cinema admissions measure the number of customers in a year and data indicates this was lowest in 1984 with 54 million admissions compared with a high of over 142 million in 2000. Closure of cinemas in the 1980s and expansion of multiplexes since also suggests the market has changed.

2a How has demand changed? (2 marks)

Cinema attendances had dramatically halved between 1980 and 1984 suggesting the market was volatile, but since then the market has more than recovered and is now showing a steady growth.

b Suggest possible causes of this change. (6 marks)

The cinema became less fashionable in the early 1980s. Television and home videos were seen as substitute goods and offered a cheaper, more attractive alternative. Matters changed when the cinema industry fought back by making better films, having more successful advertising and through raising the quality of the cinema experience with the introduction of multiplexes. This was matched by a growth in earnings, leaving people with more money to spend on leisure activities.

3 Demonstrate the change in demand using a diagram between 1980 and 2000. (3 marks)

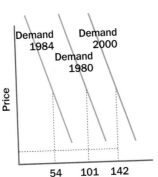

Annual cinema attendance in millions

The demand curve had shifted inwards between 1980 and 1984 meaning that considerably fewer people attended cinemas for a given price. However after 1984 the attendances grew so that by 2000 the demand curve had shifted outwards well beyond 1980 levels.

4 How might the cinema industry react to the trends in the short run and in the long run? (8 marks)

In the short run it is difficult to change the supply. Therefore during the early 1980s cinemas might have reacted by putting on less shows to lower costs or cutting prices to entice back customers. Failure of this strategy meant that some cinemas closed; as shown in the data there were over 100 less screens.
Improved attendances in the short run may have been met with cinemas raising prices or by putting on extra performances. In the long run new multiplex cinemas were built in response to the continued growing demand. Some cinemas that failed to invest may well have still closed down.

5 Demonstrate the change in supply using a diagram. (3 marks)

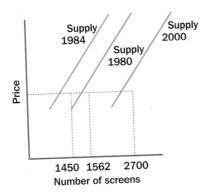

Number of screens

In the early 1980s many cinemas didn't have enough customers to cover costs and went out of business. Some became derelict and others took on different uses. The supply curve had shifted inwards. During the 1990s there was renewed investment in cinemas mainly in building multiplexes, often on the edge of cities near good road links. The supply curve had shifted outwards.

6 To what extent is there a danger of over supply in the market? (10 marks)

There is always a risk when entrepreneurs invest in new businesses that there will be over supply or excess supply. This occurs when there is too much being supplied in the market. In cinemas this may result in them being unable to fill seats on release of a new blockbuster film. Demand might go down in the short term, for example in a period of good weather. Cinemas would have more empty seats than before. A temporary over supply may be overcome by lowering prices until the market clears. There will, however, come a point when the market becomes saturated or mature. This is a long-term position of over supply. In the 1980s it was caused by a drop in demand. Today it might be caused by investors getting it wrong and simply building too many new cinema developments for the market. Finally, a new competitor in the market with a different and exciting strategy may attract customers from existing cinemas causing them problems.

7a How is easyCinema attempting to gain a competitive advantage? (4 marks)

Competitive advantage means having something more than your competitor. You might have a better product or lower costs. easyCinema feel its competitive advantage will be both. First, all bookings are through the Internet and, secondly, this will help it cut costs and it promises to pass these cuts onto the customer.

b What effect will easyCinema have on the competition should it be successful and open cinemas throughout the UK? (8 marks)

easyCinema's pricing policy is likely to create more demand for cinema goers. This is because lower prices increase demand. A proportion will be new, but some of these will be attracted from existing cinemas and easyCinema is seen as a close substitute to them. The reaction of the other cinemas will depend on how many customers they lose. They may feel they are aiming for a different type of customer. Their product, although more expensive, is better and multiplexes are well-known brands with a good reputation for comfort and service. You can also see new films as soon as they are released which fits into their heavy promotion. Many have close links with the film distributors. Some small independent cinemas may go out of business or seek a new competitive advantage such as screening specialist films.

External influences: interest and exchange rates, taxation and business cycle changes

1 What is meant by the terms 'business cycle', 'recession' and 'boom'? (6 marks)

The business cycle shows the pattern of growth and decline in the economy. It creates the fluctuation in demand for many products. During a recession demand is growing more slowly or even declining and during a boom output increases to meet rising demand. The business cycle forms a pattern over several years.

2 What decisions did Terry make during a period of economic growth? How might such decisions affect the inflation rate if adopted by most businesses? (6 marks)

Terry wanted to take on more orders. He worked out that increasing overtime would not be a sufficient measure to be able to meet deadlines. Terry introduced another shift. To attract the right staff he had to increase rates of pay and passed on the increase in costs to his customers in the form of higher prices. If other businesses were making similar decisions the inflation rate would increase.

3a National Insurance is a direct tax. Define direct tax and provide another example of it. (2 marks)

A direct tax is any tax on incomes. Income tax is such a tax. The more you earn the more tax you pay.

b Explain the effect of a decrease in direct tax on disposable incomes. (4 marks)

Reducing direct taxes such as income tax leaves employees with a greater disposable income since they are left with more money to take home. This is likely to lead to increased spending.

4 What is an indirect tax? Give two examples. (3 marks)

An indirect tax is any tax on spending. Value Added Tax is placed on most goods and services we buy. We also pay excise duties when we buy fuel, alcohol or tobacco.

5a In what ways might an increase in National Insurance affect both businesses and the economy? (4 marks)

A rise in National Insurance will mean a reduction in disposable incomes as employees pay a part of this. This may reduce spending and therefore demand for goods and services. It is a double blow to businesses because they also make National Insurance contributions. Their costs would rise. They must either reduce their profit margins or pass the increased costs onto customers in the form of price rises. The net overall effect is to increase inflation, dampen down demand and reduce growth in the economy.

b Suggest how this might affect our competitiveness against countries with lower inflation rates. (4 marks)

Higher prices will result in our products costing more to people and businesses in countries abroad. They will want to buy less from us and our exports will fall.

6 Why might the government choose to increase National Insurance at the same time as the economy is slowing down? (4 marks)

If the economy is slowing down, an increase in taxation may serve to increase the rate of the slowdown. A National Insurance tax increase reduces disposable income as workers will take home less pay and so have less to spend. On the face of it such a tax change would seem a strange choice for the government. However, if the economy is not performing so well the government will have less tax revenue and find it difficult to balance its budget. It may be forced to raise taxes.

7 Evaluate Terry's strategy of looking for new markets in Europe. (10 marks)

Terry's business may be in danger of collapsing unless he finds new markets. Looking for customers in the eurozone may give him a competitive advantage because the fall in the value of the pound has made UK imports cheaper to buy for customers in countries like France and Germany. There are some difficulties including the importing businesses needing to pay transaction costs when exchanging euros for pounds. Terry would also be wary that exchange rates could move in the opposite direction. The value of the pound may rise making his exports less competitive. He may prefer the UK to join the eurozone.

8 Explain how an increase in the UK exchange rate might affect UK businesses? (6 marks)

An increase in the UK exchange rate would mean you would get more foreign currency for your pounds. It would make imports cheaper, but exports would be more expensive for foreigners to buy. In the very short run businesses may find it difficult to change suppliers or be reluctant to do so if they believe the exchange market will soon move in the opposite direction. One way round this is to hedge your bets and reduce the effects of currency fluctuations by buying currency now for delivery at a future date. If the exchange rate stayed high then domestic suppliers may find their position less competitive against importers. The exporters may also find their demand squeezed.

9 Analyse the effect changes in interest rates will have on Terry's business and on the economy in general. (9 marks)

Terry would be concerned at interest rate rises, because converting vehicles requires him to pay for materials and labour long before he receives sales revenue. The effect would be more significant if he had a large overdraft. Higher interest rates make investment in new equipment more expensive. Higher interest rates also mean less borrowing and lower spending. He may have fewer orders as a result. In short, Terry's costs would rise, the demand for his products fall and he would be more reluctant to invest in his business. The aggregate effect of such business decisions would be a slowdown in the economy.
Interest payment is a cost to a business. Therefore an interest rate decrease has the effect of reducing his repayments and therefore his costs. Low interest rates make investment more attractive because the cost of borrowing has fallen. It also means people and organisations are more likely to borrow and spend more. This aggregate effect would be to lead to an increase in economic growth rates.

Other influences: changing population, technology and consumer laws

1 What impact will the change in demography have on

a the government (4 marks)

b the NHS (4 marks)

c NHS suppliers? (4 marks)

a. An ageing population is more expensive for the government because it increases pension payments, demand for healthcare and other facilities required by older people.

b. An ageing population will increase the demand for health services and health products as older people tend to have greater health needs. The NHS is a public sector organisation that has the major share of the health market at the customer end. It will have to supply more services if money is available from central government, become more efficient or become more selective about the services it offers.
With fewer younger people around the NHS will need to be more flexible in its approach to recruitment and retention of older employees if it is not to have a shortage of doctors and nurses.

c. The NHS is a major buyer of health supplies from the private sector. Suppliers will react to the increased demand from the NHS. Provided the government increases payments to the NHS, demand for products should rise. They may equally have difficulty finding enough staff.

2 How might the government meet increasing spending on health services? (6 marks)

One option would be to raise tax revenues. However, demographic changes require this to be raised from a smaller working population. This would place an increasing burden on future workers and businesses. An alternative is to charge for health services. This would raise revenues and serve to reduce demand, but would be politically unpopular as a good percentage of the population may not be able to afford to pay. Another option would be to encourage more and more people to take out private health insurance or even to privatise the whole service. The government might choose to do a bit of each.

3 The E-Commerce Directive is one of many laws that support the consumer. Why might some businesses welcome laws like these while others see them as yet another burden? (8 marks)

Laws are necessary to protect stakeholders like shareholders, employees and consumers. Consumer law sets out a minimum of good practice. Given an option, many businesses would not follow good practice either out of ignorance or simply because following it can add to the business costs. However, such laws will provide an even playing field. They allow consumers to receive the products they think they are buying and make it fairer for businesses like Goodnessdirect.co.uk who already look after their customer interests. Businesses that do not provide good practice before a law change will be worried about increasing costs.
Some laws are very excessive and the extra costs may be enough to force some out of business. Finally, laws need enforcing and this means local authorities setting up trading standards offices and financing these.

4 What is redundancy? How might the government minimise the redundancies that will come about through its proposed change to provide online services? (8 marks)

Redundancy occurs when the work a person does is no longer required. The contract then ends. If more and more people use online government services for tax returns, passport requests and the like there will be less need for civil servants to process forms. The government as an employer has some responsibility to its workers. It might offer to train these workers in areas where demand is increasing like the NHS. It may manage the changes over a period of time so that when someone leaves he or she will not be replaced. This means fewer compulsory redundancies. On the other hand some employees will volunteer for redundancy especially if the nature of the remaining jobs changes or if they have skills that are in demand elsewhere.

5 Why does the government wish UK businesses to embrace this technology? Why is it important for it to lead by example? (6 marks)

The broadband technology is part of the UK infrastructure. Investment in broadband will help businesses work more effectively and can help reduce their costs. Where there is strong competition these cost savings will be passed onto their customers. We can buy more with our money. This technology can open up potential markets to businesses and make them more competitive both here and abroad. The government is a major provider of services. Using online services will reduce its own costs and its actions increase the demand for broadband. This in turn will encourage companies that provide broadband, like BT, to invest in providing access to a greater part of the UK.

6 Analyse how the government might support small rural businesses that do not have access to broadband? (9 marks)

The government may offer lower business rates or taxes to businesses waiting for broadband to come to their area. This method may keep some rural businesses from moving, but it does nothing to speed up the national access to broadband. Therefore the government may prefer to offer subsidies to the companies providing fast computer access to convert telephone exchanges in rural areas.

Other influences: employment laws

1 Outline two reasons why the government wants to improve working parents' rights? (2 marks)

Improving working parents' rights helps working people with children. By doing so, more people are able to work and the cost of benefits is reduced.

2 Evaluate the effects of the new working parents' rights on a small business and a large company. (10 marks)

The new working parents' benefits will increase business costs, as businesses will have to adapt to meet the requirements. At the same time they will suffer a lack of continuity in the work place. This may place a strain on employees who have to cover the workload. Some tasks may not be covered so well and the business will be less efficient. This could be significant in a small business where the absence of one or two employees can have a large impact. Larger businesses can cope with the changes, as it will be easier for them to arrange cover and cope with job share and other flexible working requests.

3 What is an employment tribunal? (2 marks)

An employment tribunal is set up to decide whether people have been treated fairly by their employers. The tribunal for Mr Mead decided to throw out his claim, as a contract worker does not have the same rights as a full-time employee.

4 What is meant by an employment contract? What are the arguments for and against the swimwear workers' case? (8 marks)

An employment contract is a legal agreement between the employer and the employee. It lays down the rights and responsibilities of each party to the contract. The swimwear workers' union has gone to court because it believes the employer has broken his responsibility by failing to pay the workers what he owed and also by making them redundant when he then set up a similar business. It looks like he was ethically and morally at fault, but he may argue that his previous business failed and once his limited liabilities have been met he is free under the law to set up a new business. The tribunal will have to decide who is right.

Other influences: the government as a consumer, provider and constrainer

1 What is a tender? (2 marks)

In the case of the road building, tenders are the quotes given by construction companies to build the roads on behalf of the government. The construction companies will explain how they will carry out the work and what it will cost. The lowest tender will get the job as long as the government is satisfied that the work can be carried out properly.

2 Explain why the taxpayer should subsidise a private sector business such as a ferry service. (4 marks)

A subsidy to the private sector has to be paid for and it is the taxpayer who must cough up. Therefore there should be some social benefit to the community. If it were left to the free market the ferry operator would not make a profit and so there would be no service. The alternative is likely to be a longer and more expensive journey. The £1 million a year subsidy acts to reduce the business costs and so

make the service profitable. The community will gain as local trade will increase and costs and journey time between the two locations is reduced.

3a State one difference between a merger and a take over. (2 marks)

b Analyse the factors the Competition Commission might take into account to help it form a judgement about mergers or takeovers. (9 marks)

A merger is when two businesses agree to join together and a takeover is when one business buys out another. The Competition Commission is a government agency, which is charged with encouraging competition between businesses. The Commission will investigate mergers or takeovers to see if it is in the general public interest. It will look at if the merger means a business can dominate the market. In the case of GWR it was concerned that it could raise the cost of advertising because it had a local monopoly. The Commission would also look at consumer choice and if the merger would reduce costs to customers.

Other influences: the EU and the environment

1 What is meant by social costs? Provide an example of social costs from the evidence and one of your own. (4 marks)

Social costs are the costs to the business of making products plus the costs that are paid by other people and the government. Businesses can damage the environment deliberately through smoke emissions from coal-fired power stations and accidentally, as with oil spills from tankers. It is not easy to calculate social costs. For example, how do you price the traffic congestion associated with big football games?

2 Outline two of the social costs associated with the Prestige oil tanker disaster. (4 marks)

Tourism in the area is normally worth €1.5 billion and 67,000 people depend on tourism in one way or another. With bookings down 40% on last year many of the workers will be worried about their jobs especially those employed part time. In addition oyster workers have seen the price of oysters collapse as buyers reflect the fear that the oysters may be polluted.
As well as businesses being affected the local authorities have to pay for the clearing up of the beaches.

3a How is the EU intending to manage social costs? (2 marks)

b What impact will this have on businesses? (2 marks)

c Describe three other options open to governments or local authorities to manage social costs. (6 marks)

a. The EU wants to pass a law making polluters liable for their actions. This has the effect of making all costs internal to the business.

b. Most businesses will take out insurance to cover their liability and consequently their costs will increase. The business community feels that some businesses will become less competitive especially against those outside the EU who do not bear such costs.

c. There is a real danger of over-fishing in European seas and so the EU has set limits or quotas on the amount that can be fished. The EU could encourage recycling by setting targets. Taxation helps to raise costs and reduces demand. This is the prime purpose of the London congestion charge.

4 What is the purpose of pressure groups? (2 marks)

Pressure groups represent people with similar views who try to influence the decisions taken by businesses, local authorities and governments. Mast Sanity is concerned about the health effects of mobile phone masts on the local community.

5 Discuss the motives a company like Shell have by trying to minimise the social costs of its activities. (lines 38–65) (14 marks)

Big businesses have become increasingly aware of the need to satisfy a broad range of stakeholder interests especially when they are a well-known brand like Shell. Clearly they have to work within the framework of the law, but it may also make sense to be ethical. For example, Shell may very well undertake a PEST analysis. Politically the government is promoting sustainable growth, which means not putting at risk future resources. Hence Shell is researching new energy sources. Environmentally Shell is aware of pressure groups targeting it as a polluter. It is looking at its actions on climate change, biodiversity and pollution. Socially it has clear views on bribery. Shell can also use its research and development resources to produce cleaner fuels. This ethical stance makes it easier to recruit employees and provides it with a stronger socially responsible brand. The CEO sees this as being in the interest of the business and presumably its stakeholders. Not all businesses will try to minimise the social costs of their actions. Smaller businesses on the margins of survival will be very reluctant to accept any unnecessary increase in costs. They would view this as making them uncompetitive. Big companies would be showing greater responsibility if they only bought from suppliers who themselves were socially accountable.

6 Evaluate the costs and benefits of being a social and ethical business. (14 marks)

Moving towards a more social and ethical approach will often add costs to a business. For example, Shell promises not to tolerate corruption and bribery. To carry this out it will have to closely monitor its workforce. It will also risk losing business in certain countries where corruption is endemic. Being more innovative, such as in researching cleaner fuels, will increase research and development costs. However, the result might be the development of more environmental products that will give the business a competitive edge. Working with rather than against pressure groups means the company is less likely to receive bad publicity and is more likely to do the right thing first time. Being upfront and transparent requires that the

information is available to all stakeholders. Shell includes its actions in its annual report to shareholders and in published environmental audits. Pressure groups will keep a close eye and may be all too willing to publicise things that have gone wrong. For example, it looks like Shell was not too upfront when it allowed T Mobile to use its petrol stations to erect disguised masts.

7 What would happen if the government increased the restrictions of erecting mobile phone masts? (4 marks)

The risk of ill-health from living or working near masts would be reduced. The trade-off would be a poorer national coverage for users of mobile phones. The mobile phone companies may research new technology that would allow them to use fewer masts or even share them.

8 What does Unilever mean by 'the practices of suppliers must be in line with our own' (lines 80–82)? (6 marks)

Unilever needs to buy raw materials from a range of suppliers. The cost of purchasing these forms a significant part of Unilever's total costs. Unilever believes it would not be sufficient for it to be socially and ethical responsible for its own actions without its suppliers following the same practices. For example, Unilever wouldn't want to buy fish from boats that broke fish quotas or used nets that caught young fish.

End of Part 1 assessment

Paper 1: Businesses, their objectives and environment

(This is not a model answer and will have typical good and bad points.)

1 James established his business as a sole trader. State two features of a sole trader. (2 marks)

Student answer: James as a sole trader has complete control over his business. On the downside James has to face unlimited liability meaning that he would stand to lose more than just the £4000 he invested if the business were to fail.

The answer links two features of a sole trader to the case study. Other features that could be considered would include difficulty in raising finance, fewer legal constraints, lack of skills and no one to share decisions. This is a Level 1 question.

2 Outline two factors likely to affect James's ability to supply products to his customers. (4 marks)

Student answer: James needs to supply his customers with guitars, amplifiers and accessories. He may find it difficult to gain credit from suppliers as he has only just started. Because he is a small business he is likely to have to pay more for his stock. This may make his products too expensive for customers to buy. He will also be limited by the amount of space to display and store the equipment.

sellers are influenced by costs in deciding how much to supply. The answer attempts to focus on these increased costs. The question only asked for two factors to be considered. The examiner will ignore the extra reasons given. This is a Level 2 question.

3 James opened his business in 2002 and he hoped to 'make sufficient money to retire in about 20 years' time' (line 9). Analyse why James's business objectives might change over this period of time. (9 marks)

Student answer: An objective gives the business some idea of where it intends to go. One of James's initial objectives was to make enough to be able to retire in 20 years' time. This is the profit objective. It is the reward for the risk that James has taken.

He has started as a sole trader and was prepared to grow. In October the sales were high and had grown, so growth would have been a new objective. For big companies this might be measured by an increase in market share, but for James it might have been to double sales. The strategy behind this would have been to set up other shops. James would need to raise more finance and may have had to consider becoming a private limited company. In April, he was reviewing his progress in a different light. James had a range of expensive stock that was not shifting. The number of customers entering the shop in March was half that in December. He was worried about being able to pay the interest on the £25,000 loan. He was at great risk of becoming bankrupt. The threats to his business now make survival the key objective. If his business failed the receivers would sell off the stock cheaply and he would still owe the bank money.

The answer considers the three broad objectives as indicated in the evidence and has some analysis, which is required in this Level 3 question. The answer goes on to relate objectives to a possible strategy for the growth objective.

4 Evaluate the possible ways in which James might judge the success of his first year's trading (14 marks)

Student answer: Objectives, which are measurable, can be used to judge the success of any business. For James he might relate this to a number of indicators. First, he would consider the level of profit earned in the year. This information isn't given although it seems that the last few months' trading have been at a loss. James is worried about being able to pay bills such as the interest repayments on his loan. He may look at the overall sales figures and not just recent months, especially if the sales pattern is seasonal. He may be in profit for the overall year and he has survived. However, the fall in number of customers through the door might be worrying. It would indicate that he has not achieved the growth objective. Other objectives might not be so easily measured, but would be important to James. These might include the freedom to make his own decisions and shape the business. He would also want to consider the value of the business to other stakeholders such as employees. Having to make one of his employees redundant and reducing the hours of the other has helped him reduce costs, but indicates a lack of success in supporting his staff.

There is good analysis, which will lead to a high Level 3. The answer fails to reach Level 4. An evaluation requires you to weigh up the overall success of the business, e.g. I think that the overall success is limited. The business has survived, but it has fewer employees and is satisfying fewer customers. It is at risk of defaulting on payments to the bank, which has a £25,000 stake in the company through its loan. Something needs to be done to help ensure the business survives, especially given the possible downturn in the economy.

5 Discuss whether James should buy the electric guitar leads from Andy. (14 marks)

Student answer: James needs to reduce costs. Reducing costs and keeping prices the same means he has more cash available to pay the other bills like the interest payments. Alternatively by lowering prices for electric leads, demand should increase and some customers attracted into the shop by the lower prices might buy other items. Hence it is very tempting to accept the offer from Andy especially at this critical time when sales have been falling and the economy may be facing a downturn. If the public are worried about their future they may be more reluctant to spend. At first sight this would seem to support his objective of survival. However, there is a huge ethical issue here. Paying cash for the leads from Andy means that no tax is paid and this is against the law. Tax evasion is not fair on others, forcing them to pay more tax than they need in order to keep up public spending. By paying cash up front with no records James will have no comeback should the goods prove to be really bad.
Selling poorer quality leads that also might be unsafe is fooling your customers who are the lifeblood of your business. The standard of the goods must be suspect, otherwise why did the factory in Eastern Europe close down? When customers realise this they may not wish to use the shop again. They may complain to the Trading Standards Office who may then inspect the goods. Bad publicity from such actions would almost certainly lead to a big drop in customers. It is unlikely that buying these leads will have a significant impact on saving costs. I would recommend that James does not take the risk. It may provide a small short-term benefit but it has medium-term drawbacks. Rather than solve his problems this action may worsen them. Instead James should look at other ways of increasing revenues and cutting costs. He may even consider whether the rewards for running his business are enough.

The answer is balanced as it looks at the possible benefits and implications should James go ahead with this purchase. It also comes up with a sound judgement and so moves into a Level 4 type answer. The last paragraph does well to assess the impact and relate this to a time scale. It also ends by suggesting alternatives. There is some good use of relevant terms.

Marketing: Chester Zoo

1 In what ways does the zoo's marketing objectives help support its overall objectives? (4 marks)

The zoo's marketing objectives are to increase the number of visitors and what they spend. This will increase its revenues overall and the zoo will be able to spend more on supporting and promoting conservation. If marketing succeeds in getting more to attend during slack months it will help the zoo ease its cash flow especially since it will have high overhead costs.

2 In what ways is the Zoo both customer and product oriented? (4 marks)

By supporting the conservation of animals and plants Chester Zoo must be product oriented. However, the zoo's main source of income is from its customers and if their needs are catered for they will continue to visit the zoo and spend. Its market research activities focus on providing high standards of care and high quality visitor facilities that cater for all ages.

3 Discuss two promotional methods that might be suitable for the zoo to use to encourage new customers. What methods might be suitable to encourage repeat customers? (8 marks)

The zoo spent £670,000 on advertising and promotion and much of this was to encourage new customers or repeat customers. Encouraging new customers requires above-the-line direct advertising. Most visitors to the zoo have heard about it through television adverts and by promotion in regional papers. To be cost effective the adverts will start around April in time for Easter and be aimed at media watched or read by socio-economic grouping C1 and C2 who make up 70% of visitors. It is best to tempt customers to repeat a visit while they are in the zoo. This is point of sales promotion.
Below-the-line advertising may be the more effective method. For example, leaflets handed out may offer discount vouchers and visitors may be encouraged to enter a prize competition. The name and address included will allow direct marketing through mailshots.

4 What is market segmentation? How and why might the zoo segment its market? (4 marks)

Market segmentation is when different types of customers are identified. Chester Zoo might try matching customer groups to different products on offer thereby finding new market niches. For example, the zoo offers conference facilities especially in winter when there are fewer traditional visitors. The Halloween evening seems to be targeted at families with teenage children and the Safari is perhaps aimed at work social outings.

5 Explain one internal and one external factors that have influenced the rate of growth of customers to the zoo. (6 marks)

An internal factor would be the investment in new and better facilities to attract the public. Another might be an improvement in the quality of customer care. Both these should lead to an increase in demand. External factors might include the general rise in living standards, but a recession or an external shock, such as the foot-and-mouth outbreak, can have a negative effect, as can new competitors from theme parks. The marketing department needs to be aware of all this by undertaking market research and must liaise with other departments so that everybody is working towards meeting the overall objectives.

6 Assume a new marketing campaign costs £20,000 and manages to bring in an extra 3000 adults. Would it be regarded as successful? (5 marks)

The extra 3000 adults have an average spend of £12.39, which means extra revenue of around £37,000. This is £17,000 above the marketing budget. However, extra visitors will add extra costs, such as the food and beverages they buy. If these are a lot less than £17,000 then the campaign may be viewed as successful.

7 Explain why market research is important to the zoo. (4 marks)

Market research provides the zoo with essential information about how it is doing and how its competitors are performing. It also provides useful information about past and current trends in people's spending habits and these can be used to forecast future trends. The information gathered can be used to help make more informed decisions about matters such as investment, pricing and promotion.

8 How might it best carry out its research? (6 marks)

Like many other organisations, Chester Zoo targets research at likely customers. Sampling too few people will not produce accurate results. However, consulting too many can make it very expensive. The zoo employs marketing consultants to help make sure the research is sound. The primary research involves finding out information tailor-made to the businesses needs, such as what the zoo visitors feel about the facilities, where they come from, their ages, how long they stayed and what were their likes and dislikes. Secondary research collects together information that already exists. The zoo will be interested in finding out what people spend their money on and probably collect this electronically from the tills. It will also add up the number of visitors each day to provide the number of visitors per month. Other secondary sources might lie outside the organisation. Chester Zoo will want to know what its competitors charge and what facilities they offer to the customers. It will also want to know readership socio-economic groups for newspapers so it could choose the most appropriate to advertise in. Government statistics can provide useful information on spending trends as can market intelligence reports.

9 Analyse the results of past market research. (8 marks)

The majority of visitors, some 70%, are from the C1 and C2 socio-economic grouping made up of clerical, administration and manual skilled type workers. About 40% of visitors are under 15 and these are likely to be accompanied by parents or grandparents (who make up 11% of visitors). More detail on the breakdown of the average number in a family and the relationship between younger and older members would provide a more complete picture.
Over two-thirds believe their visit was very good value or excellent value and this may explain why over 60% of visitors return within 3 years. Only 13% visit the same year, however, and improvements to this figure might be a target for the marketing department.
The promotion techniques seem successful, as 54% have heard about the zoo's promotion. However, the zoo still

might aim to increase this figure. Television is the most effective way of reaching potential customers but it is expensive and the reason why some other methods might be ineffective is because little effort is made. More detailed research would help provide the real reasons here.

The monthly attendance figures are no surprise largely reflecting the traditional leisure peaks starting at Easter and slowing down in September. The worst months are in winter.

10 Why has the zoo been able to raise its prices regularly over the past 12 years? (8 marks)

Chester Zoo has increased prices from £5 to £11 in 12 years. This significant increase cannot be wholly explained by inflation. It might be that customers base prices on perceived value, especially since the zoo has such a good reputation. Chester Zoo will have been able to do this for two possible reasons. The first is that the demand for visits has increased over the years because the promotion is more effective or people have higher incomes and it is more fashionable to spend this on leisure activities. This is shown by an outward shift in the demand curve. Another reason might be that the demand is price inelastic. In this case a given percentage rise in price results in a smaller percentage drop in demand. It means total revenues will rise. This is shown by a movement of the demand curve in the diagram below. Effective promotion is one factor that may explain this, because it makes alternatives to a visit to Chester Zoo seem inferior. The promotion, however, must be combined with a positive customer experience and this requires investment in facilities. Chester Zoo must be careful about raising prices because as prices rise so demand becomes more price elastic.

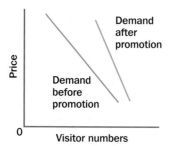

11 Produce and justify a marketing plan to increase customers who might be attracted to an event outside normal zoo hours. (10 marks)

Chester Zoo's marketing plans should meet its marketing objectives. Namely, to encourage customers to come back, get new visitors, spread them more evenly over the whole season, raise awareness of the zoo's work in conservation and sell more food, drink and souvenirs. The Halloween event might well serve to achieve all these. Tickets are priced higher than the normal entrance fee as there is a disco and supper, so they will be buying more food and drink. The price of tickets could be contribution pricing, as the fixed costs of the zoo will be accounted for in the normal entrance price. The shop will have a Halloween theme to its products. Past experience will inform the purchasing department of what to order. The creepy happenings might easily be linked to bats and a quiz may provide educational information on conservation, which then meets another

objective. Halloween is held during an out-of-season period and this should help bring in extra cash. However, promotion can be a problem as it is a period when the zoo spends less on this. The promotion can be targeted to members through mailshots. Advertising on the website and making leaflets available within the zoo during the summer period might bring in a few more customers. This may attract existing customers who are likely to be those most interested in the event. To attract new customers the zoo might advertise locally in the press and on radio. At the very least it will raise brand awareness.

Accounting and finance: The Carpet Barn

1 What is the purpose of budgets? How was the marketing budget monitored and why did it need changing? (8 marks)

A budget is a financial plan linked to the business objectives. The marketing budget is to support The Carpet Barn reach its objective of 50 sales per month and £1000 has been set aside each month for this purpose. Monitoring sales figures showed that the marketing was ineffective. Perhaps the money was not spent on the best types of promotion. Certainly Cai and Ellen thought it was insufficient and increased the budget by £3500, increasing sales by £12,000 during the three-month period compared with December and January. The owners might view this as successful since the variable costs of the extra sales came to £6000.

2 What happened to the overall budgets on expenditure and revenue over the second 6 months of trading? What might have caused the difference between the budget forecast and the actual performance? (8 marks)

The revenue forecast was too high even in the revised version. The Carpet Barn was £11,000 down on the target. Sales were lower because the demand for carpets nationally had fallen and some of the people in the town were worried about their jobs. Expenditure was £2000 less because less stock was needed although the business purchased £3500 more than was needed in the first three months. The reduction in stock more than compensated for the increase in expenses due to the new marketing campaign.

3 Using the payback method how long would it take for the investment in the computer system to have paid for itself? (4 marks)

The purchase would cost £6000, but save £4000 in wages each year. So it would take 18 months to pay back.

4 Name a variable cost for this business. (1 mark)

The cost of carpets is variable because they are dependent on sales.

5 State two fixed costs faced by The Carpet Barn. (2 marks)

The Carpet Barn pays its owners a salary and this has been fixed for the year. The marketing budget was originally fixed. The business will have to pay rent and business tax.

6 What is the contribution made by each sale? (4 marks)

The contribution is the sales price minus the variable costs or £500 − £250 = £250. This means each carpet sale contributes £250 towards covering the fixed costs of the business.

7 Calculate the break-even point. (4 marks)

For The Carpet Barn the break-even point is the amount of sales per month that will neither give it a loss or a profit. It is the fixed costs divided by the contribution. That is, £11,000 divided by £250 = 44. The Carpet Barn would need to make 44 sales per month to break even.

8 What was the forecasted margin of safety? (2 marks)

The projected sales were 50 per month and the break-even 44 per month giving a small margin of safety of 6 sales per month.

9 What would be the average overhead if sales were 40, 50 and 60 a month? (3 marks)

Monthly overhead	Sales per month		Average overhead
£11,000 divided by	40	=	£275.00
£11,000 divided by	50	=	£220.00
£11,000 divided by	60	=	£183.33

10 Use the data in the case study to explain the difference between profit and cash flow. (6 marks)

Cash flow is the movement of cash in and out of the business. For example, in January The Carpet Barn received £20,000 from sales, but paid out £22,615. Cai had to arrange an overdraft with the bank to cover the shortfall. Cash payments are made for materials, wages and other costs. They are often paid out before cash comes in from sales. In this sense a business may have a large order book that will turn in high profits but have a cash deficit. In the second 6-month period the inflow was £134,000 and the outflow was £140,400 meaning a net cash outflow of £6400, but the net profit for this period was −£2900 leaving a difference of £3500, which is because the business had increased its stocks by that amount. The actual shortage, however, was not £6400, but £3400 because the business had a carry over of £3000 in the opening balance in November.

11 Calculate the net cash flow for the month of December. (2 marks)

£20,000 came in from sales and £22,000 went out in payments resulting in a net cash flow of −£2000.

12 Calculate the closing balance in March. (2 marks)

The opening balance was negative, −£3725, and the net cash flow that month was positive at £415 making the closing balance −£3310, resulting in the overdraft facility being used.

13 In which months did The Carpet Barn need to draw on its overdraft facility? (2 marks)

From January through to April.

14 Comment on the profitability of the business. (4 marks)

The business went from a small profit of £500 in the first 6 months to a loss of £2900 in the second 6 months. Much of this loss occurred in November, December and January when sales were well down on the target. This meant that average overheads were higher. The business cannot carry on in this way. It must think about whether it can find cheaper suppliers, cut its overheads by perhaps cutting salaries or find ways of improving sales.

15 Comment on the liquidity of the business using information from the balance sheets. (4 marks)

The business has a positive working capital figure, although this has gone down from £9000 to £7200. However, much of the working capital is tied up in stocks which showed an increase from £5000 to £8500. Sometimes it is difficult to shift stocks. The carpets in the barn may not be what people want. The acid test ratio excludes the stocks in its calculation.

16 What would have happened to the working capital if The Carpet Barn had reduced the level of stocks? (4 marks)

Reducing the level of stocks by, say, £5000 would result in lower amounts owed to creditors and less being paid in the past would have increased the cash levels. The total of these two would be £5000, so the working capital would remain unchanged unless the cash was used for other purposes.

17 Equipment and the vehicles were depreciated over the 6 months. Where would the £1000 depreciation show up within the profit and loss account? (2 marks)

The £1000 depreciation would show up as expenses on the profit and loss account.

18 The decision Cai and Ellen needed to make was whether or not to cease trading. What would you recommend they do? (12 marks)

Cai and Ellen have put in considerable effort and some £4500 each of their personal savings into this venture. However the business has made a loss of £2900 in the first year. They are also liable to pay the creditors. The bank's overdraft was granted only on the basis that, as a final resort, they would have to sell their personal assets to make good the sums owed. In short, they have unlimited liability for the debts they incur.

Currently they have an overdraft with the bank of £3400 and they owe creditors £1000. On top of this they have a long-term loan of £6000 making the total short- and long-term debt £10,400.

By ending trading they would be able to sell their assets. They might receive only a portion of the value of the fixed assets and the stock. If they received half this would bring in £2750. Add the £3000 they would collect from customers who have yet to settle their bills and perhaps £4250 from the sale of stock then they would raise £10000. The £400 shortfall would come from their savings. They would lose the initial £4500 they each invested in the business although they had each earned a £20,000 salary.

With the decline in carpet sales nationally and the threat of redundancies in the town it would seem difficult other than to perhaps break even. They could earn a similar salary by working for someone else. Given these circumstances I would recommend ceasing trading. However, if they were really determined and like being their own bosses I would give them another year, but on the condition that they diversified their business to include laminate flooring. They would only need a few more customers per month to be successful. Cai could use his skills as a carpet fitter to lay laminate flooring. The Carpet Barn would need to change its name, perhaps to The Carpet and Flooring Barn and revised objectives and budgets would need to be made.

People in organisations: more nurses needed

1 What do you understand by the terms 'recruitment' and 'retention'? (4 marks)

Recruitment is the process of identifying the need for new employees through to attracting applicants and finally selecting the best ones for the vacancies.
Retention is keeping the employees with your business.

2 What is workforce planning and why is it important in a large organisation like the NHS? (6 marks)

Large organisations usually employ many people in a range of specialist posts, all of which are necessary to help them meet their objectives. It is essential that such organisations estimate the need for new recruits in the face of changes in demand and of changes in levels of staff turnover. For instance there is a growing demand for increased healthcare because we are an ageing population at a time when staff turnover has increased. Workforce planning does not stop here. It will account for how organisations cater for new technologies and new objectives. People will then require training to support them in undertaking new tasks. For example, more sophisticated operations demand different styles of nursing care.

3 What might explain the high labour turnover in the past and what has been proposed to reduce it? To what extent do you believe these proposals will be sufficient? (12 marks)

High labour turnover may be the norm for nurses in the NHS as many of them are women who take a career break to raise families. However, if working conditions worsen or pay levels are not competitive with other jobs nurses will leave for reasons of dissatisfaction. One worry the government has is losing experienced highly skilled nurses. The pay restructuring is designed to reward these employees more than others. In this way it is targeting the key shortage areas with greater financial rewards. High pay awards for all nurses would cost the NHS too much and mean that there would be less money available for equipment and medicines. It is difficult to predict how successful this measure would be without further information such as detailed labour turnover figures and data on the changes in those applying for training. The government may well need to take note of the RCN research on stress and poor morale. Perhaps the NHS needs to ensure it is providing Herzberg's hygiene factors such as having better staff room areas, and more crèche facilities. The new pay structure may provide some motivators if it encourages achievement by giving skilled staff more responsibility and a wider range of tasks through job enlargement and multi-skilling.

People in organisations: Prudential to relocate call centre

1 What do you understand by the term 'redundancy'? (2 marks)

Redundancy occurs when a person loses his or her job because it no longer exists. It might be through a change in technology, a lack of demand for the product or service or that the business is to relocate.

2 Explain why businesses like the Prudential have decided to transfer call centre work abroad. (4 marks)

Prudential has to remain competitive with other companies. It may feel that it can get better added value from the higher skilled and cheaper workforce in India or it may be worried about recruitment problems in Reading, perhaps due to a shortage of people with the skills. Labour turnover rates may be much lower in India, saving recruitment and induction training costs.

3 Analyse the concerns Prudential might have about such moves. (6 marks)

The call centre staff in India may not know about the UK culture and will need training in the soft skills areas of how to deal with UK customers. Prudential must be sure that the Indian call centre can deliver a customer care as good as or better than the UK call centre. Its induction programme will have to be very thorough and include educating the Indian graduates to the way of life of its UK customers. It must be careful about following employment laws. There is a cost to making people redundant in terms of financial payments and in terms of morale of the staff at Reading during the uncertain period between the announcement and when the redundancies have been made.

4 What arguments might the Amicus union have used in its negotiations with Prudential? How might the Human Resources Department plans be affected by the decision to make no compulsory redundancies? (8 marks)

Amicus would have wanted fairness and honesty from Prudential. Being a union that represents its members Amicus would try to negotiate a deal higher than the statutory redundancy payments. It would also have wanted Prudential to give as much notice as possible about its plans so that the call centre workers could find alternative employment. This would allow for people to volunteer to be made redundant. The negotiations with Prudential probably improved the chances of current employees transferring to vacancies elsewhere in the company. Overall Amicus felt successful in that there would be no compulsory redundancies, but of course the call centre jobs will no longer exist in Reading.
The Human Resources Department would have to encourage more voluntary redundancy, possibly through higher awards and also manage those who wished to transfer jobs within the company. Prudential would save on redundancy payments, but have extra training costs to bring these employees up to the required skills. By appointing from within there may be some concern that the posts were not necessarily being filled by the best possible staff with the most appropriate skills.

People in organisations: Amazon.co.uk

1 Identify the stages in the recruitment process described by Amazon in the article above. (4 marks)

Determine the need for posts and establish the qualities and skills it feels important for the jobs. Inform the public of these positions through the Internet. Invite them to apply. Undertake some form of shortlisting and invite those shortlisted for interviews.

2 Analyse are the advantages for Amazon using the Internet and for some positions having a phone interview. (4 marks)

The Internet is a quick, cheap and easy way of reaching a large audience. Phone interviews would be used as an additional way to the CV to shortlist further. They would quickly inform Amazon about some of the interpersonal skills of the applicants. This may be sufficient for more junior positions. Both actions help keep the costs of recruitment down, which may be significant if the business is growing rapidly or if the labour turnover is high.

3 Recommend other methods that Amazon might use to let potential applicants know about vacancies. (6 marks)

It is highly unlikely that this business will solely use the Internet to let potential applicants know, because it would

not reach a wide enough audience and this in turn would narrow the field it has for selection. It may be looking to promote internally for some positions. This rewards current employees and you know you are recruiting people who are already used to working with your culture and objectives. Hence weekly newsletters or an employment noticeboard would be necessary. A second measure is to advertise in the media locally either on radio or in the local newspaper. This will cost money but it is targeted at people who live within commuting distance. It is free to advertise in the local job centres and many of those attracted by this method would be unemployed and ready to work. For more specialist work commanding higher salaries the company may advertise in professional magazines or newspapers. These employees are more prepared to move in order to get the job. The methods chosen are likely to be cost effective and meet the relative urgency of the appointment.

4 How does Amazon structure the company? (6 marks)

Amazon structures its business by its product or service, such as books, electrical and photo departments, and also by functional departments such as customer care, finance and other administrative posts. It attempts to get staff to work in small teams and interestingly has some teams that are cross-functional allowing employees to meet others with different experiences. Amazon believes this allows for creative approaches and improves performance. It is a little like a matrix approach.
In addition all employees have to spend some time in the distribution centre especially during busy periods making sure they understand the key objective of the business of getting products to customers on time.

5 Evaluate the methods that Amazon uses to motivate its employees. (10 marks)

Amazon's financial incentives to motivate its employees include share options and fringe benefits. By offering shares in the business Amazon is both rewarding employees and giving them a small stake and incentive in the company. If the company performs well the share price will rise. However, share prices could fall and there is nothing to stop people selling their shares. Amazon also offers a range of fringe benefits including life and medical insurance after 3 months' service. Amazon may have reached a good deal with BUPA if most of the staff is young because they are less likely to claim. This benefit will be well received by employees as it demonstrates the company cares about the individual.
Its non-financial incentives to motivate link to the human relations approach to motivation. First, its cross-functional team approach suggests parallels with motivators, such as being recognised for your work and feeling a sense of achievement. It is a type of job enrichment since some of the tasks and challenges given will be beyond the current employees' experience. Such empowerment is indicated in the company's leadership style that encourages learning in an accountable environment with ideas being encouraged and rewarded. The company culture fits in with McGregor's Theory Y management attitude and it encourages employees to meet their self-esteem needs by recognising achievement and providing promotion and responsibility.
Amazon must make sure its words are put into practice,

by employing the right type of managers during the recruitment process and by undertaking surveys of its workers to see if they share the views put forward by its website. It could also check to see if there are fewer customer complaints.

People in organisations: Co-operative Bank

1 Why might the Co-operative Bank be so committed to equal opportunities? (6 marks)

The Co-operative Bank's commitment to equal opportunities may well reflect the culture and ethos of the bank. It sells itself as an ethical bank and this must apply to dealings with employees as well as customers. The culture is one of opportunity, honesty and fairness. This means it has strong equal opportunity policies in place. A second reason might be that it believes such policies, if carried out, will empower its workers who will want to perform better. A third reason is that it would wish to work within the current legislation on employment that includes areas of equal opportunities and discrimination.

2 Define the terms 'flat organisation structure' and 'flexible employee'. (4 marks)

A flat organisation structure has few levels within the organisation structure.
Flexible employees can adapt to changing circumstances. They can change the tasks and times they work to the needs of the business.

3 Evaluate the benefits and drawbacks of a flat structure to an organisation like the Co-operative Bank. (12 marks)

The flat structure fits in with the ethos and culture of the bank. It means less emphasis is placed on supervision and more on teamwork. It requires the company to adopt a more democratic approach to management so that employees feel comfortable and empowered by working in a team. Managers' attitudes will need to be similar to McGregor's Theory Y model otherwise the system will backfire and employees will just feel used. This is probably why the bank pays close attention to finding out the opinions of its employees on a regular basis for all issues. Staff training on the democratic approach and delegation will need to be a priority for all managers. With this in place the flat structure will improve communications and employees will feel more equal with their contributions valued. The reduction in bureaucracy will allow more time for discussion. Decisions will be based upon the expertise of the team as a whole.
One problem with flat structures is that there is less scope for promotion as there are fewer levels in the hierarchy. This could demotivate employees. However, the bank has other motivators in place. Teams are set up to undertake specific project work. The teams will be given responsibility and power to come up with solutions that take the company forward and enrich the employees' experiences. There must be leaders within the team who have overall responsibility and there should be clear guidelines otherwise the approach could be laissez faire and lead to decisions being made that did not fit

comfortably with the culture of the business. The democratic approach is not suitable for all types of worker and so it would pay the Co-operative Bank to look for the more flexible worker when recruiting new staff.

Operations management: Hankins Joinery

1 What is meant by the terms 'JIT stock control system' (lines 37–8) and 'cell production' (line 59)? (4 marks)

The JIT or Just-in-Time stock control system attempts to keep the costs of holding raw materials, work in progress and finished stock to a minimum by carefully scheduling the flow of materials through the production process. Materials and components are made available just when they are needed. It needs a reliable ordering system. Cell production uses teams of multi-skilled employees who work together to complete a self-contained unit of production. Each cell becomes a supplier for the next cell and is a customer of the previous one. In this way it can link in with JIT.

2 Explain how Hankins organises its production. What are the advantages and disadvantages for Hankins of operating in this way? (6 marks)

Hankins has two types of production. For bespoke or individual orders it uses job production. Although more expensive it can motivate Hankins' employees as they can use their skills to produce high quality furniture. Customers are prepared to pay higher prices for unique, quality-made products.
To supply the components to Millers and other businesses the firm will most likely use batch production as it produces a large number each of a small range of products. Once the machines have been set up this is a cheap method of production for volume runs. It may not motivate employees so much, but allows Hankins to employ people with lower skills. Due to lower prices there is a higher demand for this type of work reflected by it representing 80% of Hankins' business revenue.

3 Why does Hankins keep a large buffer stock (line 33)? What problems might Hankins face in keeping such a high level of stocks? (8 marks)

Buffer stock represents the minimum level of stocks required by the business. This seems high for Hankins, but it likes to have enough stock in to start a job immediately an order comes in. It reduces the lead time between the order being made and delivered. Hankins believes it gains a competitive advantage from this. However, holding large amounts of stock can cause a number of problems. Even with stock rotation (using oldest stock first) some of the stock of wood is likely to warp over time especially if stored under damp conditions. Also of significance are the costs of holding such a large buffer stock. It ties up working capital in having a large stock area full of stock. This can lead to cash flow problems.

4 What comparisons can you make between the size of Hankins and its main customer, Millers? How else might you compare their sizes? (6 marks)

Hankins is a much smaller business than Millers. Its sales revenue of £4 million a year is 5% of that of Millers ((£4m / £80) × 100). Hankins' workforce is 12.5% or one-eighth of the number employed by Millers. Each employee worker in Millers generates £200,000 of sales revenue compared with £80,000 per employee in Hankins. That is 2.5 times as much. Maybe Millers' stock purchases represent a greater proportion of sales than Hankins' and maybe Millers has a higher investment in capital expenditure. If much of the capital in Millers is tied up in buying stock, it may explain why it wishes to move to JIT. Therefore it would be useful to have information about the fixed assets and working capital from the balance sheet to compare the amount of capital each business employs.

Levels of profit are sometimes used to compare size, but this can be misleading because each business may have good and bad years. Looking at size alone doesn't tell the whole story. Comparing efficiency and productivity would provide a more complete picture.

5 Discuss the advantages Millers has by being bigger. How does Hankins manage to survive despite it being small? (16 marks)

A bigger business can gain considerable advantage from economies of scale. This is when the unit costs fall as output increases. It means the business has become more efficient. Lower unit costs means the business can charge lower prices and this boosts demand. By being big Millers can buy in bulk and negotiate bigger discounts. For example, the Millers order from Hankins is very important to Hankins who can't afford to lose it. Hankins will be prepared to charge less to keep the contract. Being smaller Hankins' management has to share some responsibilities, but Millers can employ more specialists. For example, it will no doubt have an expert purchasing manager and assistants who have the time and expertise to find and arrange the best deals. Millers can also employ technology more efficiently with the fixed costs of the items being spread over a much larger output. The cost of marketing Millers' office furniture in trade magazines and at displays is also spread over more sales, making the unit cost of marketing lower. It is also easier and cheaper for bigger businesses to raise finance. Millers, by making different types of office furniture and having a number of suppliers and customers, is able to spread the risk more effectively than Hankins.

Hankins can survive because it supplies components to a few businesses – it doesn't require a huge amount of marketing. It also joined other small businesses in a purchasing consortium enabling the consortium to buy in bulk. The bespoke side of the business is more suitable for job production and this cannot so easily gain from economies of scale. Big businesses can lack co-ordination and have poor motivation if not managed well. This produces diseconomies of scale. Hankins, being a small family business that attempts to empower its workers, can be more flexible when the market changes. Alternatively it can specialise in one area or with one customer, but there are risks to this.

6 Evaluate the proposal to have closer ties with Millers and accept its offer of increased orders, but daily deliveries and improved quality. (16 marks)

If Hankins decides to reject Millers' proposals it will lose half its sales revenue. Finding new markets will be difficult and the business may have to make workers redundant. On the face of it accepting the proposal has significant benefits. For example, the orders would significantly increase and Hankins would become a preferred supplier. Concentrating on just four components would mean the investment in new equipment would be more cost effective. However Hankins would require more finance and have a good business plan available for the bank. Millers may offer to buy some shares in Hankins, but this would change the emphasis of ownership. Hankins would need to be sure that Millers' own markets are strong. If Millers' market declines so will Hankins'. If Hankins dropped the bespoke side it may demotivate its more skilled employees. However, empowering the workers to come up with solutions means that hard decisions are more likely to be accepted and change more likely to succeed.

By moving to a JIT operation the level of stocks and the need for a large stock area will be reduced. The extra space released may allow the bespoke production to continue. Lower stocks means there will be less working capital required to run the business, therefore releasing capital for equipment and training to enable JIT to go ahead. The JIT operations would mean the stock room staff changing their role to include more deliveries. It would also require leaving the consortium and finding a supplier who can also deliver daily.

Working in four cells leads to more teamwork and a commitment to meet targets such as increased output, less waste and higher quality. Each team will take on more responsibility including its own quality control. By going on training courses and visiting firms operating in this way Hankins has a strong chance of making this work.

Overall I would recommend they go down this route as it has a more secure future and will make the business more efficient. Millers will have built up a strong relationship with Hankins. The main drawback is that Hankins will be dependent on one customer. If Millers fail at least Hankins' greater efficiency will give it a chance to capture new markets. In the short run Hankins will need to raise more finance. It is a risk, but one worth taking.

End of Part 2 assessment

Paper 2: Business decisions

1a Outline two methods that Tariq could use to segment his market. (4 marks)

> Student answer: Tariq has already segmented his market according to the age of his clients. He could also break it up according to gender.

> *This answer really needs a little more development, perhaps commenting on how he has segmented it according to age and briefly explain why. He could also have used their spend or the time of their visits.*

b Analyse Tariq's plans to change the target market for the salon. (8 marks)

> Student answer: Tariq plans to change the image of the business in order to capture a younger customer. The client database indicates that younger customers are prepared to spend significantly more than older ones and those aged between 22 and 40 are more frequent repeat customers. On the face of it, it seems a sensible idea to target these, but there are drawbacks and he should not just rely on this information alone and would need to weigh up the risks before spending £19,000 on refurbishment. Tariq needs more accurate data on the number of customers in each age group. However, he does know that his main customer base are people over 40. A change in image may alienate these customers and he risks losing many of them to competitors especially if he increases prices. He would be wise to consult these customers to find out their feelings. He would also need to take account of the skills and attitude of his staff and if they would feel comfortable with the changes.

> *Any analysis should take account of the case both for and against the change and this answer attempts to do that. More mention of other market research is required and greater use of appropriate business terms like primary and secondary research would improve this answer, as would a reference to staff motivation and empowerment .*

2 Evaluate the advantages and disadvantages to the business of day release as a method of training the junior member of staff. (12 marks)

> Student answer: Training staff is important in the hairdressing business to enable them to carry out necessary tasks and perform effectively. It is difficult, if not impossible, to correct any mistakes. Such mistakes will lead to a loss of customers and damage to reputation. In addition the staff need to be confident in all types of cutting. This training can be given in-house or externally – Tariq has chosen the college day release. Each system of training has its own advantages and disadvantages. By going for a day release the junior member of staff is able to learn and practise new skills gradually on customers at the college who come as volunteers. The training is off-site so errors made there will not rebound upon the business. The college will use experts to teach the latest ideas and the junior member of staff can bring these back to Style Design. The success of this would depend upon the leadership style of Tariq. He would need to encourage his employees to feel that they could contribute to the development of the business. He may do well to look at one of Herzberg's motivators by giving the responsibility of introducing good ideas to the junior employee. You cannot be in two places at once so being at college might mean staff shortages on that day and less appointments can be made. The alternative is to provide in-house training on the premises but this would tie up another employee to supervise this. Customers will also be more reluctant to have a trainee cut their hair. Day release training will develop skills, but staff also need to be trained in the house style of the business. This is especially important if Style Design is to have a new image. To achieve this the business might train its entire staff regularly by opening an hour or so later to the public on a day when business is less busy.
> To summarise, any training costs the business time and money, but Tariq wants to have a skilled staff that can also provide the customer with an excellent service that reflects the new image. External training will provide the necessary skills, but to provide a greater sense of belonging to a team and ensuring staff work in the way the business wants, it is also important to have in-house training. During these training sessions, Tariq should encourage his junior staff to share the good ideas and practices learnt at the college.

> *The answer must look at the advantages and disadvantages of external training, which means a comparison should be made with alternative methods. The evaluation should come up with a judgement that draws upon evidence from the case study and key concepts. This answer demonstrates an understanding of the importance of training and the different methods. The two-year course will also lead to a nationally recognised qualification that should ensure standards. The training will also make the junior member of staff multi-skilled, but what if the employee left after obtaining the qualification? Tariq might then feel hard done by.*
> *The answer uses the framework given in the case study, but leaves out the headings for the one-off payments that will occur in July. The answer shows the marker which figures have been adjusted and by how much. There is one error in the adding up which has meant that the final total is out by £30. Something called the 'own figure rule' will apply here and this answer would only be deducted one mark.*

3 Calculate the closing cash balance for September based on the information in Table 2 and Tariq's assumptions. (7 marks)

Student answer:

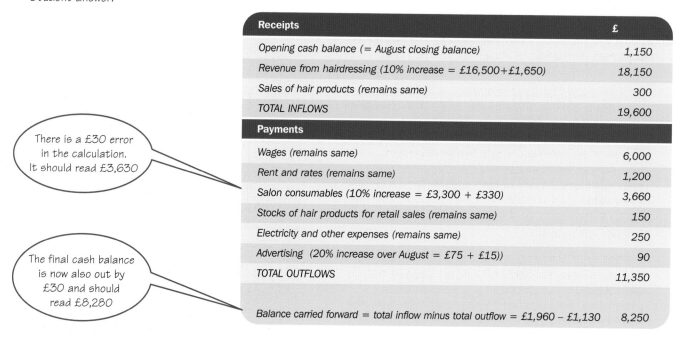

Receipts	£
Opening cash balance (= August closing balance)	1,150
Revenue from hairdressing (10% increase = £16,500+£1,650)	18,150
Sales of hair products (remains same)	300
TOTAL INFLOWS	19,600
Payments	
Wages (remains same)	6,000
Rent and rates (remains same)	1,200
Salon consumables (10% increase = £3,300 + £330)	3,660
Stocks of hair products for retail sales (remains same)	150
Electricity and other expenses (remains same)	250
Advertising (20% increase over August = £75 + £15))	90
TOTAL OUTFLOWS	11,350
Balance carried forward = total inflow minus total outflow = £1,960 – £1,130	8,250

There is a £30 error in the calculation. It should read £3,630

The final cash balance is now also out by £30 and should read £8,280

4 Evaluate the factors that Tariq should consider in deciding his stock control policy. (12 marks)

Student answer: A better stock control system would help to improve the efficiency of Style Design. The lead time of ten days means Tariq will have to wait ten days between ordering stock and receiving it. He could try to find a supplier that can deliver more quickly, perhaps within a day of receiving an order. However, that would mean selling different products when he has a local monopoly for a well-known brand. By keeping with the same supplier Tariq will need to improve his check on stocks so that he doesn't order too much stock that stands around on the shelf as this ties up working capital. Secondly, he doesn't want to run out of stock because this will turn away customers. This requires him to keep a minimum buffer stock for safety. Once the reorder level has been reached he will need to send an order to the supplier so that in ten days' time his stock on average will reach the buffer or minimum stock level. These will vary according to the product. Those selling well might be represented using the left-hand scale and those that sell less frequently by the right-hand scale on the diagram below. Since he spends over £3000 a month on stocks he may consider investing in a computer stock control system that would automatically reorder.

The answer looks at the costs and problems associated with the current arrangement. It also suggests alternatives giving reasons why. However the overall answer is too short and doesn't make a final recommendation. It could also have looked at the effect of changing market segment. The diagram is a useful addition, and relates to the text, but is not adequately labelled (see below) and explained. Diagrams can be effective if they are accurate. The student seems to have run out of time. Perhaps the answer to question 2 was a little too long.

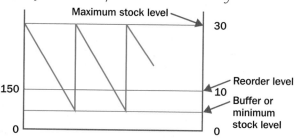

This answer would have benefited by introducing key concepts like just-in-time and stock rotation. JIT would speed up the stock and allow zero buffer levels and stock rotation would minimise products that might run past their sell by date. The answer would also benefit by providing more detail on the costs and problems of inefficient stock control. Finally, it could have considered the issues Tariq has to consider when thinking about investing in a computer control system.

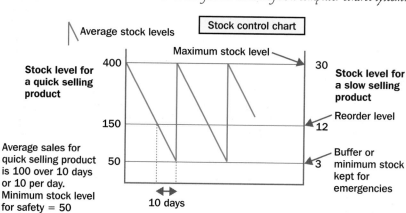

End of Part 2 assessment

Paper 3: Business behaviour

1a On a typical excursion to Innsbruck (see Table 3) there are 20 passengers. If the price charged for this excursion is £8, using break-even analysis, calculate the margin of safety. (6 marks)

Student answer: 20 passengers will produce a revenue of £160 for the excursion. The cost of the Innsbruck excursion is made up of the tour guide, extra diesel and extra road tolls and taxes, which comes to £136. The difference between the two figures is £24, which represents the revenue from three passengers and therefore three is the margin of safety. If there were three fewer passengers or seventeen passengers in total the excursion would just break even.

It is important to explain how you came to your calculations. You have not been asked to say whether this is a big margin of safety or not.

b Evaluate ways in which Thornwood Coaches could increase its profit from the OHT contract. (10 marks)

Student answer: Being paid a fixed price of £2430 will produce a profit of £400, assuming nothing goes wrong. This represents just over 16%. Any damage to the coach then the profit level will fall. Although being paid a fixed price will ensure a regular revenue the only reward for taking a full coach is that there is more chance of getting passengers to sign up to the excursions. One way to get more profit is to allow the drivers to earn an extra pound for every passenger they get for excursions. This represents a variable cost of £1 and if prices were kept the same a contribution of £7 for each passenger for the Innsbruck trip to cover the other costs of £136. It would increase the break even to around 20 passengers, but the incentive to the drivers to earn more will encourage them to promote the tour. If they manage to persuade an extra 10 more customers the profit to Thornwood will increase from £24 to £70. A similar sum may be collected from the other excursion.

Another option to increase profits is to reduce costs. Thornwood have no real control over tolls and taxes or the amount of diesel used and I'm not sure what comes under miscellaneous.

This leaves cutting wages or the drivers' lunch allowances. Both of these may lead to drivers quitting. A third way is to try to renegotiate the contract with OHT, but OHT may say no and look for alternative sub-contractors.

When there is lots of competition it is difficult to increase profits. Increased efficiency is only possible at the expense of drivers' incomes. Encouraging drivers to promote excursions seems the best bet.

It is easy to start to look for ways outside the contract, but you should avoid this. Hence profits can be increased only by increasing revenues or reducing costs. The answer given sensibly makes use of the work on break-even analysis.

2 With reference to appropriate motivational theory, evaluate monetary and non-monetary ways in which Thornwood Coaches could motivate its drivers. (16 marks)

Student answer: Herzberg believed that job dissatisfaction would occur if a business lacked hygiene factors. These included the pay and working conditions. Thornwood Coaches may have to alter these if its employees were dissatisfied. Thornwood Coaches would be sensible to pay attention to the feelings of its staff, especially if the views of Linda and Rob are typical of the other drivers. First, however, it would need to find out how motivated its employees were. It might look to see if there is an increase in labour turnover or absences. Asking drivers their feelings is an important part of two-way communication.

However, it is not that simple to put hygiene factors in place. Profit margins are already felt to be too low so it would be difficult to use monetary ways to increase the motivation of its drivers. Wages at £38 per day are not high for a long day, but they do receive fringe benefits in terms of free accommodation and food. Providing uniforms would be one cost-effective way of providing hygiene factors.

To make employees do their best Herzberg believed there must be motivators. It is this area that Thornwood Coaches can work on. Recognition of your effort and responsibility are two motivators that could be put into place if Thornwood Coaches took on board Linda's idea about keeping some of the revenue from getting customers to go on excursions. This would be job enrichment and the extra responsibility would encourage them to make an effort to get more on each excursion and also to provide an excellent service. This would be an example of empowerment. It would also provide them with a financial reward that given the explanation in the answer to question 1b) would also increase the profits for the business. It will encourage further initiative from employees. I would recommend trying this out.

The section on job enrichment could be developed to describe what it is. For the motivators to work it will need the managers to be democratic in approach. This would lend itself to McGregor's Theory Y type manager. Clearly the question could be answered using any suitable motivation theory.

3 Discuss suitable promotional methods that Jayne Oaks could use if OHT introduces fly-drive coach holidays. (16 marks)

Student answer: The fly-drive holidays would be an extension of the product range. It would be attractive to the 19–39 age ranges, which is the company's growth market segment. Hence any successful promotion should be aimed primarily at this group. However, such promotion methods should be cost effective.

The company would do well to continue with its existing above the line promotion by sending mailshots to existing customers using its database. This is cost effective as it targets likely customers who will then buy directly from the company. Using travel supplements in the better quality newspapers will be more important when selling higher value holidays. Brochures at travel agents will allow information to reach a wider audience. A well-designed website that can be easily accessed and with online booking would appeal to the target audience and once set up is cheap to run.

The image OHT presents will be important in attracting customers once they have heard about the fly-drive holidays. It should promote its emphasis on quality by making the public know about its awards. For example, these should be on the front page of any brochure or website.

OHT might offer discounts for early bookings. This would help the cash flow, but might reduce the profit margin. Another strategy might be to offer people a discount when they book their next holiday soon after the completion of the first. This would give secure bookings and deposits in the bank at an early date. It could also throw in free excursions as a loss leader. Another alternative is to make an arrangement with taxi firms, bus and rail travel to offer a discount for travel to the airport. This has the advantage of not costing OHT money and increasing business for the other public transport businesses.

To launch the holidays OHT will need to use some below the line promotion techniques. Asking for customer feedback is an example of good public relations. OHT could sponsor events, but its limited size suggests this is not a serious option.

The second to last paragraph looks more like pricing rather than strictly promotion. Some distinction should be made between direct and indirect marketing, the latter being to use intermediaries like travel agents to sell holidays. It is important to give both advantages and disadvantages of a strategy when the question says 'discuss'. This answer will only score low level 3 because the majority is not specifically about fly-drive coach holidays – it could apply to promotion of any product.

4 Evaluate the extent to which management of capacity is important in the context of the case. (10 marks)

Student answer: OHT has to cover its overheads as well as the costs of paying a fixed price to the coach business it sub-contracts to. Those coaches that run with significant empty seats may just be covering the fixed price and not contributing to overheads. Those running at full capacity will, and so it is important to ensure that it has enough sales staff and marketing strategies to increase sales. OHT might try to separate its market by offering big discounts to late bookings where sales have been poor.

The seasonal nature of holidays affects both OHT and the sub contract firms. They will be paying for overheads all year, but receiving most income in the spring and summer. Winter ski visits, more short breaks to European cities, and day trips to UK towns might provide a way of reducing the cash imbalance in non-peak seasons.

A coach not working on any day is an inefficient use of resources, because it is not generating income. The coach is not being productive. Coach companies want to raise capital productivity as it makes them more competitive and they will earn more profit from the investment in their coaches.

OHT needs to manage capacity utilisation by ensuring that it fills as many seats as possible on each coach because it pays a flat fee to the sub-contractor and needs to generate as much revenue as possible to cover these costs, the overheads and make a profit. This is not so important to Thornwood because it is paid a flat rate; however, many people are on the coach. Thornwood is more concerned with ensuring that its coaches are used for as many days as possible.

Management of capacity is difficult and the ideal situation is that coaches are used all the time and full up. The case study looks at under-capacity, but remember there is a danger of not having enough capacity to meet demand during peak periods. Can OHT call on reserve coach companies to fill in if demand is high and are there enough hotel beds? Disappointed customers who are told that trips are full may not bother to try to book again next year.

Index